Leisure Education

Theory and Practice

Jean Mundy
Florida State University

SAGAMORE PUBLISHING
Champaign, IL 61820

Book Design: Kathryn J. Meyer
Production Manager: Susan M. McKinney
Cover Design: Deborah Bellaire

ISBN: 1-57167-035-1

Printed in the United States

Table of Contents

Chapter 1: Philosophical Considerations in Leisure Education 1

Chapter 2: Leisure Problems of People 29

Chapter 3: Leisure Education Models 49

Chapter 4: Implementing Leisure Education in Recreation and Leisure Systems 67

Chapter 5: Leisure Education Program Planning 101

Chapter 6: Leisure Education Units for Implementation 111

Chapter 7: Leisure Eduction Facilitation Techniques 223

Chapter 8: Issues and Special Considerations 251
- *Feature A*: for Persons with Disabilities 252
- *Feature B:* for Persons in Correctional Facilities 270
- *Feature C:* for Older Adults 279

Appendices 287
Author's Page 315
Index 316

Publisher's Note

Due to expired copyrights, pages 295-300 have been removed from this publication.

Philosophical Considerations in Leisure Education

Chapter Overview

This chapter provides an introduction to the concept of leisure education. It deals with a rationale for leisure education as a component of recreation and leisure services, a definition of leisure education, the goal of leisure education, what leisure education is and what it is not, and contrasts the differences between leisure education and traditional recreation services.

The concept of freedom is explored along with selected internal and external factors that can influence a person's perception of freedom as well as the issue of internal motivation as an aspect of leisure. The remainder of the chapter focuses on various philosophical perspectives of leisure education, making a case for the individual developmental model or intrinsic determination approach as the conceptual framework of the author.

Introduction

For a number of years, the primary emphasis and focus of the field of recreation, parks, and leisure have been on the provision of recreation activities, areas, and facilities. If there was any educational emphasis, it was on developing knowledge and skills needed for participation in recreation activities. As a profession, we have assumed that possessing knowledge and skills about recreation activities, as well as opportunities for participation, will lead to enriching, enhancing leisure lifestyles. Therefore, we have taught people the following:

- what the term "infield fly" means—but not what the term "leisure" means,
- to value sportsmanship—but not to value leisure in their lives,
- how to exercise for their health—but not how to attain leisure,
- to follow our plans and enroll in our scheduled programs—but not how to make their own leisure decisions and plans,
- to value fitness because we sponsor National Fitness weeks to raise people's awareness of the fitness aspects of their lives—but not to value leisure because we do not sponsor National Leisure weeks to raise people's awareness of the leisure aspects of their lives.

It is clear that this emphasis is not enough to aid a vast majority of people in developing meaningful, enriching leisure. It is not that the focus has been wrong; rather, it has been incomplete in light of the goal the field has maintained for the enhancement of the quality of life through leisure. If we go back to the Boston Sand Garden and the New York Settlement houses as the beginning of the modern recreation movement in the United States, the 100 years of our field's existence give evidence that our limited focus has not been effective. Essentially, people

- are unaware of what the term leisure even means,
- have problems with leisure in their personal lives,
- know a variety of recreation activities but don't have meaningful experiences in their free time,
- have leisure patterns that are predominantly home-based, passive, and restricted to a few easily accessible experiences.

It is not surprising that this situation exists given the past limited focus of the field, the underlying assumptions under which we have operated, and the traditional systems of delivering services that we have devised.

As a profession, we have assumed that the primary socializers in our society—the family unit and the schools—are developing the basic leisure ethos, attitudes, and behaviors in the people we serve. Since we assumed that the basics were in place, our concern and role have centered in supplementing and complementing the family and the schools' roles by providing programs, services, facilities, and leadership to facilitate participation. However, regardless of what may once have been, today the world is a very different place. It can no longer be assumed that people have the basics needed for satisfying recreation and leisure.

Children are growing up with fewer recreation and leisure skills and less appreciation than ever before. Schools are being pressured into a "back to basics" movement because children are showing that they cannot read, write a complete sentence, do fundamentals of mathematics, or recite what countries border the United States. Numerous schools are eliminating art, music, band, interests clubs, intramural and interscholastic sports participation, and even recess in order to spend all of their time on scholastic subjects. Current economic problems will only hasten and expand such cutbacks in areas that are perceived by many as "frills."

The family unit in our country is not necessarily in a position to pick up what the educational system is eliminating in relation to recreation and leisure. When one considers the number of dual working-parent families, single-parent families, and the economics of after-school care, the development of positive leisure attitudes, interests, and skills may well be severely curtailed. When time and money are scarce and parents feel that life is hurried, harried, and stressful, then the leisure development of children will generally take a back seat to keeping one's head above water.

If the leisure development of people is going to occur in our society in any systematic way, the recreation, leisure, and park movement must assume the leadership responsibility for accomplishing this goal. The schools will not/cannot do it. They will continue focusing on academics for the foreseeable future. The family systems' emphasis will probably continue to be limited as they continue to place emphasis on economics and taking care of basic maintenance and living tasks. Also, when one considers the fact that a child's basic value system is set by ten years of age, it is apparent that leisure education must begin at an early age. If we don't educate for leisure, who will?

In relation to our traditional systems of delivering services, there are three distinct differences between how we deliver recreation services and leisure as experiences and how we need to proceed in the future. These differences, I believe, are counter to the leisure development of people and need alteration.

First, the delivery of recreation and leisure programs and opportunities as they are currently provided in most settings tend to be activity-oriented. Leisure, however, is experience-oriented—the experience being an internal, psychological condition regardless of the external, behavioral activity. Second, recreation programs and opportunities as they are currently provided tend to be organized and structured, whereas free time and leisure are without structure and organization, except what the individual may choose to bring to them. Finally, recreation programs and opportunities tend to be leader-initiated, leader-planned, and leader-provided, whereas leisure is self-initiated, self-planned, and self-provided. Clearly, the understandings, knowledge, and skills needed for activity participation are different from those needed for the development of enhancing and enriching leisure experiences.

The incongruent and divergent program emphases and delivery systems can partly explain the differences in the way people function in various settings. For example, it is not uncommon for children to be in a variety of recreation and leisure programs and possess skills for participation, yet these same children at home express feelings of boredom with nothing to do. The field's past approach could also explain why some patients in therapeutic recreation programs without leisure education components function well in the therapeutic setting but not at home. Once they leave therapeutic recreation programs, their leisure patterns revert to what they were before their involvement in the programs, and they remain unable to handle this aspect of their lives effectively because they were not exposed to leisure education.

In order to respond to the current leisure needs of people in our rapidly changing society, we, as a profession, need to begin our own "Focus on *Leisure* Fundamentals" movement. Our "Focus on Leisure Fundamentals" movement is what leisure education is all about. It is simply helping people develop the attitudes, knowledge, skills, and behaviors for satisfying leisure.

Leisure: A Definition

Views and definitions of leisure have little uniformity and even less consensus in the field. The wide variance in the field's philosophical orientation, with its resulting controversy and confusion among leisure scholars and practitioners, offers a potential block to the implementation of leisure education. Iso-Ahola's (1980) research on the definition of leisure, however, provides an empirical basis for a definition of leisure that transcends individual interpretations of the concept of leisure. Therefore, the definition of leisure used in this book is a state characterized by a sense of freedom and internal motivation in self-selected experiences (Iso-Ahola). Iso-Ahola's work also reveals that for most individuals, leisure, as defined here, is achieved in non-work—or more accurately, nonemployment—time.

Leisure Education: What Is It?

The term *leisure education* carries diverse connotations. To some, the phrase means teaching lifetime sports, while to others it is viewed as imparting information regarding leisure throughout the education system. Leisure education has been viewed traditionally as teaching knowledge and skills about a variety of activities or as the process of educating individuals for leisure by providing opportunities for participation through recreation programming and after-school programs. The most common approach in leisure education has been that of imparting, or teaching, what is "worthy" or "wise" use of free time.

Leisure education, as the term is used here, can best be described in terms of process, rather than simply content. It is viewed as a total developmental process through which individuals develop an understanding of leisure, of self in relation to leisure, and of the relationship among leisure, their own lifestyle, and society. Leisure is viewed as a process because the programmatic aims are for individuals to go through a process of determining the place and significance of leisure in their own lives and for facilitating a leisure lifestyle development that is compatible with their own values, needs, and goals.

Other definitions of leisure education include one set forth by the Leisure Education Advancement Project (LEAP) of the

National Recreation and Park Association. The LEAP definition views leisure education as a process whereby people recognize leisure as an avenue for personal satisfaction and enrichment, become familiar with an array of leisure opportunities, understand the impact leisure has on society, and make decisions regarding their own leisure behavior (Zeyen, Odum, & Lancaster, 1977). Neulinger (1981) has stated that leisure education should impart "knowledge that is relevant to the leisure domain—as it pertains to the individual, to the individual's immediate environment, and to society at large" (p. 185). According to Peterson and Gunn (1984), leisure education is "a broad category of services that focuses on the development and acquisition of various leisure-related skills, attitudes, and knowledge" (p. 22).

The following differentiation is offered to further clarify the concept of leisure education as it is used in this text:

Leisure Education Is

- a process to enable individuals to achieve leisure in their lives,
- a total development process to enable individuals to enhance the quality of their lives through leisure,
- a process to enable individuals to identify and clarify their leisure values, attitudes, needs, and goals,
- an approach to enable individuals to be self-determining, self-sufficient, and proactive in relation to their leisure lives,
- deciding for oneself what place leisure has in one's own life. Coming to know oneself in relation to leisure,
- relating one's own needs, values, and capabilities to leisure and leisure experiences,
- increasing individuals' options for satisfying quality experiences through leisure,
- a process whereby individuals determine their own leisure behavior and evaluate the long- and short-range outcomes of their behavior in relation to their goals,
- developing the potential of individuals to enhance the quality of their own lives in leisure,
- a movement in which a multiplicity of disciplines and service systems have a role and a responsibility.

Leisure Education Is Not

- a new name for recreation or recreation services,
- a watered-down, simplified version of a recreation and parks professional preparation program,
- an attempt to replace an individual's set of values with "our" set of values; a focus upon the value of the recreation profession,
- the communication of predetermined standards concerning what is "good" or "bad," "worthy" or "unworthy" uses of free time,
- a focus on getting people to participate in more recreation activities,
- teaching only activity skills and providing recreation programs,
- a program to undermine the work ethic,
- a responsibility of the schools alone,
- restricted to what educators, but not leisure professionals, should do.

The goal of leisure education is to enable individuals to enhance the quality of their lives through leisure. This goal, translated into a conceptual model, takes leisure education out of the realm of merely providing information regarding recreation opportunities, developing skills for leisure activities, providing leisure opportunities through programming, or teaching what is a "worthy" use of leisure. It is the goal that makes leisure education different in focus, emphasis, process, and content.

In order to further clarify and differentiate leisure education from traditional recreation services, Figure 1.1 contrasts the two areas by their designed program focus and objectives. There are some areas under the leisure education side, such as those in the self-awareness category, that may be a *by-product* of recreation involvement. However, in most traditional recreation programs and services, these areas are not generally a stated programmatic aim nor a planned outcome.

Figure 1.1
Contrast Between Leisure Education and Recreation Program Focus

Leisure Education	Recreation
A. Content/Objectives	
Leisure Skill Development	Recreation/Leisure Activity/ Skill Development
-Activity skill development	
-Decision making	
-Problem solving	
-Planning	
-Evaluation	
Leisure Resources	Recreation Participation
-Activity opportunities	-Bring together people with similar interests
-Personal resources	-Provide affordable activities
-Family and home resources	-Provide facilities
-Community resources	
Leisure-awareness	
-What is leisure?	
-Benefits and outcomes of leisure involvement	
-Forms of leisure involvement	
-Concept of personal responsibility in leisure	
Self-awareness	
-Current leisure interests, involvement, and satisfaction	
-Current leisure attitudes, expectations, and behaviors	
-Actual and perceived abilities and limitations	
-Relationship among life needs, goals, and aspirations with leisure involvement	
B. Primary Focus	
Learning Self-direction	Leader-directed/controlled or Open Participation
Long-term/Long-range Outcomes	Temporary/Immediate Outcomes
Leader Facilitated	
C. Participant Outcomes	
Ability to Enhance Own Quality-of-life in Leisure	Satisfying Use of Free Time
Positive Life Decisions Beyond Supervision and Direction	Mental Development through Leisure Involvement
Satisfying Use of Free Time	Physical Development through Leisure Involvement
Learning to Use Resources, Self, and Community	Social Development through Leisure Involvement
Mental Development through Leisure Involvement	Emotional Development through Leisure Involvement
Physical Development through Leisure Involvement	
Social Development through Leisure Involvement	
Emotional Development through Leisure Involvement	

The philosophical foundation of leisure education presented here is based upon the following premises. The remainder of this chapter and the programmatic implementation in the subsequent chapters revolve around these constructs:

1. The essence of leisure is freedom; therefore, leisure education must, above all else, facilitate individual self-determination.

2. The leisure experience is a uniquely individual experience; therefore, the individual should be the primary focus: recipient of the values, evaluator of the outcomes, and agent of the leisure education process.

The Concept of Freedom in Leisure

In dealing with the concept of leisure as a state of perceived freedom and internal motivation in self-selected experiences, professionals need to understand in more depth the issue of freedom as it relates to leisure because "perceived freedom is the critical regulator of what becomes leisure and what does not" (Iso-Ahola, 1980, p. 189). Freedom of choice is the most widely recognized prerequisite for experiencing leisure (Bordin, 1979; Ellis & Witt, 1984; Tinsley & Tinsley, 1986). Tinsley and Tinsley state, "Individuals will not experience leisure if they believe they are required to engage in an activity, either as a direct requirement or less directly as an expectation . . . ." Since educating for leisure is intricately tied with this perceived state, professionals must be able to deal with the concept and facilitate its attainment with individuals with whom they are working. The question of to what depth this can and should be done by leisure professionals will be explored in a later chapter.

The Concept of Freedom

Freedom is a feeling of being in control of one's own actions (Csikszentmihalyi & Graef, 1980). Freedom exists when there is a minimum acceptance of external constraints and controls and of external rewards and punishments controlling one's behavior and actions. Tied in with this concept is the individual's realization and perception of this control in his or her own life. If this perception and realization of the state of control does not exist, then the feeling of freedom does not exist.

One may easily ask: Is a person ever really free? Isn't freedom just an illusion? Aren't significant choices and decisions already determined for us by the external world and circumstances? Aren't we relegated to simply responding to the forces acting on us? These questions go to the very heart of a significant and long-standing controversy regarding human behavior and its relationship to the environment. Environmental determinists like Skinner contend behavior is determined by the world acting on the person (Skinner, 1977). He views behavior as being determined by external contingencies to which the individual responds. Libertarians, on the other hand, believe in freedom of the will (Yalom, 1980). The majority of empirical research reviewed by Bandura (1978) supports the position of reciprocal determinism. That is, the individual influences his or her environment and, in turn, the environment has an impact on one's behavior.

It is evident that there are external contingencies influencing our lives that cannot be negated. Genetics, society, family, and the environment in which we live all exert influences upon our lives. For example, an individual may have a disabling condition, an unfortunate family background, or inadequate education, to name a few of these types of constraints. However, to the libertarians, this does not mean people have no responsibility or choice in what they make of the adversity and their attitude toward it (Yalom, 1980). It is how the individual perceives and deals with adversities and problems that is important.

The concepts of freedom of will and of personal responsibility for one's life are at the very core of leisure behavior and leisure education. The philosophical position of the practitioner on this issue will affect the entire leisure education process. The approach outlined in this book is from the perspective of reciprocal determinism. An individual's perception of freedom is affected by both internal and external factors. A select few of these factors require a more detailed examination.

Selected Internal Factors Influencing the Perception of Freedom

Perhaps the most significant factor affecting the individual's perceived feeling of freedom is the person's own belief system regarding locus of control. Locus of control refers to one's belief regarding control and responsibilities in one's life. It asks whether the individual believes that he or she controls (and is responsible for) events in life or believes that control is determined by external factors. Locus of control, by its very nature, affects the perception of the individual regarding freedom. An internal locus of control tends to give one more of a sense of personal freedom than does an external locus of control. An "internal" (with an internal locus of control) basically feels that she controls her life, possesses a sense of personal power, is responsible for her life and her choices, and directs her efforts toward mastering her environment (Mischel, Zeiss, & Zeiss, 1974). This leads to feeling free and in control of one's own actions and life. That is not to suggest individuals with an external locus of control cannot obtain a sense of freedom. It does mean that a sense of freedom may be more difficult and slower in coming to "externals" than "internals."

"Externals" feel they are controlled by what happens to them that is external to themselves. Answers, solutions, guidance, support, and approval are seen as needing to come from the external world (Mischel et al., 1974). Responsibility for one's life as it is currently being lived is not a personal response but a response to all of the demands, obligations, controls, and restrictions other people and circumstances impose on the individual and over which the individual has no real control or influence. Since these people feel their lives are basically controlled by external forces acting on them, they do not feel they are responsible for their lives and what happens to them, even though they are the ones making the choices. They tend to blame other people and events, positive or negative, for what is transpiring in their lives. In this orientation to the world, it is easy to see why one would face enormous difficulty in perceiving a sense of freedom as fully and completely as does the internal person. It should also be recognized that one's orientation can change from external to internal locus of control. While the origins of locus of control can be traced to the early family environment, there is evidence in psychotherapeutic literature that shifts from external to internal locus of control can and do occur (Dua, 1970; Gillis & Jessor, 1970).

Figure 1.2 illustrates locus of control statements as they relate to and may be expressed in leisure.

Figure 1.2
Locus of Control in Relation to Leisure

External Views	Internal Views
I don't have time for leisure.	I will have to make time for leisure.
I have to . . . ; I should . . .	I choose to . . .
What do you recommend, think, suggest?	Here is what I am going to do.
I can't.	I won't; I'm not.
My enjoyment of leisure is dependent on other people.	I can enjoy my leisure on my own.
The time I have for leisure is determined by my family and my work.	I am responsible for making time for leisure.

A second internal factor that influences perceptions of freedom is how individuals choose to interpret events and experiences in their lives. Albert Ellis (1987) contends that emotions are caused and controlled by thinking. His approach views emotions as stemming from *self-talk*—that is, internal messages we give ourselves to interpret life's events. According to Ellis, what individuals tell themselves regarding a situation becomes their thoughts and emotions in that situation; it becomes, for them, their reality. For example, if a person interprets an event as "awful," there will be negative feelings associated with the event. On the other hand, if the person judges the event to be "wonderful," the emotion will be positive. Thus, if an individual tells herself "I don't have a choice," "I have to," or "I should," the accompanying feelings will be ones of little, if any, sense of freedom or satisfaction. On the contrary, we can choose what we think. What we think (our *self-talk*) determines what we feel and influences our behavior. Therefore, by learning to control our self-talk, we can control our perceptions and feelings and, thus, influence our own sense of freedom.

A third internal factor that influences an individual's perceived sense of freedom encompasses other psychological encumbrances, both conscious and unconscious, that interfere with the perception of freedom, choice, decision, and will. As an example, for reasons often unclear or unknown even to the person, the individual may be involved in responsibility-avoiding behavior. Yalom (1980) identifies some of the most common responsibility-avoiding defenses as displacement of responsibility to another, denial of responsibility, compulsivity, avoidance of autonomous behavior, and decisional pathology. These types of psychological encumbrances, along with things like guilt, worry, fear, anxiety, and helplessness, can operate to the point of interfering with any perception of freedom.

Selected External Factors Influencing the Perceived Sense of Freedom

As we go through life, we are generally involved in striving for goals, whether these be related to work, family, relationships, or personal accomplishments and achievements. Since many of our goals may carry contingencies, we are placed in the position of making decisions of whether or not we want to pay the price to attain the goal. Frequently, the contingencies run something like this: "If you want to do that, then you must first do this." Physicians in this country do not simply decide they want to be doctors, open their offices, and begin practice as licensed physicians. They must first complete college and medical school. A college education and medical school are contingencies to being a physician. These contingencies carry the price of being willing to accept external controls, directives, and constraints. Medical students choose to live by a system of external rewards and punishments until their goal is achieved. The same type of situation can occur in relation to other life decisions we all make. For example, if a person wants to scuba dive, they must be able to swim, enroll, and successfully complete a scuba certification program. Likewise, they must have the fiscal resources to dive, which includes money to rent or purchase equipment, to travel, and to obtain nautical conveyance to diving sites.

Decisions can be expensive. To choose one path may mean having to give up something else. It may mean relinquishing options. Therefore, if we act responsibly in relation to our decisions, it can mean that although we choose our course of action, our freedom to make other choices and decisions are lessened, at least for the time being. This can lead to a decreased sense of freedom.

Research has also identified other factors that influence a perceived sense of freedom. For example, Harvey (1976) found the sense of freedom is greater when one perceives that decisions are made between pleasant alternatives rather than unpleasant ones. Iso-Ahola (1980), on the other hand, states, ". . . instead of saying that the potential pleasure of activities increase perceived freedom, it is more accurate to state that competence-elevating activities enhance the sense of freedom" (p. 197). His rationale for this statement comes from the fact that "liking" is related to perceived competence because activities that help satisfy a person's need for competence are greatly preferred over those that don't (p. 197).

The number of choices an individual has, as well as the equality in the attractiveness of options, has also been shown to increase perceived freedom. While excessive choices can be confusing, perceived freedom is higher for a larger number of choices than for a smaller number of choices (Harvey, 1976). Likewise, perceived freedom has been shown to be greater when the alternatives are similar in attractiveness and offer similar benefits or gains (Harvey; Steiner, 1970).

Perhaps one of the most critical external factors influencing a sense of freedom is time. The amount of time people feel they have is related to the contingency decisions they have made, as well as to the number and extent of general obligations and responsibilities they have assumed in their lives. It is also related to abilities, such as organization and the effective and efficient utilization of time.

Four concepts are of particular importance in leisure education because, when dealt with by the participant, they can produce substantial benefits. These four concepts consist of the following:

1. Time is one resource that is equally distributed. Each of us has the same 24 hours in a day. No one has more time than anyone else.

2. Time and what we do with it is a matter of the choices we make.

3. We can never get "more time." We can only change the decisions we make regarding how we choose to use the time we have.

4. Time is emotionally neutral. Our feelings about time are influenced by the choices we make and the experiences we have as a result of those choices.

Leisure and Internal Motivation

Motivation can be defined as a driving force behind behavior. It is what causes one to behave as he does. While one's motivation can be considered internal or external, in reality it is generally a combination and interaction of both. Internal motivation as a component of the state of leisure has been addressed by numerous writers (Neulinger, 1974; Gray & Greben, 1974; Csikszentmihalyi, 1975; Iso-Ahola, 1980). Internal motivation refers to those motivations primarily arising from within an individual, as opposed to the external or extrinsic reward that one may achieve.

Internal motivation is one of the commonly recognized conditions for leisure and leisure experiences (Kelly, 1982). Largely, internal motivation is critical to leisure because it has been shown to be associated with more enjoyment (Csikszentmihalyi, 1975, 1978; Csikszentmihalyi & Graef, 1979) and higher levels of effect and involvement (Csikszentmihalyi, 1978).

The Controversy

Because of the potential for both positive and negative behavior during free time, one of the major philosophical controversies in leisure education relates to the approach to be used to educate for leisure. Free time provides for people the optimum availability of discretionary behavior. During leisure, individuals have the opportunity to live more by their inner directions, motivations, and needs, and with less restrictions and external controls, than in any other situation. In essence, one is free to make choices and decisions and thus to engage in the widest ranges of human activity life affords. The individual has the freedom to choose meaningful avenues of human experiences that are at the moment compatible with his or her inner feelings and needs. Free time allows one to be freely and uniquely one's self. As Brightbill (1966) has so aptly stated, "tell me what you do when you're free to do as you wish and I will tell you what kind of person you are" (p. 1).

It is during free time that individuals have the maximum opportunity to affect the quality of their lives in a positive or a negative direction. The positive potential for human life that is available during free time, contrasted with the numerous negative, neutral, and destructive uses of free time, has contributed to a controversy regarding the approach to educating for leisure.

Just as we have dealt with internal and external loci of control and motivation, there are two similar basic approaches that can be utilized in leisure education—the *extrinsic determination approach* and the *intrinsic determination approach*. *Extrinsic determination* refers to an individual or group who focuses upon instilling a predetermined set of leisure values and attitudes in people through leisure education. *Intrinsic determination*, in contrast, approaches the leisure education process from the standpoint of facilitating each person's ability to think through, evaluate, and make his or her own leisure choices and decisions. It also helps individuals to understand the impact of their choices on their individual lives, on others, and on society.

Advocates of extrinsic determination tend to believe that there are universal leisure attitudes, values, behaviors, and tastes that are necessary to gain the full benefits of leisure. They believe the task and goal of leisure education is to impart these predetermined qualities to children and adults alike and to convince the participants that these precepts are the proper parameters of leisure behavior by which to live. Extrinsic determinism assumes that these attitudes, values, and behaviors are universally right, good, satisfying, and enhancing for everyone. Therefore, the approach for transmitting these predetermined "sets" is through moralizing, inculcation, indoctrination, and persuasion. The assumption behind the extrinsic approach, stated by Simon, Howe, and Kirschenbaum (1972) runs like this:

> My experience (and professional training) has taught me a certain set of values, which I believe would be right for you. Therefore, to save you the pain of coming to these values on your own, and to avoid the risk of your choosing less desirable values, I will effectively transfer my own values to you. (p. 16)

External deterministic writers point out that the approach is becoming less effective because of the bombardment of conflicting values and behaviors being urged upon people from parents, teachers, friends, peers, bosses, co-workers, and others. The writers also say that people are not prepared to make their own responsible choices because "they have not learned a process for selecting the best and rejecting the worst of what is being urged upon them" (Simon et al., 1972, p. 16).

Another problem with the extrinsic determination theory identified by Simon et al. (1972) is that "it results in a dichotomy between theory and practice; lip service is paid to the values of the authority, while behavior contradicts these values." It "frequently influences only people's words and little else in their lives" (p. 17).

The "wise" or "worthy" use of leisure is one of the predominant goals of leisure education that emanates from the extrinsic determination approach. As usually occurs, what is considered wise or worthy leisure experiences, behaviors, and choices are based on norms or on others' judgment, and are normally handed down or passed onto people who are then urged to accept these standards and to live by them. Individuals are not provided opportunities for decision making regarding what they consider wise or worthy leisure choices and experiences, as is done with occupations and careers. They are likewise not generally provided with learning experiences to develop the skills needed for making their own responsible choices, as is done with health or family issues.

Other proponents of the extrinsic determination position believe, as does Neulinger (1974), that leisure education is ". . .

a conscious, systematic effort to bring about an attitude favorable toward leisuring . . ." (p. 158), and that the function and purpose of leisure education is to change people's attitudes in a predetermined direction. Kabacs (1965) also has focused on exposing elementary school children to the concepts and values of leisure as well as on methods of shaping their attitudes toward discretionary time. Staley (1976) said about people, "We need to help them change their attitudes toward the creative, self-actualizing use of leisure in the process of discovering their own significance" (p. 3). This concern for changing people's attitudes toward leisure carries with it the unstated assumption that current attitudes need to be changed to predetermined, "better" attitudes—in that, at best, people's attitudes are not developed enough to effectively contribute to meaningful leisure experiences. Although there may be some validity in this last statement, such a gross over-generalizational and indoctrinational approach should not be the springboard and primary goal of leisure education. Attitudes may, and most probably will, change as a result of the leisure education process.

Other supporters of the extrinsic philosophy see leisure education programs as being important to and inextricably tied with the fate of society and, therefore, advocate the development of attitudes, behaviors, and values that would benefit society. Jacks (1932) was a strong proponent of leisure education as an instrument of social change. Ragnathan (1954) maintained that a change in the character of a nation's leisure could change the character and efficiency of that nation, making leisure education no incidental task in any culture. Staley (1976) says, "Helping to shape a new culture for a new civilization is indeed one of our most critical problems and exciting challenges" (p. 3). This book takes a different approach.

Although it is recognized that leisure education can make significant contributions to both individuals and society, the focus upon the individual should take precedence over social purpose. The benefits of leisure and, therefore, leisure education, belong predominately to each person and only secondly to society. If leisure education focuses upon developing within each person the potential to enrich and enhance the quality of life in leisure, it follows that there will be positive societal benefits. The converse is not necessarily true, as can be seen historically when nations have subjugated the individual will to serve the national and societal interest.

Harmin, Kirschenbaum, and Simon (1973) observe that people do not need more values imposed upon them. They believe individuals do need to learn skills that will help them to deal with the multiplicity of problems and alternatives in today's complex society. "For this reason it is more effective to teach the process of valuing than it is to teach one set of values" (p. 32).

Responsible and worthy leisure experiences are definitely desired outcomes of the leisure education process. However, this outcome should come about as a result of individual determination and evaluation of one's own leisure choices, decisions, and values, not from "peer pressure, unthinking submission to authority, or the power of propaganda" (Simon et al., 1972, p. 16). Wise or worthy use of leisure as the principal focus and goal of leisure education to the subjugation of individual outcomes related to quality of life is contrary to both the essence of leisure and to leisure as a uniquely human experience.

Nevertheless, this change should be an outcome or byproduct of a process in which individuals examine, think through, and evaluate information—as well as their own goals, values, and attitudes—in order to determine if they would be able to reach the goals and the quality of life they desire in leisure with their current attitudes and values. This approach is vastly different from that of predetermining what are good and bad attitudes regarding leisure and then setting out to change people's attitudes or values systems to coincide with someone's idea of good or desirable leisure attitudes. Professionals who believe that leisure education programs should benefit the social order first and foremost also fall in the extrinsic camp.

There are three basic approaches that can be utilized in helping to foster the intrinsic determination of leisure behavior, attitudes, and values in people: 1) maintaining a laissez-faire attitude, 2) modeling, and 3) active facilitation. The approach of *maintaining a laissez-faire attitude* leaves people on their own to do and to think whatever they want without any intervention. The problem with this approach is that when people are left on their own, they may experience a great deal of conflict and confusion (Simon et al., 1972). Many people do want and need assistance, even though they may not want someone to tell them what they should think, how they should behave, and what they should value.

Modeling is a second approach that can be utilized in intrinsic determination. Through modeling, it is supposed that if one leads and lives an exemplary leisure life, those with whom one comes in contact will want to adopt and imitate this behavior. Although modeling acknowledges the importance of a living example, people are exposed to conflicting models (Simon et al., 1972), again without the tools or skills to determine what they want to accept or reject.

The *active facilitation approach*, as it is called here, advocates the intrinsic determination of one's own leisure interests, behaviors, attitudes, values, and choices as a result of the systematic facilitation of decision-making skills and opportunities to think through and evaluate leisure issues. This approach is the most compatible with assisting individuals to attain a sense of freedom and internal motivation, which is the essence of leisure. It attempts to enable people to 1) develop a cognitive, conscious awareness of their own behavior and beliefs, 2) establish criteria for leisure decisions and issues, and 3) develop skills related to enriching self-determination and meaningful control over their leisure lives.

In the active facilitation approach, there is active intervention; facilitators share and declare their own values, attitudes, choices, interests, and reasoning. However, the content, or answers, to personal leisure questions is not the central focus of active facilitation; rather, enabling people to go through the process of determining their own answers is the central focus. Therefore, active intervention into the process of intrinsic determination is non-judgmental of others' decisions and answers in terms of saying, "You are wrong," "That isn't good," "You shouldn't do that—what you should do is . . . ." Because there is sharing and declaring of one's own ideas, beliefs, and reasoning, the emphasis is changed to "I would not make that choice for the following reasons," "That is not an outcome or 'price' I would be willing to pay," "Because of what I value I could not do that," "I disagree with you on that because . . . ." The focus is on expressing one's own feelings, beliefs, and opinions—not on judging and attacking another's beliefs and actions. With the active facilitation approach, as with all other approaches in the end, the final answers and actions are up to the individual alone and may or may not coincide with one's own ideas of right-wrong, good-bad, or desirable-undesirable.

From a professional standpoint, utilizing the intrinsic determination of one's leisure life system, the role of any professional is not to have the answers to what people can and should do in leisure and what they should and should not value and believe. Such an approach may have been conceivable in 1946 when Anna Mae Jones developed a leisure education plan for the New York City schools to "... habituate youth to the worthy use of leisure" (Jones, 1946, p. 1). Nevertheless, at this point in our development as a society, approaches other than practitioners teaching or imparting their own set of values, attitudes, and behavior to others are available and are of more value.

In keeping with the nature of leisure as a uniquely individual phenomenon, the role and responsibility of the professional should be to focus on enabling people to find their own answers. In the extrinsic approach, someone else's values dictate how a person should live. In the intrinsic approach, the capacity of each person to live and function independently, proactively, and meaningfully in leisure is developed. There is a proverb that one often sees on posters: "If I catch a fish for a man, I can feed him for a day. If I teach a man to fish, he can feed himself for a lifetime." The aim in leisure education is to teach each person to fish—to enhance and enrich each individual's life far beyond the bounds of the professional's limited contact with each person. The ultimate success will be achieved when people can function independently and meaningfully because of professional expertise—rather than in spite of it—in living rich, full lives that include meaningful, enhancing leisure experiences.

In order to operationalize the varying concepts of leisure education, numerous approaches or models of leisure education have been developed. While there are various ways these models have been classified in the literature, one recognized classification, which parallels and emanates from the intrinsic and extrinsic approaches discussed here, breaks the models down into individual developmental models and socio-professional models (Mundy, 1990).

The Individual Developmental Models and the Socio-professional Models

The *individual developmental models* have as their primary focus the development of the individual regarding the leisure aspects of his or her life. These models approach the leisure education process from the

> standpoint of facilitating each person's ability to think through, determine, and evaluate his or her own leisure choices, behaviors, and decisions, as well as to understand the impact of these choices on his or her life, individual life, other people, and on society at large (Mundy, 1990, p. 19).

While these models focus upon the individual, "they operate within a cultural context where other cultural values, such as family values which may supersede individual values, can be taken into account" (p. 19). The role of the professional in these models is to act as a facilitator to enable people to determine, clarify, and evaluate their own answers to leisure-related questions, rather than to provide answers for people.

Socio-professional models of leisure education are models that primarily focus upon leisure as a social phenomenon first and the individual second. Socio-professional models tend to focus upon cognitive and theoretical understandings of leisure and its place and value in the lives of people and societies in general. These models are more informational in their orientation than applied (Mundy, 1990).

Socio-professional models operate from the following premises:

1. Leisure is inextricably woven into the fabric of society and, therefore, needs to be of benefit to society and utilized as an instrument of social change, political influence, and support for the delivery of services.

2. There are professionally predetermined, universally applicable leisure attitudes, values, behaviors, and tastes that are needed if the full benefits of leisure are to be realized by individuals and societies.

Socio-professional models approach educating for leisure by transmitting information on leisure and predetermined "sets" of attitudes, values, behaviors, and tastes through persuasion, moralizing, inculcation, and indoctrination. The role of the professional in the leisure education process is to act as the expert disseminator of information regarding leisure and leisure behavior. The professional is the authority with answers to people's questions. There are two aims of socio-professional models of leisure education. One aim is to have people understand leisure and its importance and value in order for them to exert political and economic influence to help professionals accomplish their leisure goals. A second aim is for individuals to understand leisure and its place and value in the lives of individuals and society and to be able to accept and incorporate those attitudes, values, behaviors and tastes that professionals feel must be promulgated in order to attain enhancing leisure. While the first aim may be a by-product of individual developmental models, it is not their primary aim.

Because of the foci and aims of the two models of leisure education, the individual model of leisure education holds the most potential for international application. While neither model is "culture-free," individual developmental models, by design, allow for the expression and appreciation of differences between and among individuals as well as cultures (Mundy, 1990, p. 20).

The intrinsic approach, and an accompanying individual developmental model, are the philosophical and applied basis of leisure education that is utilized in this text. In summary, this approach and model were chosen for the following reasons:

1. Philosophically and operationally, they are the most compatible with the concept of leisure.

2. They acknowledge and utilize the individual's personal needs, interests, and concerns as a basis of personal leisure development.

3. They acknowledge the individual's right to be self-determining in leisure and the process of leisure education.

4. They ask questions and provide information rather than providing "instruction" in the form of leader-determined answers.

5. They provide opportunities for clarification of personal leisure issues and values rather than imparting the facilitator's own values in the form of should's and ought-to's.

6. They develop the individual's skills in recognizing, assessing, evaluating, and acting in ways that are personally satisfying and socially responsible.

7. They are cognizant that externally promulgated values, choices, behaviors, and tastes can diminish one's feeling of freedom, internal motivation, and satisfaction, which are the essence of leisure.

8. They provide for on-going self-development and growth.

The Ultimate Challenge

A discussion of quality of life is often nebulous and often connotes a grandiose, lofty ideal that one hopes will occur somewhere, somehow; but, the results are often incapable of being measured or documented by the professionals involved. However, enabling individuals to enhance the quality of their own lives through leisure can be accomplished. It can be accomplished, first of all, because the experience of leisure itself, by its very nature, has the capacity to enrich and enhance one's life (Campbell, Converse, & Rodgers, 1976; London, Crandall, & Seals, 1977). Secondly, it can be accomplished because it is a philosophical ideal that can be translated into a programmatic structure, although working toward this end will, in many instances, necessitate breaking from traditional program means that have been utilized.

There are two dimensions of the quality of life concept that professionals must examine closely and must develop the techniques to impact upon. One dimension is the physical environment with which planners, sociologists, and environmentalists have been concerned. A second dimension involves psychosocial factors and conditions in one's life. These factors include the social, emotional, physical, spiritual, aesthetic, and material aspects of life. This dimension has primarily fallen into the behavioral science domain. Both of these dimensions of quality of life are open to change and can be positively influenced by professionals in leisure services.

The first dimension, the physical environment, refers to the qualities or properties of community life that contribute to quality living for the citizens of that community. These attributes often include pleasing business and residential areas that are clean, safe, and interesting environs; aesthetically pleasing public and private structures and buildings; quality educational, health, and human services; landscaped streets and highways; quiet wooded parks and greenbelts; and a socially, culturally stimulating atmosphere (Crohn, 1982). Research has shown not only that people prefer these kinds of physical-social environs but also that these types of environs are associated with living "the good life." Therefore, the physical leisure environment of the total community becomes an important aspect of the quality of life. The leisure professional can help influence this aspect of the environment through the quality of leisure programs, services, areas, and facilities provided for her clientele.

The psychosocial factors and conditions related to people's perceptions of their quality of life are also open to change and can be facilitated through planned intervention techniques and strategies. Through systematic and purposeful program design that takes into account the unique needs and interests of people, participants can be helped to achieve personal, social, emotional, physical, and aesthetic goals *that the individual perceived as quality enhancing*. Again, the focus and approach to life enhancement resides in enabling individuals to learn how to select, modify, and change elements of life through their decision-making capacity and the development of leisure skills. It is critical that people develop the knowledge and skills to enhance the quality of their own lives through leisure because, in the final analysis, the only person who can ultimately determine what and how experiences enhance life is the individual living the experience, feeling the emotions, and sensing the sensations. Although there may be external behavioral indices that act as windows through which one can catch glimpses of the internal dynamics in operation, such clues are indicators at best.

In conclusion, it is not the intention or purpose of leisure education to enable people to live continually at a "peak" or "high." This is too unrealistic an expectation. Life in general is far too variable and complex to sustain such a level of existence for extended periods of time. Therefore, the aim of leisure education is to enable people to reach a relatively higher plateau, to have leisure experiences that fall in the upper level of the satisfying, enriching, enhancing end of the life continuum and to be able to attain this level of satisfaction through one's efficacy.

Chapter 1 References

Bandura, A. (1978). The self-system in reciprocal determinism. *American Psychologist, 33*(4), 344-358.

Bordin, E.S. (1979). Fusing work and play: A challenge to theory and research. *Academic Psychology Bulletin, 1*(1), 5-9.

Brightbill, C.K. (1966). *Education for leisure-centered living.* Harrisburg, PA: Stockpole.

Campbell, A., Converse, P.E., & Rodgers, W.L. (1976). *The quality of American life: Perceptions, evaluations, and satisfaction.* New York: Russell Sage Foundation.

Crohn, L. (1982). *Consideration for establishing a positive community climate.* Portland, OR: Northwest Regional Educational Laboratory.

Csikszentmihalyi, M. (1975). *Beyond boredom and anxiety.* San Francisco, CA: Jossey-Bass.

Csikszentmihalyi, M. (1978). Intrinsic rewards and emergent motivation. In M.R. Lepper, & D. Grene (Eds.), *The hidden costs of reward* (pp. 205-216). Hillsdale, NJ: Lawrence Erlbaum & Associates.

Csikszentmihalyi, M., & Graef, R. (1979). Feeling free. *Psychology Today, 13,* 84-85.

Csikszentmihalyi, M., & Graef, R. (1980). The experience of freedom in daily life. *American Journal of Community Psychology, 8*(4), 401-414.

Dua, P. (1970). Comparison of the effects of behaviorally oriented action and psychotherapy reeducation on intraversion, extraversion, emotionality, and internal vs. external control. *Journal of Counseling Psychology, 17,* 567-572.

Ellis, A. (1987). The impossibility of achieving consistently good mental health. *American Psychologist, 42*(4), 364-375.

Ellis, M., & Witt, P. (1984). The measurement of perceived freedom in leisure. *Journal of Leisure Research, 16*(2), 110-123.

Gillis, J., & Jessor, R. (1970). Effects of brief psychotherapy on belief in internal control. *Psychotherapy: Research and Practice, 7,* 135-137.

Gray, D., & Greben. (1974). Future perspectives. *Parks and Recreation, 9*(6), 26-33.

Harmin, M., Kirschenbaum, H., & Simon, S.B. (1973). *Clarifying values through subject matter: Applications for the classroom.* Minneapolis, MN: Winston Press.

Harvey, J.H. (1976). Attributions of freedom. In J.H. Harvey, W.J. Iches, & R.F. Kidd (Eds.), *New directions in attributions research* (pp. 73-96). Hillsdale, NJ: Lawrence Erlbaum & Associates.

Iso-Ahola, S. (1980). *Social psychological perspectives on leisure and recreation.* Springfield, IL: C.C. Thomas.

Jacks, L.P. (1932). *Education through recreation.* New York: Harper.

Jones, A.M. (1946). *Leisure time education.* New York: Harper.

Kabacs, G.H. (1965). Automation, work, and leisure: Implications for elementary education. *The Vocational Guidance Quarterly, 13*(3), 202-205.

Kelly, J.R. (1982). *Leisure.* Englewood Cliffs, NJ: Prentice Hall.

London, M., Crandall, R., & Seals, G.W. (1977). The contribution of job satisfaction to qualify-of-life. *Journal of Applied Psychology, 62*(3), 328-334.

Mischel, W., Zeiss, R., & Zeiss, A. (1974). Internal-external control and persistence: Validation and implications of the Stanford Preschool Internal-External Scale. *Journal of Personality and Social Psychology, 29*(2), 265-278.

Mundy, J. (1990). Education for leisure across cultures. *World Leisure and Recreation, 32*(4), 19-22.

Neulinger, J. (1974). *The psychology of leisure.* Springfield, IL: C.C. Thomas.

Neulinger, J. (1981). *The psychology of leisure* (2nd ed). Springfield, IL: C.C. Thomas.

Peterson, C.A., & Gunn, S.C. (1984). Therapeutic recreation program design. Englewood Cliffs, NJ: Prentice-Hall.

Ragnathan, I.R. (1954). *Education for leisure.* London: G. Blunt & Sons.

Simon, S.B., Howe, L.E., & Kirschenbaum, H. (1972). *Values clarification.* New York: Hart.

Skinner, B.F. (1977). In A. Bandura (Ed.), *Social learning theory.* Englewood Cliffs, NJ: Prentice-Hall.

Staley, E.J. (1976). The struggle for significance. *Leisure Today Journal of Physical Education and Recreation.* Washington, D.C.: American Alliance for Health, Physical Education and Recreation.

Steiner, I.D. (1970). Perceived freedom. In L. Berkowitz (Ed.), *Advances in experimental social psychology.*

Tinsley & Tinsley. (1986). A theory of attributes, benefits, and causes of leisure experience. *Leisure Sciences, 8*(1), 1-45.

Yalom, I.D. (1980). *Existential psychotherapy.* New York: Basic Books.

Zeyen, D., Odum, L., & Lancaster, R. (1977). *Kangaroo kit: Leisure education curriculum.* Washington, D.C.: National Recreation and Park Association.

Leisure Problems of People

Chapter Overview

Chapter Two outlines selected problems people have with life in general and suggests possible origins of these difficulties. Problems are described as well as showing how they may be manifested in leisure-related ways. Some of the problems addressed are lack of conscious awareness of leisure, low self-esteem, negative leisure socialization, inertia, the inability to discriminate along a continuum, preconceived expectations, locus of control, boredom, and lack of time.

Introduction

Frequently, when discussing the fact that one is in the field of recreation and leisure, people will make comments such as "You need to tell me how to get some leisure," or "I try to stay busy because I get bored when I have too much leisure." All too often, comments such as these, from friends or from participants, elicit a flip or superficial response. In the past, professionals in the field may not have taken such comments as seriously as the individual with whom one was conversing meant the comment. If serious responses were given, they tended to be simplistic and superficial answers such as "work fewer hours" or "take up a hobby."

Today, we realize that people do have problems with leisure. In order for recreation and leisure personnel to facilitate the development of meaningful and satisfying leisure lives, it is necessary to understand some of the problems people have with leisure. It is likewise important to be acquainted with some of the possible origins of these problems and how they may be manifest in leisure.

It should be pointed out that many leisure problems are simply problems people may have with life in general that are manifested in leisure-related ways. While there may be some difficulties that could be categorized as only leisure problems, these are few indeed. Also, as with all behavior, there can be diverse behavioral manifestations stemming from the same cause. One person may respond to fear with rage, while another may withdraw into himself. Along this same line, one behavior can stem from many differing causes or precipitants. For example, rage can come from fear, from anger, or from frustration of needs. Therefore, this chapter will deal with the most prevalent manifestations and the most frequently identified sources of problems people may have with leisure. No attempt will be made to cover all of the possible options.

A Lack of Conscious Awareness of the Leisure Aspect of Life

There are people who are unaware, at a conscious level, of the leisure aspect of their lives. Without such an awareness, an individual's ability to make leisure a meaningful and viable part of her life can be seriously diminished. The lack of conscious awareness can stem from several different causes. For example, there are individuals who periodically or continually live on "automatic." They are creatures of habit who live by routine and by reacting to external forces or stimuli. They are not consciously aware of, in tune with, or sensitive to what is happening with and to their lives. Some of these individuals "just never think about leisure." They are even unaware of when they have the potential for leisure. They simply go through the day with a low conscious awareness of what is happening with and to their lives.

People can also be unaware of leisure because it has not been brought to their attention in such a way that they understand the term and its meaning as a part of their lives. They may not have the verbal label of "leisure" to attach to experiences or they may not know to which experiences to attach the label.

For other individuals there are, in their estimations, more pressing, compulsory demands for their time and attention. They don't think about what is not clamoring for their immediate attention or action. Leisure is frequently crowded out and not a part of their conscious awareness or their lives.

Low Self-esteem

Few problems have more diverse behavioral manifestations than low self-esteem. It is also an area of difficulty that can produce almost totally divergent behaviors stemming from the same root. The following are examples of some of the ways low self-esteem may affect the individual in leisure-related ways.

At its most basic level, low self-esteem can make people think they are unworthy and undeserving of leisure as well as of the fun and enjoyment that may accompany it. This can cause them to not take time for leisure nor to seek enjoyable and enriching experiences. In other instances, a sense of guilt can be generated when the person takes time for himself or when the person has too good a time. Individuals with low self-esteem may not believe in the value of some of their abilities, talents, capabilities, or judgments. Also, they don't like to stand out in a group or to be noticed for fear of judgment and ridicule; therefore, they may not try new experiences or not participate in other experiences around certain people or groups. When complimented on an accomplishment, a performance, or admirable ability, there may be a negating of the worth of the task and disclaimers regarding its value or importance. This can be expressed through phrases such as "I can't do that" or "Oh, that's nothing . . . anyone could do that."

Because individuals with low self-esteem believe themselves to be unworthy and of little value, their behavior is heavily outer/other-directed. Such persons may feel that other people (particularly those perceived as significant others) possess more worth than they. In turn, they will tend to be overly responsive to valued others. In some instances, such individuals will even give up their own leisure. They will do what other people want them to do and what they think others expect of them in leisure. In return, they mistakenly think they will receive love, respect, security, or the like. Individuals who are overly responsive to external, outer-directed influences are particularly vulnerable to societally transmitted expectations. The "have to's," "should's," "musts," and "ought to's" will have a tendency to dominate much of their decision-making process. It is quite common to hear "I don't even have leisure because there are too many things I have to do." As was mentioned in the introduction, this same type of behavior can have other origins, such as social learning, which will be discussed shortly.

Low self-esteem can also be one of the causes of overcommitment. It is difficult for people with low self-esteem to say "no" or be uninvolved in whatever is going on. They do not want people unhappy with them for saying "no" nor do they want to be left out. They may also fear not being asked again. Being in on everything, staying busy, and having too much to do says, "I'm valuable. I'm important. I'm needed."

These examples highlight only a few of the most frequently encountered difficulties with low self-esteem as they are manifest in leisure. Again, the reader should keep in mind that these same behaviors may have roots other than difficulties with self-esteem and that may produce additional types of behaviors that have not been enumerated.

Social Learnings

Every individual undergoes a process of socialization whereby the social agents in society (i.e., parents, teachers, peers, television, etc.) pass along the accepted norms of behaviors, values, customs, traditions, and role expectations of the society within which the individual resides. It is an attempt to develop the individual into the type of social being that the culture, group, or subgroup believes should exist. The difficulties that arise relating to leisure tend to be twofold: 1) negative leisure socialization and/or 2) socialization that is counter to the development of positive leisure lifestyles. In the first instance, a person receives messages that, in essence or actuality, communicate that "Work is the important thing in life. Play is childish and not important in real life." In the second instance, there are not necessarily negative messages related specifically to leisure. It is simply the transmission of values, beliefs, and behaviors that are not conducive to, or are contrary to, leisure living.

An example of these for adults would be the messages that are communicated regarding the "successful" person, the "dedicated, conscientious" student, the employee "who is going places." These communications, in essence, say that success is measured by an individual's position, status, salary, possessions, and how busy a person is, how much in demand a person is, and how much responsibility a person is given. Also, today there is "job image": how one is perceived to regard her job and how work has been tied to messages regarding work behaviors. The messages say that long work hours equate with dedication to the job and a high level of motivation, aspiration, and seriousness regarding work. For numerous individuals in American society today, this is contributing to more time being spent working, on and off the job. While these types of messages do not say outright that leisure, recreation, and play are not an important part of life, they imply that if you want to be successful, you won't *take* time to play . . . you won't *have* time to play.

Numerous problems people have with leisure are directly related to their social learning from the societal messages they have received as a part of their socialization. Other problems, such as guilt and worry, may be spin-offs from one's social learning. When an individual internalizes values and behaviors that are not conducive to meaningful leisure and then goes counter to those values and behaviors by playing, guilt and worry can occur. Guilt, it should be noted, is one of the most frequently encountered problems related to leisure.

According to Wayne Dyer, in *Your Erroneous Zones,* guilt is viewed as someone else's idea of how we should behave that we have internalized (1976). Another view of guilt is real or imagined transgressions. Whichever view of guilt is held, it is evident that part of the dynamics involve one's socialization regarding how you "should" behave and how life "should" be lived. For example, an individual may have received messages that the "good" mother does everything for her family, sacrificing her own wishes, time, energy, and interests. If she then wants to engage in some experiences to meet her own needs and has to forgo some of the family obligations, she may sense a feeling of guilt because she believes she is committing a transgression against the family she loves and values. Only after we have reevaluated many of the standards and expectations that we have learned in light of our own value system and how we decide *we* want to live our life can we determine whether or not our transgressions are real or imagined.

Overchoice is another difficulty that an individual may have that can stem from societally transmitted messages. We may feel that we or our children need to try to do it all, see it all, or have it all. This belief system can be associated with work, family, and free time, all of which can impact leisure. It is not uncommon in our society for parents to have their children in numerous recreation activities or to attempt to see and do everything during a vacation. This can lead to feeling pressured, rushed, and harried, even during times when one has the option to set one's own pace. Overchoice can also be a manifestation of compulsive activity, which is attempting to mask loneliness and perceived meaningless.

Societally, transmitted messages can also be responsible for lessening enjoyment and satisfaction from leisure experiences. This stems from the basis of selection of one's experiences. An individual may select experiences because they are in vogue—the fad—due to their reference group affiliation or because of the individual(s) who may be involved in the experience. When factors other than the enjoyment, enrichment, and satisfaction of the experience take precedent, the possibility of diminishing the quality of the experience is increased. It can also cause inactivity because of difficulty in making choices.

Inertia

As you may recall from physics, *inertia* is the tendency of matter to remain stationary (or continue in motion) unless acted upon by an outside force. The focus of this fourth problem area will be the "tendency to remain inert or stationary." It is being called *inertia* because of how people generally describe their difficulties. You may hear phrases such as, "I really would like to do something besides just sitting home and watching television. However, I am just too tired and burned out to do anything." Others may say, "There is nothing that I find that is interesting or fun" or "There is a lot I think would be nice to do, but I'm just not motivated to do anything. I'm drained at the end of the day."

While it is possible that many individuals are involved in physical labor as a part of their jobs, there are far more people whose sense of physical fatigue is due to sedentary, stressful, high-tension, high-anxiety situations. Frequent expressions of fatigue that are restricting without any apparent physical problems or exertion can be caused from the aforementioned sources. Therefore, what one may be dealing with is actually stress, tension, and anxiety that are verbally expressed and physically felt as fatigue.

Inertia can also occur when the perceived payoffs of an experience do not appear to be worth the apparent effort . . . or any effort. In instances like this, the individual may have received little previous satisfaction from leisure and, therefore, cannot relate to or anticipate receiving satisfaction in the future. Inertia, which can be associated with lessened motivation, can result from frustration, depression, feelings of helplessness, and feelings of hopelessness. These feelings can be temporary in nature and not indicative of pathology, or they can be associated with emotional disorders. In both instances, however, the individual may have a lessening of motivation to do anything in leisure and have a lowered level of aspiration regarding leisure and life in general. When working with people evidencing inertia, the professional should be aware of some of the possible causes of this behavior. The apparently simple explanation of fatigue does not necessarily reflect the problem.

The Inability to Discriminate Along a Continuum

An individual's lack of ability to discriminate along a continuum can produce all or nothing thinking. The individual sees and judges people or situations in terms of polar opposites. A particular leisure experience will be judged as either good or bad, fun or boring. The person's own abilities or performances can be viewed also as good or bad, right or wrong. The person does not tend to see levels, gradations, and variations. Things are viewed as either black or white with only a theoretical awareness of any gray areas. In their own mind, degrees do not tend to exist.

The person who has difficulty discriminating along a continuum will also tend to generalize one characteristic or attribute to their total self or to a situation or activity. A person may say, "I don't care about leisure because I don't care about playing games" or "I don't want any leisure because I can't stand to be idle." When this occurs, the person is generalizing about leisure being associated with only one kind of experience. The same type of generalization can also occur in the selection of leisure experiences that may be new and yet untried. For example, one may state, "I don't think I would like macrame because I tried ceramics once and I didn't like it. I'm not an artsy-craftsy person." In this instance, the person has cut off a multitude of leisure options based on one experience in a program category.

People who have difficulty with continuum differentiation will also tend to view themselves and others as sets of consistent and unchangeable traits. That is, they tend to believe, "You either have it or you don't." This thinking is applied all the way from "having" talent, skills, knowledge, competence, and looks to will power. Phrases like, "I can't do that; I don't have any talent" or "I'm just not one of those lucky people who can be at ease in a crowd," express this mind set. These individuals do not tend to see behavior and characteristics as learned skills, decisions, and behaviors that are situation-related. This same type of thinking can affect each person's beliefs and attempts at change in each person's life. They may not even attempt change or abort attempts if success is not instantaneous. The inability to discriminate along a continuum can block meaningful leisure experiences for people. And unfortunately, it will frequently occur before the person has even tried or explored a possible area of potential enjoyment and satisfaction.

The Presence of Preconceived Expectations

Most people, when anticipating an event, will conjure up in their mind's eye a scenario of what they think the event may be like. This "mind picture" may range along the continuum from positive to negative. The picture that is in one's mind is frequently the basis of decision making in leisure . . . even if and when that picture is inaccurate and has no basis in fact; it is a preconceived idea of what is expected.

Preconceived expectations can also be problematic during a leisure experience. If the actual experience does not measure up to the anticipated and preconceived experience, the person may abort the experience, stay in the experience but psychologically abandon it, anticipate another experience that will come after that one is over, or begin remembering past meaningful experiences. Preconceived expectations can rob people of the joy of living in the here and now. People will tend to go from one experience to another searching for experiences that will fit their images. Since many of the images and expectations are from media and advertising, more frequently than not, the preconceived expectations will far outdistance reality. When this situation exists, the person's primary style of living is searching for what they have been told life and experiences should be like rather than utilizing their own powers of self-determination through decision making to impact upon their own experiences and to help make their experiences and lives what they want them to be.

Negating Responsibility for Self: Lack of Internal Locus of Control

When an individual negates responsibility for himself, it may be manifest in several ways. One of the ways is when individuals blame other people, situations, circumstances, and just plain luck for why they are what they are, and how they behave. If they do not have leisure, it is the boss's fault for being so demanding that they can never take time off from the job. If they don't enjoy a party, it is because the people who were invited were bores.

Another way of negating responsibility for self or in manifesting a lack of internal locus of control is when individuals do not exercise the control and opportunities for self-determination that exist within their lives. They do not exercise the control they do have through their decision-making abilities because they really believe they cannot affect their own lives. They feel what happens (or does not happen) in their lives is due to other people, situations, or circumstances that they cannot control. These individuals have lacked opportunities for affecting and controlling their own lives through their own decisions and choices. Their environments have not been ones in which to experience mastery. Therefore, the person will tend to wait for good things to happen to them or seek positiveness in sources outside of themselves. They believe what they want out of life is out there hiding somewhere and if they look hard enough, and are lucky enough, they just may stumble across it. They feel they are merely passive recipients of what life has to offer. They believe events, circumstances, and other people control their lives.

Of all of the problems people have that are manifest in leisure-related ways, there are few others that have more of a profound impact upon the individual's capacity for meaningful leisure experiences that can enhance the quality of life than not utilizing their own capacity for self-determination through the choices and decisions they can make.

Boredom

Boredom is one of the leisure problems that has been identified and discussed in considerable detail and is, therefore, familiar to recreation and leisure professionals. Boredom is a condition resulting from stimulation deficit or overload. Since overload is also associated with overchoice, which has already been discussed, stimulation deficit will be the focus of this discussion. It is most frequently associated with doing the same thing, in the same way, with the same people, in the same environment, with no variation over time. The nature of the human nervous system demands variety, stimulation, and novelty that is perceived as meaningful. When deprived of such variety and stimulation, feelings of discomfort and unpleasantness occur. Boredom results when the individual does not adjust or regulate his or her behavior to offset the perceived sameness of daily experiences.

The work of Iso-Ahola (1984) gives a significant insight into some of the factors associated with boredom and leisure. Iso-Ahola says that first and foremost among these factors is the lack of awareness of the psychological value of leisure, not a lack of awareness of leisure opportunities. He states, "This finding would seem to underscore the importance of leisure education in making people cognitively conscious of the potential of leisure to enrich their lives" (p. 11). Iso-Ahola also found that having a leisure ethic, a large repertoire of leisure activity skills, a high degree of self-motivation, and fewer constraints lessened perceived boredom in leisure. From this study, Iso-Ahola concluded that one must be psychologically prepared for leisure in order to decrease the chances of perceiving leisure as boredom. These findings further underscore the importance of leisure education, which aims at preparing people for satisfying leisure.

Another state that is frequently described as boredom is related to frustration of needs. Boredom may be felt when a need exists concomitantly with a preconceived expectation for fulfilling that need. If the preconceived idea of what will fill that need is not an available option at that point in time, the person may be highly agitated and frustrated and say he or she is "bored" or that they "don't have anything to do."

People will also say they are bored when they feel a need stirred and they want to do something but they are unable to identify what they want to do. This condition can result because 1) they can't identify the need they are feeling and thus don't know what would fulfill it, 2) they don't know the options that are available, or 3) none of the options they can think of are appealing at that moment. Again, the person can become agitated and frustrated. Boredom can be seen to contain an active and agitated state. It is not necessarily a passive condition.

Lack of Time

In today's world, perhaps one of the most frequently expressed problems people are aware of with leisure is their real or perceived lack of time. The real or perceived lack of time is often tied to other problems such as social learning and negating responsibility for self (lack of internal locus of control). Many people are choosing to use their time on activities in which they place high value and ones they perceive will contribute to attaining their goals, such as careers and career advancement, for which they have been socialized. Other are caught in the "have to's" and "should's," which can lead to feeling they "have to" do all of the things that currently fill their time and lives.

There are other individuals who do not realize their time and their lives are under their control and that it is their responsibility to make their life what they want it to be. This lack of an internal locus of control makes people believe their time (and their lives) are under the control of other people, such as their bosses, and cannot be influenced.

Lack of organizational skills and skills for the effective and efficient use of time also lead to feeling the time crunch. These individuals take more time to get the same tasks accomplished that an organized and efficient person can accomplish in half the time.

It must also be recognized there are individuals, such as single, working mothers, for whom the lack of time is very real. For this group of people, their time is devoted, of necessity, to daily living and subsistence tasks. In most instances, they have the sole responsibility for making a living, child rearing, keeping the home, and personal, family, and home maintenance.

When dealing with expressed problems of lack of time, it is necessary to determine with the client the actual nature of the problem before it can be dealt with effectively. Is it a lack of internal locus of control? Is it the person is choosing to respond to societally transmitted messages? Or is it a matter of lack of organization or a very real lack of time due to their life circumstances. The answers to these questions will aid the practitioner in providing the most beneficial assistance.

Intervention Strategies

In addition to understanding problems people may have with leisure, it is also necessary for facilitators to be familiar with possible strategies and techniques that can be used to help people deal with problems they may be having. The following section identifies each of the problems discussed and suggests possible intervention strategies that may be effective in addressing the problems.

Problem: Lack of Conscious Awareness

Possible Interventions

Help participants:

1. to understand how much of life can be lived on "automatic" as opposed to "consciously."

2. to understand that to be consciously aware of our time and our lives, in order to make the most of both, may require a conscious effort to do the following:
   - to remain "aware" in the here and now and project and plan future events.

3. to understand the term leisure; which in turn will help to understand opportunities that exist, or that can be made to exist, for leisure.

Problem: Low Self-esteem

Possible Interventions

Help participants:

1. to use basic self-esteem strategies for increasing self-esteem in general.

2. to understand, reevaluate, and clarify for themselves the following:
   a. other people's expectations and demands,
   b. their belief system about feeling the need to meet others' expectations and demands,
   c. their belief system about overcommitting and overchoice.

Problem: Socialization

Possible Interventions

Help participants:

1. to understand the process of socialization and how it affects our belief system and behavior.

2. to reexamine, reevaluate, and clarify the following:
   a. negative leisure messages,
   b. messages that are not conducive to, or are at odds with, developing a satisfying leisure lifestyle.

3. to understand the origins of guilt and worry and how they are affected by socialization:

a. To understand guilt is related primarily to events in the *past*. These events are over and there is nothing that can be done to change the past; all we can do is move past the event, putting it behind us and make changes in our future behavior.
b. to realize guilt can also arise when contemplating a future action. In these instances, participants need to reexamine, reevaluate, and clarify the standards or expectations they have learned in light of their current values to determine which they want to maintain and which they want to change or discard.
c. to understand that worry is concern about *possible, future* negative consequences. Since much of what we worry about never comes to pass, it wastes energy to worry and take no action.
d. to realize worry can be useful if it leads us to plan and to take action regarding whatever is troubling us. Once we take all of the steps we can to prevent *possible,* negative consequences, that is all we can do. At this point we need to let go of our worry by consciously choosing non-worry thoughts and moving ahead so we do not waste energy on situations we cannot control or predict.

Problem: Inertia

Possible Interventions

Help participants:

1. to determine the possible source(s) of inertia:
   a. stress, tension, anxiety,
   b. frustration, depression.

2. to understand the link and physiological processes involved in stress, tension, and anxiety, leading to feelings of physical fatigue.

3. to explore large muscles and vigorous exercise that they may enjoy and would probably do, which could decrease feelings of physical fatigue.

4. to explore and develop skills in meditation and relaxation as alternatives to, or complementary to, exercise.

5. if depression or other psychological problems such as feelings of helplessness or hopelessness appears to be at the root of the inertia, to suggest someone trained to deal with these issues work with the individual or refer him or her to an appropriate professional.

Problem: The Inability to Discriminate Along a Continuum

Possible Interventions

Help participants:

1. to understand all-or-nothing thinking (seeing things in terms of polar opposites rather than along a continuum).

2. to provide experiences that focus on rating, ranking, or scaling issues, actions, behaviors, talent, skills, knowledge, and competence. For example: "On a scale of 1 to 10, how would you rate. . . ?" "Which choice do think is the most desirable?" "Rank the following on how important they are to you."

3. to deal directly with the issue that what may be perceived as "natural" talent or abilities is most often simply hard work and practice. You may want to share a personal vignette similar to the following for discussion:

   > I once said to a friend of mine who played the piano beautifully, "I would give anything to be able to play the piano like you." She replied, "Evidently anything except the hours of practice time it takes."

   Explore the ideas that
   a. We may wish for something but not enough to work for it. We would like it if someone could just sprinkle "pixie dust" on us and all of a sudden our wish would come true with no effort or energy on our part;

b. When we wish for something, and we do not back up by action; we are in essence making a choice or decision to *not* pursue it, for whatever reason.

4. to select a priority learning of their choice that they are willing to devote time and energy to developing. Assist them with planning, scheduling, evaluating, and supporting their efforts. Help participants focus on their progress along a continuum.

Problem: Preconceived Expectations

Possible Interventions

Help participants:

1. to understand the origin of many preconceived ideas such as advertisements and fiction on TV and in books. Discuss examples of preconceived ideas such as what Christmas (or any other holiday) or the perfect mate is supposed to be like and the origin of these ideas. Then help participants look at the reality of such situations.

2. to understand the possible impact of unrealistic preconceived ideas that become our expectations:
   a. causes us to search for "idealized," usually unrealistic, experiences, situations, and people;
   b. causes us to not enjoy what is "real" because we think there *should* be something closer to our idealized expectations;
   c. tends to cause us to search for the idealized, preconceived expectation;
   d. tends to cause us to not enjoy here and now experiences, situations, and people;
   e. tends to cause us to wait and search for the idealized rather than taking responsibility and using our personal power to effect our experiences and our lives.

Problem: Lack of Internal Locus of Control

Possible Interventions

Help participants:

1. to understand the dynamics in internal and external locus of control and how they are manifest in one's life (refer to Chapter 1).

2. to understand that one's locus of control can be changed.

3. to understand their own locus of control and its resulting beliefs system:
   - Dramatic shifts in consciousness have occurred in participants simply by being presented an alternate view of their own power for self-determination and self-responsibility.

4. to recognize the role of their own choices and decisions in life events and how other choices may have produced different results.

5. to practice alternative belief systems through:
   a. self-talk,
   b. vocal communications; for example, changing "I don't have time for leisure" to "I am not using the time I have for leisure."

6. to practice identifying options and possible outcomes of different options as a part of their decision-making process.

Problem: Boredom

Possible Interventions

Help participants:

1. to develop an awareness of the psychological value of leisure through value clarification so they can be consciously aware of the potential of leisure to enrich their lives.

2. to understand that boredom often occurs from doing the same thing, in the same way, with the same people in the same environments, with little or no variation over time:

    - to learn how to add variety to their daily lives in order to offset perceived sameness of their daily routines.

3. to understand the vast array of experience that can be considered leisure. Participants frequently perceive leisure experiences as only recreation activities.

4. to develop a repertoire of leisure interests and skills.

5. to develop an awareness of leisure opportunities in their areas of interests.

6. to tune into and become consciously aware of needs they may be feeling and what leisure experiences may help them satisfy those needs.

Problem: Lack of Time

Possible Interventions

Help participants:

1. to work on developing an internal locus of control.

2. to understand their time is under their control and that time and what we do with it is a matter of the choices we make.

3. to analyze their current time use patterns.

4. to clarify their values and priorities regarding how they want to spend their time.

5. to develop time management skills.

6. to develop organizational skills.

7. to develop and carry out a new time-use plan.

Chapter 6 on leisure education units provides some specific learning experiences related to the interventions outlined above. The reader should refer to the units in that chapter for more complete explanations and details on some of the interventions listed.

Summary

Many leisure problems are simply problems people may have with life in general that are manifested in leisure-related ways. It should be remembered that as with all behavior: 1) there are diverse behavioral manifestations stemming from the same problem, and 2) one behavior may stem from different precipitating causes.

Some of the problems addressed include a lack of conscious awareness of leisure, low self-esteem, negative leisure socialization, inertia, the inability to discriminate along a continuum, preconceived expectations, locus of control, boredom, and lack of time. There are strategies and techniques facilitators can use in helping people deal with problems they may be having with leisure. Aiding in the resolution of leisure problems is a responsibility the field must accept if it is to facilitate the leisure development of people.

Chapter 2 References

Dyer, W.W. (1976). *Your erroneous zones.* New York, NY: Avon Books.

Iso-Ahola, S. (1984). *Leisure and boredom: An analysis of causes and effects.* Paper presented at the NRPA Leisure Research Symposium. Orlando, FL.

Leisure Education Models

Chapter Overview

Conceptual models of leisure education are outlined in this chapter of the text. The models are divided into curriculum models and models using a systems planning approach for leisure education. The curriculum models were primarily developed to be used in school systems. These models include the Scope and Sequence of Leisure Education, the NRPA Leisure Education Advancement Project Model (LEAP), and the Leisure Education Curriculum developed by the National Curriculum Development Commission for the State of Israel.

Peterson's Leisure Education Content Model and two models developed by Mundy are the models using a systems planning approach for leisure education. Also, these models were specifically developed for use in recreation and leisure service systems.

Introduction

In order to develop leisure education programs that will enable people to both enrich and enhance the quality of their lives through leisure, conceptual models of leisure education can prove to be useful. Such models provide a programmatic guide and blueprint for the development of leisure education objectives, learning experience, and strategies.

Several contemporary conceptual models of leisure education have been developed since 1975. Each model reflects the individual model builder's perception of the goal of leisure education, as well as what they believe a program to educate for leisure should contain. While there is variety within the models, the common elements are numerous. The leisure education models tend to fall into two categories: 1) curriculum- or school-based models and 2) models using a systems planning approach. Systems models are ones developed using designations of major program components with each component broken into further levels of specificity called subcomponents. Each component and subcomponent provide the foundation upon which input, process, and output descriptions are designed.

Curriculum- or School-based Models

One contemporary curriculum is entitled, "The Scope and Sequence of Leisure Education." This model was developed by leisure service faculty and graduate students at Florida State University in cooperation with Florida State Department of Education personnel. The model (Figure 3.1) is comprised of 107 objectives arranged sequentially under six categories: 1) self-awareness, 2) leisure-awareness, 3) attitudes, 4) decision making, 5) social interaction, and 6) leisure activity skills.

The Scope and Sequence Model was developed by taking advantage of the advances in instructional design. The instructional design approach stipulates that in order to formulate any comprehensive educational program, one must first identify the goals of the program in terms of terminal objectives or behaviors. Terminal objectives refer to the behaviors an individual should exhibit as a result of the instructional process. A review of literature and the National Policy and Position Statement on Leisure Education (SPRE, 1972) served as a springboard upon which the goals for the Scope and Sequence Model were formulated. The goals for the model are that, as a result of leisure education, an individual will be able to 1) enhance the quality of life in leisure, 2) understand the opportunities, potentials, and challenges in leisure, 3) understand the impact of leisure on the quality of life individually and the fabric of society, and 4) have the knowledge, skills, and appreciations that enable broad leisure choices. From the stated goals, a breakout process was then employed to identify objectives that were necessary to accomplish the stated goals. Through this process it was found that the first goal was the predominate one. It was also apparent that this goal (to enhance the quality of one's life in leisure) makes leisure education new in focus, emphasis, process, and content. It is this goal that took leisure education out of the realm of 1) merely providing information regarding leisure, 2) developing knowledge and skills related to recreation activities, or 3) of just providing leisure opportunities through programming.

The Scope and Sequence Model presents a comprehensive set of objectives for a leisure education program—pre-kindergarten to retirement. The horizontal axis identifies six broad categories of a leisure education program: self-awareness, leisure-awareness, attitudes, decision making, social interaction, and leisure skills. The vertical axis presents progressive levels of objectives to be achieved. The objectives are divided into intervals according to areas of focus and suggested grade level and life cycle stages. By reading across the page, it is possible to discern the objectives to be achieved at any one stage of development that are common in focus. Figure 3.1 shows an example of the Scope and Sequence. The entire leisure education program can be found in the Appendix.

Notice that the Scope and Sequence Model encompasses not only the period during which one would be within educational systems but also periods throughout one's life. Also, some objectives would be generically appropriate for school age children, adults, or retirees, alike, whereas others would not be developmentally and intellectually appropriate. For example, both elementary children and adults may need to be aware of their own leisure and recognize the outcomes of their leisure choices. However, the methods and techniques utilized to obtain the objectives would differ greatly, as would the level of learning sophistication. On the other hand, adults will probably not need to identify life activities of group members such as one's family, friends, schoolmates, and so on. As with any developmental process—objectives, methods of presentation, as well as levels of sophistication and difficulty must be carefully selected and planned to meet individual or group needs, interests, and developmental levels. So it is the case with leisure education and the use of the Scope and Sequence Model. It was developed to be a guide, a tool, and a catalyst to facilitate the education-for-leisure process. Therefore, its use was to focus upon the selection

Figure 3.1
The Scope and Sequence of Leisure Education

Focus	Levels	Self-awareness	Leisure-awareness	Attitudes	Decision Making	Social Interaction	Leisure Skills
Awareness of life activities of self and the familly	Pre-K	Understands the role of self in family activities	Identifies own activities	Recognizes the various activities of the family	Is aware of making choices	Attends, takes turns, begins to share	Participates in leisure experiences in a variety of program areas
		Expands knowledge of self as an individual and as a group member	Identifies life activities of group members (family, school, etc.)	Appreciates activities of each member of the family unit	Is aware of the choices of self and others	Identifies elements that contribute to successful interaction with another individual	Identifies specific leisure activities and relates them to program areas
Leisure and leisure choices and experiences	Level I	Is aware of one's own leisure	Defines the meaning of leisure	Appreciates varying forms of human endeavor	Recognizes the decision-making process in relation to leisure	Identifies possible outcomes, varying types of social interaction and behavior	Develops basic skills and simple tool handling related to preferred leisure experiences

of appropriate objectives according to individual needs and the subsequent development of appropriate learning strategies and activities. (Grade and general life cycle references are shown for the purpose of *example only.*)

It should also be pointed out that since leisure education is viewed as a lifelong, continuous process, there are objectives that, while emphasized at a specific interval, are generic and important to achieve throughout life. An example of such an objective is found under the decision-making area in the last interval (retirement); the individual "chooses from a multitude of leisure choices, those most personally enhancing." Although this is particularly relevant as a *focus* during retirement, it is equally desirable and important during all phases of life.

Validation of the Scope and Sequence Model

Once the goals and accompanying objectives were formulated for a model of leisure education, pre-kindergarten to retirement, a joint meeting of Leisure Service and Studies faculty and educators from the State of Florida Department of Education was held. During this meeting, the educators, representing elementary and secondary education, analyzed the model for age appropriateness, developmental sequencing, wording of objectives, and compatibility of objectives with the stated goals of leisure education. Based upon the changes and refinements suggested, the Scope and Sequence Model in its present form was established. Closely following this meeting, the Society of Parks and Recreation Educator's Leisure Education committee held their first meeting in Tallahassee, Florida. During this two-day meeting, the committee reviewed and further analyzed the Scope and Sequence Model from a leisure frame of reference. Upon completion of the validation of the Scope and Sequence Model, experimentation was begun at Florida State University Developmental Research School with two randomly-selected, matched, first-grade classes. Because of the reading level of the students, all questions on the pretest and post-test had to be administered verbally. The following selected results of the 48 pretest interviews are particularly interesting.

One question included in the interviews with first-grade children was, "Tell me what the word *leisure* means. You may not have heard the word before, but what do you think it means?" In response to this question, the subjects showed not only varying ideas of what the word meant but also varying levels of sophistication and understanding. Selected answers in order of levels of comprehension were as follows: "I don't know," "I think it means nothing," "It is a break in the skin," "Something you carry a dog around on," "Doing things," "It means activities," "Coloring," "Play time," and "It is a time when I can choose what I want to do."

When the first graders were asked, "Who teaches you how to do some of the things you choose to do in leisure?" the responses overwhelmingly named in order of frequency of reply were the following people: mother, daddy, and my teacher. Not one child mentioned any type of leisure service personnel, although 80% of the children were involved in some form of organized recreation and leisure program. A probing technique was utilized in order to determine if the respondents perceived recreation personnel as being associated with teaching them how to do things they choose to do in leisure. Still, the respondents did not associate recreation personnel and departments with learning. On further probing, one comment was particularly revealing. A first grader was asked, "If the recreation people don't teach you things you can do in leisure, then what do they do? What is their job?" After thinking for a minute, the child said, "They are secretaries." He was then asked why he thought they were secretaries. He answered, "Well, they come out and play with us for a little while and then they go back and do their work at their desk. They are secretaries."

The most comprehensive curriculum model (K-12) was developed as a part of the Leisure Education Advancement Project (LEAP) of the National Recreation and Park Association. The entire curriculum is build around eight goals designed to be infused into the school curriculum regardless of the grade level or subject matter. The infusion process means that the goals and learning experiences can be incorporated into any grade level or subject matter. They were not designed to be a separate content area but instead an integral part of the entire educational process. The eight goals are as follows:

1. The student will understand that most life experiences can be leisure experiences. They can be active or passive, indi-

vidual or group, physical or mental, planned or spontaneous, anticipatory or reflective.

2. The student will understand that because leisure time is increasing, leisure—as well as work—must be viewed as a very important source of self-worth and dignity. It also influences the quality of life—even actual survival.

3. The student will understand the effects that dynamic interaction among natural and physical environments, social institutions, and individual lifestyles have on leisure opportunities, choices, and behaviors.

4. The student will identify, understand, and evaluate leisure resources available in the community, state, and nation; the student will develop appreciation for various modes that individuals have of utilizing these resources.

5. The student will recognize that leisure experiences are neither good nor bad. The value assigned is a matter of personal and societal judgment. He will recognize that leisure experiences are chosen because they seem appropriate to the individual.

6. The student will appreciate those intangible qualities of leisure experiences that transcend an individual's physical existence yet are experienced on the emotional and spiritual plane.

7. The student will recognize and evaluate the consequences each person's use of leisure has on human, social, constructed and natural environments. The student will recognize that each person is ultimately responsible for her own leisure as well as for influencing the community to suggest leisure opportunities.

8. The student will understand the potential of leisure as well as work, family, and other social roles in developing a life plan to insure continuing personal growth and satisfaction.

This curriculum model, contained in the "Kangaroo Kit," includes goals, objectives, learning activities, and strategies. It is divided into two volumes. One volume is for K-6 and the other volume is for grades 7-12 (Zeyen, Odum, & Lancaster, 1977). Woodburn (1978) developed a curriculum resource guide for teachers as a part of a Canadian leisure education project out of the Ministry of Culture and Recreation. Woodburn's approach suggested strategies for teachers to use in the classroom to focus on leisure. He outlined teachable moments, drawing leisure concepts out of subject matter, learning through recreation and leisure experiences, and focusing on leisure as a topic; all are viable means of educating for leisure.

The latest contemporary curriculum model was developed by the National Curricula Development Commission for the school system in the State of Israel. The Leisure Education Curriculum is a framework for leisure education within educational systems and encompasses kindergarten through twelfth grade.

The Leisure Education Curriculum is organized around three clusters of objectives: 1) objectives in the areas of knowledge, understanding, and awareness; 2) objectives in the areas of behavior, habits, and skills; and 3) objectives in the areas of emotions and value-oriented attitudes (Ruskin & Sivan, 1995). The goal of leisure education within this curriculum model is "to help the individual, the family, the community, and society achieve a desirable quality of life through wise use of leisure time" (Ruskin & Sivan). They recommend that leisure education be dealt with as an independent subject in the educational system as well as incorporated into different subjects that are a part of the total school curricula.

While these curriculum models were designed for teachers to use as guides for curriculum development, professionals in leisure and other disciplines can utilize the material to educate for leisure in their systems and their populations.

Models Using A Systems Planning Approach

The most widely recognized model of leisure education designed specifically for therapeutic recreation systems was developed by Peterson (1984). Peterson's model focuses upon leisure education as one of the three components of therapeu-

Figure 3.2
Peterson's Leisure Education Content Model

Leisure Awareness - 1.0	**Social Interaction Skills - 2.0**
1.1 Knowledge of leisure	2.1 Dual
1.2 Self-awareness	2.2 Small group
1.3 Leisure and play attitudes	2.3 Large group
1.4 Related participatory and decision-making skills	
Leisure Resources - 4.0	**Leisure Activity Skills - 3.0**
4.1 Activity opportunities	3.1 Traditional
4.2 Personal resources	3.2 Nontraditional
4.3 Family and home resources	
4.4 Community resources	
4.5 State and national resources	

tic recreation services. She conceptualizes leisure education as "a broad category of services that focuses on the development and acquisition of various leisure-related skills, attitudes, and knowledge" (p. 22). Figure 3.2 outlines the components and subcomponents of Peterson's model.

Peterson's model is based on a normalization concept. "Non-disabled individuals were studied to determine components of successful leisure involvement" (p. 25). Based on her investigation, the four general categories of leisure-awareness, social interaction skills, leisure resources, and leisure activity skills emerged as skills necessary for "leisure ability." Peterson states, "A cognitive understanding of leisure, a positive attitude toward leisure experiences, various participatory and decision-making skills, as well as a knowledge of, and the ability to utilize, resources appear to be significant aspects of satisfying leisure involvement" (p. 22).

Peterson's Leisure Education Content Model is generic in nature. It can be used in community settings with nondisabled populations as well as in clinical setting with persons with disabilities. Likewise, it is not designed for any specific disability or any specific clinical agency. The application of the model to any specific group or setting is up to the individual practitioner.

The Author's Leisure Education Models

Model building is a continuously evolving process. The experimentation and utilization of a model provides input regarding its usefulness and the critical and nonessential elements. It points out what is missing and what is superfluous. The following models have undergone such a process.

The first non-curriculum model developed utilized a systems planning approach. The program design in the Systems Approach (Figures 3.3, 3.4, & 3.5) is organized around five major program components, with each component broken into further levels of specificity through the use of subcomponents. Each component and subcomponent is accompanied by input and output descriptions. Processes to achieve the stated output or outcomes are not delineated, since there are many and varied processes that could be utilized to reach the outcomes.

In this model, although it was realized that decision making and social interaction could be contained within the leisure skills component, they were pulled out as separate components because of their importance in the leisure experience.

The 13 years of use with this model has led to revisions, additions, and deletions. The original model (1987) was organized into five major program components. However, the five components in the latest model have been reorganized into four program components: 1) leisure awareness, 2) self-awareness, 3) leisure skills, and 4) leisure resources. The previous components of decision making and social interaction were placed under leisure skills as program subcomponents. Figures 3.6A-C outline a new configuration, with progressively more specifically delineated subcomponents and potential behavioral outcomes. The most specific level of objectives, with accompanying suggested learning experiences, can be found in Chapter 6. Chapter 6 is where this latest model is translated into specific program units that can be used by practitioners in their leisure education programs. It is recommended the reader take an initial look through this chapter in order to more clearly understand the focus of the individual subcomponents in the model.

Figure 3.3
Leisure Education Components

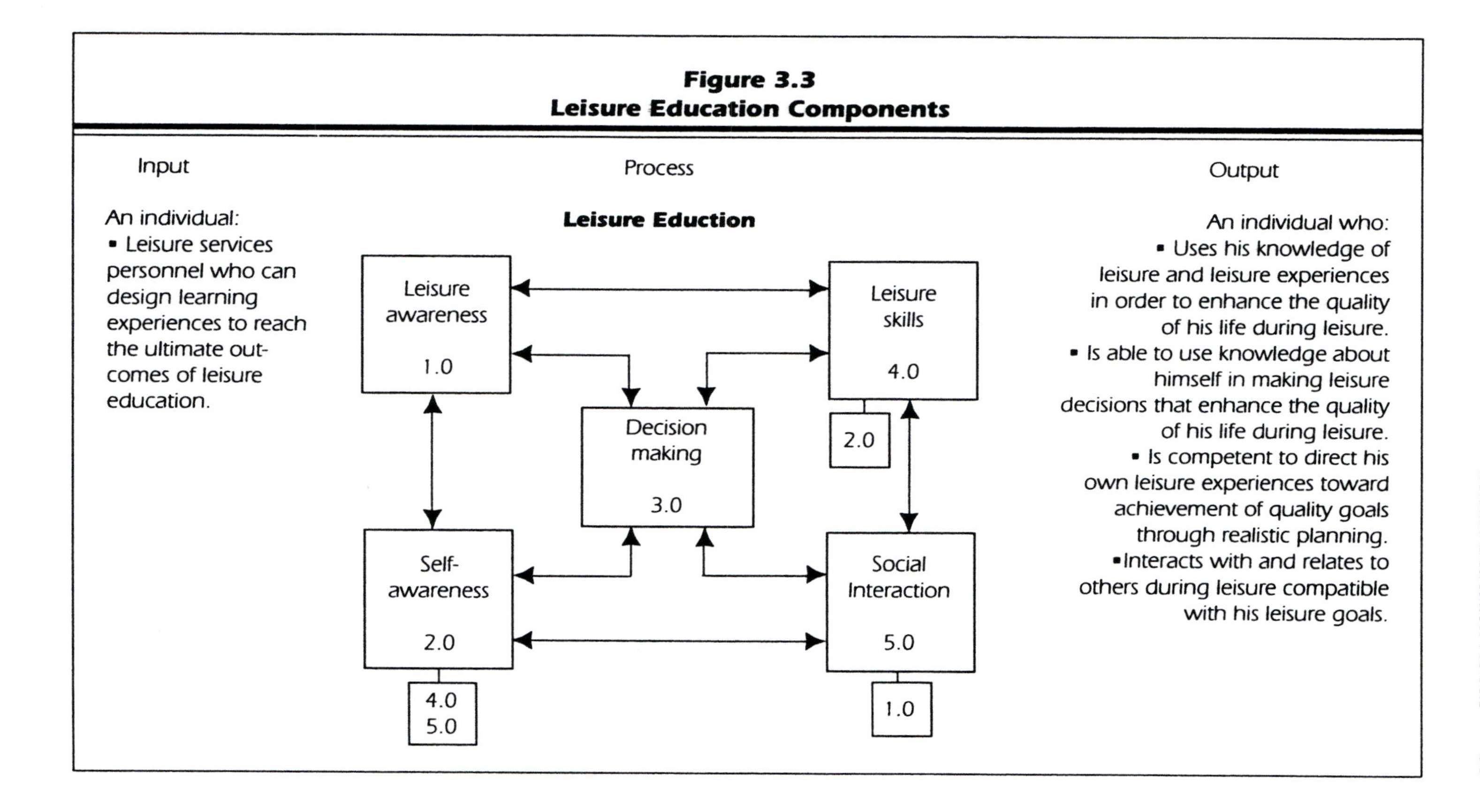

Figure 3.4
Leisure Education Components and Subcomponents

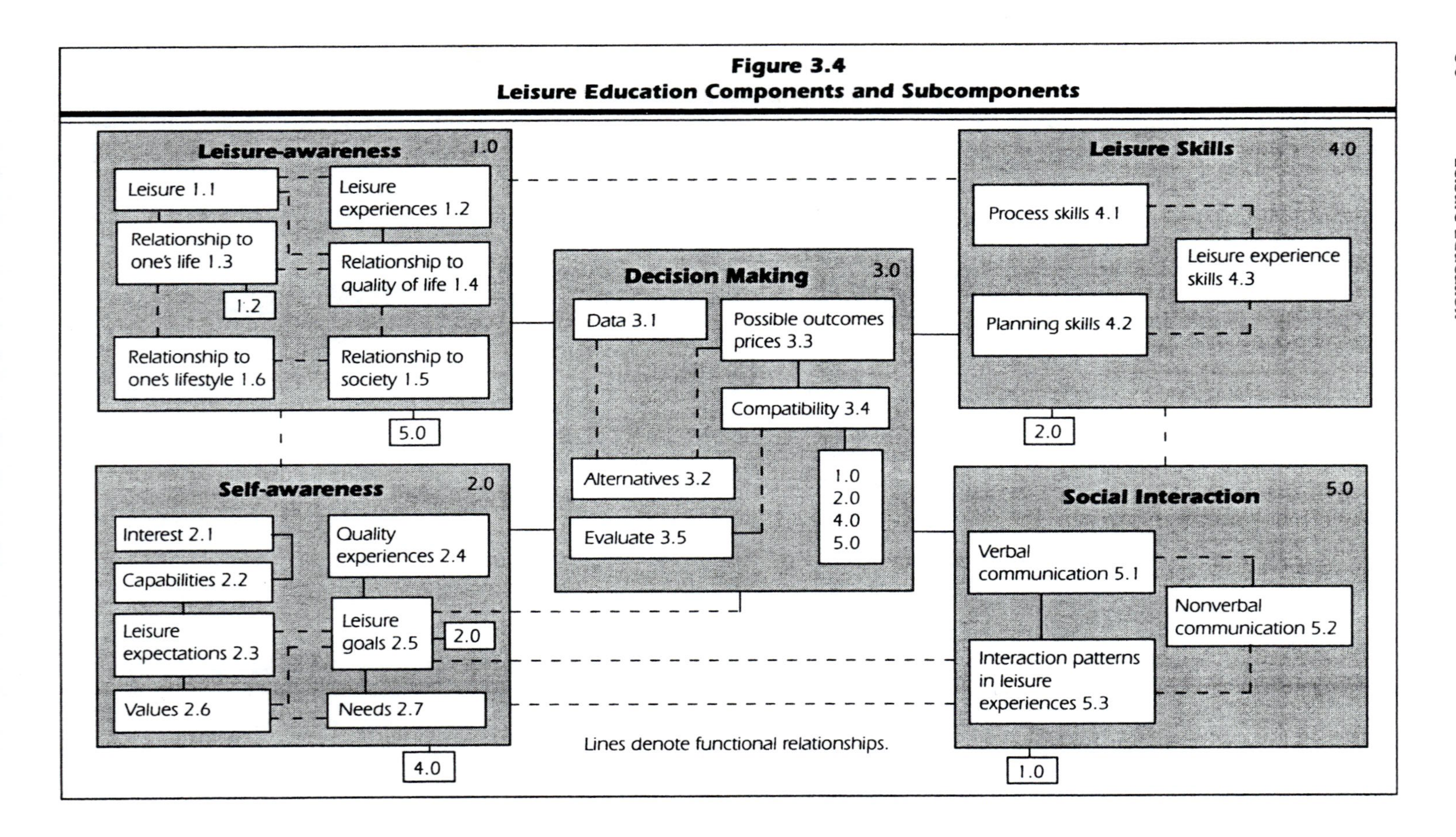

Figure 3.5
Input, Process, and Output of Leisure Education Subcomponents

Input	Process	Output
An individual:	Leisure awareness	An individual who:
Personnel trained in educating for leisure		Knows what leisure is Identifies a variety of leisure experiences Describes the relationship of leisure to his life Relates leisure to her lifestyle Relates the relationship of leisure to the quality of life of the individual Explains the relationship of leisure to fabric of society
An individual who:	Self-awareness	An individual who:
Knows what leisure is Can identify a variety of leisure experiences		Is satisfied with her leisure interest and its scope Has capabilities compatible with his level of aspiration Identifies realistic leisure expectations for self Identifies elements of quality leisure experiences for self Chooses leisure experiences compatible with individual values Can modify elements of leisure experiences to be more compatible with her own expectations, interests, capabilities, etc.
An individual who:	Leisure skills	An individual who:
Knows what leisure is Can identify a variety of leisure experiences		Uses planning and process skills for leisure and leisure experiences

Figure 3.5 Cont.

	Leisure skills	An individual who: Can perform basic entry-level skills in a variety of leisure experiences Has acquired advanced skills for self-selected leisure experiences
An individual who: Knows what leisure is Can identify a variety of leisure experiences Can perform basic entry-level skills in a variety of leisure activity clusters Can identify own present leisure interests, expectations,and goals	Decision making	An individual who: Identifies, gathers, and applies information regarding leisure and leisure experiences Identifies alternatives and uses them in making decisions related to leisure and leisure experiences Identifies possible outcomes of leisure choices Makes leisure decisions compatible with awareness of self Evaluates leisure decisions
An individual who: Knows what leisure is Can identify a variety of leisure experiences Can perform basic entry-level skills in a variety of leisure activity clusters Can identify own present leisure interests, expectations,and goals	Social interaction	An individual who: Identifies and uses types of verbal and nonverbal communications that contribute to reaching her leisure goals Identifies, selects, and uses patterns fo social interaction in leisure experiences compatible with his awareness of self

New Configurations

Figure 3.6A
Leisure Education Program Components and Potential Behavioral Outcomes

Program Components	Behavioral Outcomes
Leisure awareness	Uses knowledge of leisure and leisure experiences to enhance the quality of an individual's life through leisure.
Self-awareness	Is able to use self-knowledge in making leisure decisions that enhance the quality of life through leisure.
Leisure Skills	Possesses the leisure skills to direct life and leisure experiences toward the achievement of relaistic, self-determined goals.
Leisure Resources	Utilizes leisure resources for enhancing and enriching leisure experiences.

Figure 3.6B
Leisure Education Program
Components and Subcomponents

Leisure awareness

Definition of Leisure
Perceived freedom
Internal motivation
Self-selected experiences
Self-responsibility
Leisure experiences
Relationship to one's life
Relationship to one's lifestyle
Relationship to quality of life
Relationship to time

Self-awareness

Interest
Values
Attitudes
Motivation
Satisfaction
Capabilities
Needs
Leisure expectations
Goals
Outcomes
Leisure constraints

Leisure Skills

Decision making
Problem solving
Value clarification
Planning
Evaluation
Leisure activity skills
Social interaction
Behavioral change techniques

Leisure Resources

Personnel
Products
Equipment
Places
Community
Environmental

Figure 3.6C
Leisure Education Program Subcomponents and Potential Behavioral Outcomes

Leisure awareness	Behavioral Outcomes
Definition of Leisure Perceived freedom Internal motivation Self-selected experiences Self-responsibility Leisure experiences	Understands the concept of leisure and is able to apply it to one's life.
Relationship to one's life, lifestyle, quality of life, and time	Relates the concept of leisure and its relationship to other areas of one's life.
Self-responsibility	Acknowledges and accepts personal responsibility for leisure.
Leisure experiences	Identifies a variety of potential leisure experiences.

Self-awareness	Behavioral Outcomes
Interest Values Attitudes Capabilities Needs/Motivation	Understands how one's interests, values, attitudes, capabilities, and needs interact with and impact leisure experiences.
Satisfaction	Identifies current level of leisure satisfaction and the factors that contribute to or detract from it.
Expectations	Identifies realistic leisure expectations for self.
Goals	Determines and reconciles life with leisure goals.
Outcomes	Identifies and understands current and desired outcomes for leisure.
Constraints	Understands leisure constraints and ways to deal with them.

Figure 3.6C Cont.

Leisure Skills	Behavioral Outcomes
Decision making Problem solving Evaluation	Utilizes decision-making, problem solving, planning, and evaluation processes to achieve leisure goals.
Value clarification	Clarifies value issues in relation to leisure goals.
Planning	Is competent to realistically plan for leisure and leisure experiences.
Leisure activity skills	Possesses activity skills for self-selected leisure experiences.
Behavioral change	Utilizes techniques to facilitate desired behavioral change.
Social interaction	Possesses social interaction skills needed for leisure satisfaction.
Leisure Resources	**Behavioral Outcomes**
Personal Community Environmental	Identifies and utilizes personal, community, and environmental resources for leisure and leisure experiences.
Products Equipment Places	Evaluates and utilizes leisure products, equipment, and places for worth and usefulness and their contribution to leisure goals.

Chapter 3 References

Peterson, C.A., & Gunn, S.C. (1984). *Therapeutic recreation program design.* Englewood Cliffs, NJ: Prentice-Hall.

Ruskin, H., & Sivan, A. (Eds.). (1995). *Leisure education toward the 21st century.* Department of Recreation Management and Youth Leadership. Provo, UT: Brigham YoungUniversity.

SPRE. (1972). National policy and position statement on leisure education. Washington, D.C.: National Recreation and Park Association.

Woodburn, R. (1978). *Curriculum resource guide for teachers.* Canadian Leisure Education Project. Ministry of culture and recreation.

Zeyen, D., Odum, L., & Lancaster, R. (1977). *Kangraroo kit: Leisure education curriculum.* Washington, D.C.: National Recreation and Park Assoc.

Implementing Leisure Education in Recreation and Leisure Systems

Chapter Overview

The purpose of Chapter 4 is to develop an awareness of a wide variety of implementation opportunities and strategies that can be used in our current systems of operation. The ideas are generic in nature, although certain strategies may fit certain systems better that others. Implementation strategies are divided into infusion strategies and direct strategies.

Infusion strategies deal with infusing a focus on leisure into recreation and leisure activities and programs while *direct strategies* clearly focus on some aspect of leisure in and of themselves. Infusion strategies include infusing leisure content into 1) existing games or activities, 2) expressive art forms, or 3) special events, themes, and productions. It also outlines how to infuse experiences specifically designed for leisure education into recreation and leisure programs, using teachable moments and established processes and procedures to focus on leisure.

The direct strategies described in the chapter offer an array of straightforward means of focusing on some leisure education goal or objective. The direct strategies predominantly emphasize how public agencies, in particular, can go about educating the general public regarding leisure. Again, it is important to emphasize how these strategies could be used in a variety of different systems, not only public systems. In order to help students gain a clearer understanding of how the suggested implementation strategies may fit into existing program structures, two tables are included that summarize the strategies that are appropriate and applicable to age and special population groups and various forms of programs.

The last part of the chapter presents a new and different conceptualization of how recreation and leisure services could be reorganized to emphasize the leisure education function of a public system. This is the author's vision of how she would structure a system whose primary goal was to educate the citizens of a community regarding leisure.

Introduction

Educating for leisure within recreation and leisure service systems may be unfamiliar to some practitioners, so the question arises as to how it can be implemented within existing systems. The purpose of this chapter is to suggest implementation opportunities that exist and strategies that can be utilized in our current systems of operation. The ideas presented are not restricted to use in any one system, organization, or institution exclusively. While certain strategies may fit certain systems better than others, they are designed to be generic in nature. In addition, some of the strategies may fit the personal styles of professionals more than others. For example, some face-to-face leaders may be comfortable in inserting leisure education games into their programs but may feel uncomfortable dealing with more in-depth issues through value clarification experiences and discussions. The object of implementing leisure education is not attempting to fit round pegs into square holes. Each system and professional needs to assess its clients' needs and its own current operations to determine what implementation strategies can be used in light of its goals, personnel, and operating structure.

Various implementation strategies and experiences differ in their designed or innate capacity to accomplish leisure education objectives. The continuum of learning runs from leisure awareness to in-depth leisure learning. For example, some experiences are designed in such a way as to simply have people become consciously aware of leisure—to "think leisure." Other experiences, such as value clarification experiences, may go into depth regarding some aspect of leisure as it relates to one's own life. Both types of experiences are valuable and have their place. Each serves a different purpose. It is important to recognize the varying capacities of experiences as program implementation is undertaken, so that a realistic picture is gathered of what is really being accomplished by the systems. How our efforts can be misconstrued was brought home through a conversation with a practitioner in a public recreation and park system who was excited about their "program" to educate their community regarding leisure. When asked about their program in order to get additional ideas, it was related that their program consisted of free bumper stickers saying, I LOVE LEISURE. While bumper stickers can be an excellent way to bring leisure into people's conscious awareness, in and of themselves they will not educate a community regarding leisure. Another issue related to implementing leisure education is the practitioner's own expectations regarding what may or may not be accomplished. Unrealistic expectations and the desire to accomplish more than may be possible in a system can lead to frustration before some efforts are even begun.

For example, practitioners in public recreation and park systems frequently ask, "How can we reach all of the citizens in our community and really educate them about leisure in their own lives?" The reality is that in most communities you cannot reach everyone to the extent and depth you may feel is warranted. Therapeutic recreation personnel will frequently say, "I work in a short-term, acute-care facility. Our patients are with us for only three or four days. How can I educate them regarding leisure in that short a time?" The answer is that you can't. You can't if the expectation is a totally leisure-educated person. It may sound simplistic, but it is true—we can accomplish only what we can accomplish. In any setting we need to decide, based on identified client needs and priorities, what we can realistically accomplish and help people accomplish in relation to the leisure aspect of their lives. As with other areas of our program and service operations, we must select and prioritize the goals and objectives that we believe are the most important to focus upon for various client groups.

Likewise, as with other program offerings, it is important to offer a variety of opportunities from which people can self-select, based upon their own needs and interests. For example, a public system may offer an assessment package consisting of assessing clients' leisure interests, motivation, and satisfaction. The client comes in, takes the assessments, consults with one of the professional staff on the interpretation of the results, and leaves. Or, a six-week, in-depth class on "Time for Yourself: How to Get It, How to Keep It, How to Enjoy It" may be offered.

Implementation Strategies

Implementation strategies can be broken into infusion and direct strategies. Infusion strategies insert leisure education goals and objectives into ongoing programs, activities, services, processes, and procedures. In contrast, direct strategies clearly focus upon some aspect of leisure in and of themselves. These strategies include activities, programs, and services directly and primarily related to leisure education goals and objectives. The following are examples of both indirect and direct strategies for the implementation of leisure education.

Infusion Strategies for Educating for Leisure

For most recreation and leisure professionals, one of the easiest means of beginning to bring an awareness of leisure to participants is through infusing a focus on leisure into recreation and leisure activities. Many activities are open for content or theme suggestions. These include activities such as games, crafts, art, drama, and dance, to name a few. This strategy involves the following: 1) inserting leisure content into existing games, 2) using games and activities that have been developed specifically for leisure education, 3) inserting leisure content into expressive art forms, 4) using leisure as a focus for themes, special events, and productions, 5) using teachable moments, and 6) using processes and procedures.

Infusing Leisure Content Into Existing Activities

Any leisure activities that are open for content or theme suggestions can have a leisure theme as a focus. Games like Charades or Password, drawing, painting, collages, some art and craft activities, creative dramatics and dance, all lend themselves easily and meaningfully to inserting leisure content into the context of the activity. The following are examples of inserting aspects of leisure into recreation or leisure activities:

Charades

This version of Charades is played like a regular game of Charades. The difference is that by adding categories related to leisure activities, the participants "act out" or try to guess what leisure experience the person is depicting.

Procedures (4 to 16 participants): Divide the game participants into two teams. In turn, each team decides on a leisure activity or experience to be acted out for the other team to guess what the leisure experience may be. One or more people on the team may be used to portray the experience. No verbalization or prop can be used in the portrayal.

Members of the other team try to decipher the actions of the person acting out an experience in order to guess the specific activity that is being shown. Members of the team trying to guess the activity may guess out loud at any time. As soon as the activity is guessed, the "guessing" team then selects and acts out an activity for the other team. Some leisure experiences can be guessed rather quickly, so a time limit or a limit of two or three guesses may be used to make it a more challenging game, particularly when adults are involved in the game.

Infusing Leisure Content into Expressive Art Forms

Art and certain craft projects, whether they be on a playground or in a structured class, can have leisure as a theme, focus, or suggested content. For example, through drawing, painting, or collage making, participants could depict through illustrations things such as what follows:

- what you think illustrates what society views as a "successful" person,
- on one sheet of paper, how you think your mother (or father) wants you to spend your leisure; on another sheet of paper; what you want to do during your leisure,
- how you would feel in leisure if you were involved in an experience that would involve new people, high risk, or a high level of competition, etc. You may want to focus upon the whole body, just the face, or show your feeling through the use of colors and the strokes and motions you make in your illustration.

Abstract finger-painting for children or acrylic painting for adults can be an excellent medium through which participants can express feelings associated with various situations. Some situations that could be included are as follows:

- how you feel on a Friday afternoon,
- when you are on vacation,
- when you do something in your leisure that someone wants you to do,
- when you must hurry,
- when you have to stay in your house because of the weather.

Activities like spatter painting, block or potato printing, silk screening, and similar processes can be utilized to depict an individual leisure symbol, coat of arms, or favorite leisure experience.

The area of drama, like art and some crafts, also lends itself nicely to theme or content orientation. This is particularly true of creative dramatics or creative improvisation. One would only have to go through the content in this chapter to find a wealth of interesting situations or themes that could be utilized in creative dramatics. Act out or depict any of the following situations:

- irresponsible leisure choices and their outcomes or consequences,
- how never being able to say "no" would affect you, your leisure, and others,
- how joining a league would affect you, your leisure, and others,
- a scene that would dramatize how leisure-oriented people would behave, the choices they would make, and what you think their attitudes would be,
- a scene where one of you want to learn or try a new leisure experience but just never seem to pursue it,
- scenes from your own leisure that show the experiences and the levels of satisfaction shown in the "Hierarchy of Leisure Experiences."

Dance and creative movement is an avenue that can be utilized for the open expression of feelings through movement. Moods, feelings, and emotions have long been articulated through movement in general as well as creative, expressive movement forms. Certain theme orientations that would be applicable to the area of creative movement are as follows:

Walk the way you would walk:

- when you are happy,
- when you feel good about yourself or something you have done,
- when you have lost a game,
- when you feel "leisurely,"
- when you feel rushed or hurried,
- when you are unconcerned with time.

Move to show how you feel:

- when in leisure,
- when you feel free,
- when you feel controlled or boxed in,
- when you feel powerless,
- when you are hopeless,
- when you feel like you have done something wrong,
- when you are excited and anticipate something wonderful will happen,
- when you have had an experience that makes life worth living—a peak experience.

The modalities of games and the expressive art forms are experiences that are a part of almost all leisure programs. Although professionals often suggest themes, content, or a focus for these activities, leisure as a focus or theme, in and of itself, does not tend to be included. Yet these modalities lend themselves to the meaningful, logical inclusion of leisure as suggested content or orientation. The vast repertoire of leisure and recreation activities that allow for or require a theme or content offer previously untapped potential to create a heightened awareness of leisure within program offerings. Rather than suggesting that a participant draw a picture of their dog Pokey, suggest that they depict what they would like to do in leisure; rather than moving like a hippopotamus, they can move to express how they feel in leisure; rather than acting out a conversation between two trees, participants can dramatize the outcomes of what they would consider an irresponsible leisure choice or decision; children can be taken on a "canoe trip" rather than a "bear hunt."

Infusing Leisure Content in Special Events, Themes, and Productions

One of the primary advantages of infusing leisure content into special events, themes, and productions is the vast number and cross-section of people these activities reach. They tend to be high-impact, high-visibility events that can frequently reach individuals who may not otherwise be engaged in our leisure systems. The following are a few suggestions:

- The Department of Leisure Services in the city of Cerritos, California, initiated an annual city-wide "Leisure Fair" for residents of all ages. All of the public, private, and nonprofit agencies and businesses in the community that were leisure-related were invited to participate. The fair included demonstrations of *leisure activities*—opportunities for visitors to try activities of their choice, displays of leisure products, distribution of information on community leisure opportunities and resources, and even computerized interest inventories. This special event was highly successful, drawing citizens not only from the city of Cerritos but also from surrounding communities.
- Like most cities, the city of North Miami had always had a theme for its summer playgrounds program. One summer, North Miami used "Hobbies" as its theme. While hobbies were the overall theme, children were exposed to the concept of leisure, making up songs, poems, and playground productions about leisure. They also shared their hobbies with others and explored a variety of new activities in which they may have had an interest but had no experience.
- Productions, such as the one performed by the Tarpon Club at Florida State University, provide an excellent

example of using leisure as a theme. One leisure services graduate student was a member of the FSU Aquatic Art Club. She had to choreograph an aquatic art number for their annual production and she chose leisure as a theme. The production contrasted work and nonwork time through music, movements, and facial expressions.

Infusing Leisure Awareness Experiences Developed Specifically for Leisure Education into Recreation and Leisure Programs

In the activities outlined in the previous section, a focus on leisure could be inserted into the theme or content of the experience, along with other content. The examples of experiences in this section have been developed to focus almost exclusively on leisure. The purpose of these activities is to utilize them in the same way any other recreation activities would be utilized: the content just happens to be devoted to leisure and leisure-related topics. Again, additional examples can be found in the Appendix, as well as in Stumbo and Thompson's text (1986). Here's an example of a leisure-awareness depiction:

Meet Your Match

The purpose of this game is for players to match their answers to leisure-related questions with other participants' answers. The game activities highlight the commonality and variation that exist among people regarding what outcomes or feelings they attach to various experiences in leisure.

Procedures: There is one leader who asks the questions, gives the words, and generally keeps the game going. Three to eight participants can play at one time. The game consists of three rounds of questions, each round comprised of four questions or words each. Each round of questions is related to a different topic. The topic for round one is "What do you get out of the following experiences?" Round two relates to "What do you do in leisure that gives you the following feelings?" Round three is "On a scale of one to three, how would you rate the level of enjoyment or satisfaction that you receive from the following? (1 = low level, 3 = high level)".

The questions or words for each round are placed on separate pieces of paper in three different boxes. Questions are then drawn by the leader and read to the participants. As a question is used, it is taken out of play. The leader then repeats this process for each round of play.

Each player lists the names of all other players on a piece of paper. This sheet will be the "tally sheet" to record the number of times a player matches answers with other players.

As a question is asked or a word given, each participant writes down his answer on a separate sheet of paper. After everyone has recorded their response, the papers are then shown in order for players to "meet their match(es)." Each player then makes a tally mark by the name(s) of the person(s) whose responses match his own. At the end of play each person then sees which players answer(s) are most similar to his own.

The following list contains suggestions for the three rounds of play to show possible examples.

Round One	Round Two	Round Three
Fishing	Excitement	(The list of experiences in round one can be used again.)
Hiking	Fear	
Photography	Joy	
Camping	Happiness	Dancing
Sailing	Contentment	Playing golf
Carpentry	Stimulation	Playing an instrument
Taking a class	Boredom	Attending a concert
Walking	Fun	Eating out
Contemplation	Accomplishment	Having a party
Gardening	Pride	Being out-of-doors
Reading	Discomfort	Volunteer work
Shopping	Relaxation	Watching a sunrise
Talking with friends	Prestige	Playing with a pet
Cooking		

(Developed by Sharon Sofford, graduate student, Florida State University, Leisure Services and Studies.)

Infusing Leisure Education Into Teachable Moments

Recreation, park, and leisure professionals have numerous opportunities to infuse a focus on leisure, as well as to develop leisure skills, through the way in which situations are handled to utilize "teachable moments." We have tended to focus our attention upon the actual activities and people's participation in these activities. We have not tended to view the total contact time with participants as a gestalt. Therefore, the seemingly informal contacts and interaction opportunities that exist to discuss or focus upon leisure have not been viewed and used as openings to educate for leisure. However, a myriad of teachable moments exist through our informal conversations with participants to bring leisure into their conscious awareness and utilize it as a focus of interaction. Almost all of us use conversations with participants to establish rapport, to show our interest in them as people, and to learn more about them. However, just as we have not utilized leisure activities that are open to a leisure content, we have not availed ourselves to the openings in our conversations to talk with people about leisure.

In addition to infusing leisure into our conversations with participants, we can also modify the *way* we go about the practice of our profession. For example, the skills of problem solving, decision making, planning, and evaluating can be transformed from leader actions to participant actions. Presently, personnel are trained and expected to perform these functions for the individuals and groups with whom they work. These are individual skills people need to develop and exercise in relation to their own time and leisure; professionals can facilitate further development and application by having participants perform these tasks for themselves. The development of these skills does not have to be done in a formal, instructional manner. In fact, the most effective approach would be to focus upon skills as the situations arise and the need for them is apparent at a particular moment. Whether the participants are children on a playground, participants in a judo or floral arranging class, team members, 4-H Club members, or Golden Age Club members, as much of the decision making, problem solving, planning, and evaluating as possible should be done by the participants. All too often, the leader's skills in these areas are honed as a result of their practice; participants' skills may be unaffected, however, because most tasks are done for them by leaders. It is particularly important to facilitate the development of the aforementioned skills when working with children and persons with disabilities.

Two examples from actual experiences illustrate how the facilitation of these skills can be accomplished in practice. Box hockey was a particularly popular activity on a children's playground one summer. Because the playground had only one box hockey set, many arguments and fights resulted. Inevitably, the children would run to one of the leaders and ask her to make the two children playing box hockey give it up so that they could have their turn. The typical scenario on a playground would be for the leader to go over to the children playing and, in their best first-grade voice, demand that the children stop playing and let the next children take their turn. While such action may exercise or further develop the leader's skills in resolving playground conflict, the children involved have no additional insight into how to resolve conflict on their own without running to the leader. In educating for leisure, this situation would constitute a teachable moment and could be used to develop the skills of the children involved in problem solving and conflict resolution rather than the leader's solution.

The scenario as it was actually played out by a skilled facilitator revolved around working with the children on the issues of "What are some of the ways we can resolve conflicts and arguments when they arise?" (examining the advantages and disadvantages of each option) and "What is the main problem here and what are some of the potential solutions?" The main problem identified by the children was that there were not enough box hockey sets for the number of people who wanted to play. The solution they pursued was to "barter" with the district playground supervisor for more box hockey sets in lieu of new balls and bats for softball, which were provided every season whether they were needed or not. Their bartering was successful, which reinforced the entire process.

A second example involved working with a group of mentally retarded teenagers in a state facility. These teenagers were slated for community placement within two years. The recreation therapists at the facility did all of the planning, organizing, and implementation of the programs for this group of teenagers, who had no responsibilities associated with their programs except to show up and participate if they chose to do so. The participation of this group began to drop off severely. The leader informed the group that, since there was apparently little interest in the program, it would be discontinued. After about three weeks, the group was bored, came to the leader, and asked that she begin the program again. She informed them that she would, but with one change. They would have to assume joint responsibility for planning, organizing, and implementing the program. They agreed, not really realizing what was involved.

The group began the project by deciding they wanted to have a cookout and to take a trip to some caverns nearby. With the assistance of the leader, they decided on the menu, the activities, and who was responsible for each task. When the day of the trip arrived, the teenagers gathered the equipment, supplies, and food together for the outing. Although there was a picture checklist for the food to be included, in the excitement, the hot dogs were not packed. The leader checked with everyone to see if everything they needed was packed. Although she was assured they had everything, she knew the hot dogs were missing. After she asked one last time if everything was ready, everyone got on the bus for the trip to the caverns. When it came time for dinner, the hot dogs were nowhere to be found. The group had to eat pickles and potato chip sandwiches for dinner.

Most leaders would have intervened with the group and assumed responsibility once the hot dogs were found still in the refrigerator. However, the group would have learned far less regarding responsibility and consequences had the leader stepped in and rectified the situation.

Two critical points need to be made regarding the development of participant skills in decision making, planning, and other crucial activities. First, the transition from leader-determined to participant-determined operations is a process that needs to occur along a continuum. In most systems, a drastic, abrupt change is likely to develop into chaos. When participants lack practice in problem solving and planning or have role expectations of having everything done for them, the transition can most effectively be accomplished through small steps. Successive approximations toward participant-determined operations allow for development and practice of the necessary skills as well as shifts in role expectations.

A second critical point to be aware of in the transition from leader-determined to participant-determined operations is that transition and participant determination both require more time, energy, and planning in the initial stages. It is frequently much faster and easier for leaders to operate the way they always have—by doing everything themselves. However, once the transition has taken place, participants have developed valuable skills and have become able to function more independently, requiring less staff time in the final analysis.

Utilizing Processes and Procedures

Every leisure system has established processes and procedures that are a part of their system's operation. These processes and procedures can be used to help create a conscious awareness of leisure and leisure experiences for participants. Most systems have some type of intake procedure, whether it be registration through registration forms or client intake evaluations, or interviews in therapeutic recreation. Registration forms or membership forms can be revised to include a few well-chosen questions to facilitate a conscious awareness of leisure and important factors surrounding upcoming participation or membership. The following form (Figure 4.1) illustrates the type of questions that could be added to a registration form or membership application, along with other information needed by the agency.

Figure 4.1
Recreation and Parks Department Registration Form

Name ____________________ Leisure Class/Activity ____________

Address ____

1. Which of the following do you want to get out of participation in this leisure experience? (Circle all that apply.)

   a. develop a skill in an area of interest
   b. meet new people; socialize
   c. personal enjoyment
   d. self-improvement
   e. have something to do
   f. a change of routine

2. What personal goal do you have that you hope this class will help you reach?

3. What are some other areas of leisure interests that you may want to pursue but have not?

4. Approximately how many hours of free time do you have per week?

Our department has professional staff trained to help you have more leisure and get more enjoyment and satisfaction out of your leisure. If you are interested in this free service, please call 555-2252 for an appointment.

The city of Dartmouth, Nova Scotia, Parks and Recreation Department used their on-site registration process to raise peoples' leisure awareness by setting up display booths depicting leisure activities that were available in the community. These booths also provided information on the activities and how to become involved in them.

Evaluation procedures at the end of a program or class can also include questions to help participants think through and evaluate the results of their experience. The questions included on the evaluation form are examples only. There are many possibilities for including additional or different questions. Figure 4.2 presents a sample Recreation and Parks Department Evaluation Form.

Figure 4.2
Recreation and Parks Department Evaluation Form

Leisure Class/Activity ______________________________

1. On your registration form, you indicated what you hoped to get out of participation in this class. Please rate the ***degree*** to which you received each of the following. Circle the number that corresponds to your answer.

	Very Much	**Somewhat**	**Little**
a) developed or further developed knowledge and skill in my area of interest	3	2	1
b) met new people and had an opportunity to socialize with them	3	2	1
c) personal enjoyment	3	2	1
d) self-improvement	3	2	1
e) something to do	3	2	1
f) a change of routine	3	2	1

Figure 4.2 Cont.

2. To what degree do you feel that participation in this class helped you to reach the personal goal(s) you had in taking the class? 3 2 1

3. In terms of personal enjoyment and satisfaction, how does this leisure experience rate in relation to your other leisure pursuits?

   a) It was more enjoyable and satisfying than my other leisure experiences.
   b) It was as enjoyable and satisfying as my other leisure experiences.
   c) It was less enjoyable and satisfying than my other leisure experiences.

4. Which of the following statements reflect how you feel about this leisure experience?

   a) I found I don't really enjoy it.
   b) It is OK but it isn't something I would care to pursue.
   c) It is fun; I really enjoyed it.
   d) It is really great; I love it.

5. Which of the following are descriptive of your experience?

   a) I enjoyed the people and interacting with them as much as I did learning and doing ____________________.
   b) I enjoyed learning and doing ____________ more than I did interacting with other class members.

6. Would you like additional information or more advanced work in this area? ____ yes ____ no

7. Would you like information on how to continue to pursue advanced work on your own? ____ yes ____ no

Note: Our department has leisure interest, motivation, and satisfaction inventories with people trained to interpret them to help you get the most enjoyment and satisfaction out of your leisure. If you are interested in taking one of the inventories and talking with our staff, please detach the bottom of the page and return it to the instructor.

- -

Name ______________________________

Address ______________________________

______________________ Phone ____________

Direct Strategies for Educating for Leisure

As was mentioned earlier, direct strategies involve activities, programs, or services that are clearly identified as being leisure-related. They are straightforward means of focusing upon some leisure education goal or objective.

There are numerous ways an agency or organization can directly focus upon leisure and can facilitate the development of the leisure lifestyle of its clientele and help them with individual leisure problems. My experience educating the general public regarding leisure reveals that people are very interested in the leisure aspects of their lives. They feel they do not have enough time to do what they want to do. They do not give themselves permission to do things for themselves that do not include the family; they feel guilty when they take time for fun and enjoyment when maybe they "should" be working harder to get ahead in today's tight economy; they have preconceived ideas of what weekends, vacations, and holidays "should" be like and, therefore, do not know what to do when they are alone and end up being lonely and depressed. These issues, as well as numerous others, are leisure-related. The primary problem I have seen over the years is that people are vitally concerned with and value the leisure aspect of their lives, but they do not know or understand that their concerns are leisure-related. They may not have the verbal label of leisure to attach to their issues, concerns, or behaviors. In most instances, they do not understand the concept of leisure, particularly as it relates to their lives. Therefore, they frequently simply exclaim that they don't have leisure and dismiss the problem. They may proceed to tell you that they don't have time for their souls to catch up with their bodies; that they live hurried, harried lives; that anxiety, tension, and stress are making them ill. But they are not connecting any of these concerns with "leisure." All of this is to say that today, if an agency advertises classes or workshops on leisure education *by those titles,* they may attract few people. Individuals who have had the most success in attracting working adults to sessions, classes, or workshops have used catchy, problem-oriented titles for pressing concerns that people are experiencing, then related those problems to leisure. Successful titles have included: "Time for Yourself: How to Get It, How to Keep It, and How to Enjoy It"; "How to Survive the Holidays"; and "Reducing Stress Through Your Free Time."

Activities Specifically Developed for Leisure Education

Numerous games and activities to educate for leisure have been specifically developed by professionals in the field. These activities were designed to be used in the same way any other recreation activities would be used; the content just happens to be focused on some aspect of leisure. "Meet Your Match" and "Leisure Auction" are examples of these types of experience and can be found, along with numerous others, in Chapter 6.

Class and Workshop Suggestions

- Offer classes or workshops in the regular schedule of programs on topics such as "Time for Yourself: How to Get It, How to Keep It, and How to Enjoy It." Additional titles are suggested throughout the remainder of this chapter.
- Have a brown-bag luncheon series in the business district to attract the business community. The same type of program can be offered for company personnel either over lunch or as a part of their work time. Many employers encourage self-development and lifestyle development sessions because of the positive benefits such training has for employee morale and productivity.
- Offer pre-retirement leisure lifestyle planning sessions for corporations and governmental agencies.
- Plan and conduct class sessions for elementary and secondary students on leisure in the schools. The city of Cerritos, California, had one of its staff members available as the city's public school leisure instructor.

General Suggestions

- Designate a "Leisure Week" and plan accompanying events to heighten leisure awareness.
- Use leisure as a summer parks and playground summer theme. This was successfully implemented in the city of North Miami with children making up songs, skits, and the like, about leisure.
- Have leisure awareness bulletin boards in all of the centers or facilities.
- Organize a "Leisure Fair" for the entire community. Include representatives of all the private businesses and not-for-profit agencies that have leisure programs, products, or services, as well as your own agency. Cerritos, California, has a Lei-

sure Fair every year that includes demonstrations of various activities, opportunities to try experiences or activities, leisure interest inventories that people could take, and community leisure resource handouts. Some businesses display boats, recreation vehicles, bicycles, home exercise machines, and other recreation and leisure equipment.

- Develop a "home page" for the agency on the internet. Today this is an effective, inexpensive, and easy to develop option for any agency to reach potential and current clients. A home page could include a calendar of events, schedules, and special announcements, and could acquaint readers with community leisure opportunities and leisure resources. Additionally, the home page offers an excellent opportunity to include tips on leisure and leisure education activities for children and adults. For example, activities such as leisure interests, motivation and satisfaction inventories, and flow chart information processing of leisure outcomes all hold a natural appeal for adults and would adapt to internet communication easily. The internet is no longer a playtoy. It has become a major communication network for numerous people worldwide.
- Offer or find sponsors to provide free leisure interests, leisure motivation, and leisure satisfaction assessments for the public.
- Provide a leisure counseling service available on a referral or appointment basis. Currently, there are leisure professionals called in for consultation or individual sessions by psychotherapists to work with individuals, couples, or families on leisure issues and problems.
- Institute a telephone leisure "hot-line" to provide information on what is happening in the community on any given day. The city of North Miami established such a service for their citizens and called it "Dial-A-Happening." Anyone could call 893-FUNN 24 hours a day, seven days a week, to find out what was happening in the community that might be of interest to them. The recreation and parks department in North Miami instituted this service at no additional cost by using one of the lines coming into the department as their "Dial-A-Happening" line. They also used an answerphone they already had to provide the information. This service was so popular and got such heavy use that the department

had to break out additional lines for various interests, such as sporting events and participation, special events, and the arts.

- Establish a community leisure resource center. This could include books, videos, and cassette tapes on "How-to topics," such as how to improve your golf or tennis game or any leisure activity that is available. The center could also have an equipment checkout system so that people could rent equipment such as racquetball equipment, to see if they like the game before investing in their own equipment. The city of Cerritos established such a resource center in their city library. The staff identified all of the recreation- and leisure-related activity books and videos that were already available in the library as a part of the center's offerings. They also made equipment rental available to the public, using equipment they already owned. One popular idea was "Picnic Baskets" and "Beach Baskets." These baskets contained self-selected equipment that people could check out for their picnics or outings at the beach.
- Sponsor a leisure activity exploration day or weekend. The purpose of this event would be to allow people to explore leisure experiences they have never tried without having to sign up for an extended eight- or ten-week session on something they may or may not enjoy. This type of event would help people to expand their leisure interests and options quickly and easily.
- Compile a leisure recipe book or card file. The recipes could include recipes for boredom, loneliness, and stress; what to do on a cold, rainy day; what to do when there is nothing good on television; how to get back in touch with your family; and other pertinent topics.
- Use leisure awareness as a focus for departmental promotional programs. For example, the recreation and parks department in California developed their own Leisure Anagram. The anagram included words on the benefits or outcomes of leisure and leisure experiences. The anagrams were given out to elementary school children, and the children identifying the most words in the anagram received a coupon for a free activity offered by the agency.

The ideas and strategies that have been discussed thus far have been ones that could be utilized by professional personnel within their service systems. Considering the percentage of any potential client population that may not enter the system for services, it is evident that outreach techniques that are effective in reaching large numbers of people within a given population are needed by public agencies. One of the outreach strategies that holds the potential to reach the largest and broadest segments of the population is the media.

Media Utilization

National and multinational studies (Robinson, 1990; Szalia, 1972) show that people spend a large percentage of their free time with the mass media. Kubey and Csikszentmihalyi (1990) reported that in the United States, nearly half of people's free time was devoted to watching television alone. As a profession, we have decried this use of free time. Rather than fight it, perhaps it is now time for us to begin to utilize this same, yet other, media to present additional options for enriching, enhancing leisure experiences. Television has become one of the primary socializing agents within our society. It is not unusual for children to spend more time with their televisions than with their families, their teachers, recreation and leisure personnel, and even their peers. All one has to do is to watch an evening of television to see the implicit leisure messages contained within the commercials: weekends are made to drink beer; after the work day is over, it's off to the bar where everyone is socializing, happy, and having fun; the reward one gets for climbing to the top of the mountain is a tub of iced beer flown in by helicopter to celebrate the achievement. Where are *our* messages for people to consider? We need to become masters of the 60-second spot to begin to reach a large portion of the world.

Our justification for not utilizing some media, particularly television, has been the expense. There is no denying the expense. However, public service announcements are free to many leisure agencies. Also, it may well be time for us to rethink our priorities regarding the distribution and allocation of funds to the various goals of our agencies. Media messages may need to begin having a higher priority in our goals and resources.

Suggestions for using mass media for reaching out to our publics regarding leisure are not about advertising our agencies' program offerings, listing class or league schedules, or publishing the scores of league play. Although these are legitimate activities in their own right, what is being advocated here is using mass media to heighten the public's awareness of leisure itself, not the recreation, park, or leisure system. These efforts may include messages such as "A full life includes a leisure life" or "If you don't have leisure, you are not using time you have available for leisure . . . because time and what you do with it are a matter of the choices you make."

Television and Radio Suggestions

- Develop 60-second spots to be used as radio and television public service announcements or as paid spot announcements. The city of Detroit has done this successfully. Ongoing spots on "Leisure in Your Life" could also be developed.
- Have your local cable station feature a leisure education program such as "How to Get the Most Out of Your Vacation," "How to Survive the Christmas Holidays Without the Blues and the Blahs," "Getting Control of Your Time and Your Life." These could be videotaped and offered by your department on a free loan basis for home viewing. The audioscript portion could be recorded for distribution on cassette tapes.
- Have your local television stations, cable company, and radio stations run a daily leisure calendar of events on what is happening in the community, brought to you by your local recreation and parks department.
- Become a regular guest on local morning or noon talk shows on various leisure themes like boredom or how to help your children find something to do when they think there isn't anything to do. **Note:** Several times I have been interviewed on how to handle holiday depression for our local radio station. One of the interviews was picked up by the radio network in Florida and run statewide. Associated Press, UPI, and the *National Inquirer* also picked up the interview content and ran it nationwide. This is incredible coverage from a five-minute interview!
- Run a daily column on community leisure happenings.
- Volunteer to write a "Leisure Lines" column for your daily newspaper to run once a week on leisure topics similar to the ones mentioned above.

Departmental Publications Suggestions

- Develop a leisure resource guide to your community, alphabetically listing leisure experiences. Include all public, private, and not-for-profit offerings. The city of Cerritos in California developed such a guide with the assistance of volunteers and field work students. If someone was interested in hot air ballooning, they could check the guide and find a listing of the operations offering this experience, along with their addresses and telephone numbers. These Cerritos Leisure Resource Guides were made available to the citizens of the community at no cost. Once the information is compiled on a computer, it is very easy to change and update the material. The city of Austin, Texas, developed a similar guide that was included in the newcomers' "Welcome Wagon" package, along with free coupons for recreation and parks department events or classes.
- Produce and distribute handouts, brochures, or self-instructional learning packets on leisure-related topics such as "Getting Beyond the Guilt to the Fun" or "Getting the Most Enjoyment from the Free Time You Do Have."
- Provide consumer information on leisure equipment, supplies, toys, and products for knowledgeable, safe purchase.
- Develop and distribute leisure coloring books for young children (careful not to sex stereotype activities).
- Develop and distribute leisure workbooks for school-age children on topics such as "What to Do When There Is Nothing to Do."
- Develop and distribute a booklet on "Fun and Free." This could include all of the things you and your staff identify that people can do at home or in their community as free leisure experiences.

Oral Presentation Suggestions

Recreation and leisure personnel are always being asked to make presentations to civic, educational, and community groups of all types. A director of recreation is asked to speak to the Women's Club; a supervisor is asked to talk to a class; a director of therapeutic recreation services is asked to be a part of an in-service training program for new hospital personnel. In addition to promoting one's own agency, these opportunities can be utilized to involve people in "mini-experiences" related to their own leisure. A series of leisure education activities such as those found in this chapter and Chapter 6 can be included to help groups look at their own leisure, their own thoughts and feelings on leisure, as a part of or as the entire presentation. The success of these mini-sessions has been tremendous. They are participatory, directed at understanding one's self, and of great interest to the participants. Once an agency lets it be known that it is available for such presentations, opportunities become plentiful.

In order to assist those who may be unfamiliar with leisure education to gain a clearer understanding of how the aforementioned implementation strategies may fit into their existing program structure, the following tables and examples are offered. Table 4.1 shows what implementation strategies can be used in programs that are organized around age and special population groups.

Table 4.1
Implementation Strategies Appropriate for Age and Special Population Groups

STRATEGIES:

Infusion	**Children/ Youth**	**Adults**	**Seniors**	**Disabled**
Leisure Content into Existing Activities	X	X	X	X
Expressive Arts	X	X	X	X
Special Events, Themes, & Productions	X	X	X	X
Leisure Education Activities	X	X	X	X
Teachable Moments (how situations are handled)	X	X	X	X
Processes and Procedures	X	X	X	X

Table 4.1 Cont.

STRATEGIES:				
Direct	**Children/ Youth**	**Adults**	**Seniors**	**Disabled**
Classes and Workshops	X	X	X	X
Media	X	X	X	X
Departmental Publications	X	X	X	X
Oral Presentations	X	X	X	X
Leisure Counseling	X	X	X	X
Leisure Assessments	X	X	X	X
Computer-assisted Instruction	X	X	X	X

It is apparent from viewing Table 4.1 that all of the implementation strategies are appropriate and can be included in programs for each age group or special population group. The strategies of inserting leisure content into existing activities would, of course, depend on the type of program that was being offered.

While it is easy to see how the implementation strategies can be applicable for inclusion into programs for age groups and special populations, it is frequently more difficult to visualize how specific strategies can be included into the different forms of programs offered by an agency. Table 4.2 outlines the implementation strategies applicable to various forms of programs. The X denotes that the strategy is applicable to the program while an * signifies the strategy is applicable depending on the type and content of the program. For example, inserting content into existing activities would be appropriate in a drawing class but not in a guitar class. Also note that direct leisure education strategies are not included in Table 4.2. That is because infusion strategies insert leisure content into existing programs and activities while direct strategies are programs, classes, and services provided by the department that are *in addition to* the department's offerings.

Table 4.2
Implementation Strategies Applicable to Various Forms of Programs

STRATEGIES:

Infusion	**Play-grounds**	**Classes**	**Special Events**	**Leagues**	**Tourn-aments**	**Camps**
Leisure Content into Existing Activities	X	*	*			X
Expressive Arts	X	*	*			X
Special Events, Themes, & Productions	X	*	*			X
Leisure Education Activities	X	X	*			X
Teachable Moments (*how* situations are handled)	X	X	X	X	X	X
Processes and Procedures	X	X	*	*		X

It is evident from viewing Table 4.2 that the form of programs least open to the inclusion of leisure education are those related to sports leagues and tournaments. Beyond using process and procedure and teachable moments, including a focus on leisure per se does not fit the form of current programs in this area. Again, it is not the intent to try to educate for leisure where it is not appropriate and applicable. There are many avenues that are open to implementation of which an agency can take advantage.

To illustrate how some of these strategies can be interwoven into the fabric of existing forms of program, the following examples are drawn from actual experiences of practitioners involved in leisure education.

Slimnastics Classes

The instructor for this class was one of the professionally trained recreation directors of a community center who taught a slimnastics class. She began the class using the registration form listed earlier in this chapter. From this form she found the participants were interested in the class for self-improvement and to meet new people and socialize. She then structured the format of the class to begin each class session with a leisure education activity to afford the participants an opportunity to socialize and get to know one another.

For example, the first day of class she used a Leisure Mixer, whereas on subsequent days she used activities such as Meet Your Match, Week at a Glance, and Leisure Outcomes. During the one break in the class, she would choose various discussion topics related to leisure. Anyone who has run a slimnastic class knows the drop out rate can be as high as 50%. In this class, there was no participant drop out. The instructor finished the class using the evaluation form suggested in this chapter. The evaluations were all excellent and over half of the class stated an interest in the leisure inventories that were mentioned at the end of the form.

Playgrounds and Camps

Playgrounds and camps offer many excellent opportunities for including leisure education as a part of the program. These two forms of programs can use every one of the infusion strategies listed above. They offer exceptional opportunities for developing skills in assuming personal responsibility, decision making, problem solving, and social skills through the way the leaders work with the youth and through direct instruction in these skills.

Also, numerous playgrounds and camps have added leisure education activities, accompanied by short discussions, as a part of their planned schedule of activities. For example, an after school playground program for at-risk youth scheduled a variety of activities in sports, art, music, and leisure education each afternoon.

A Different Conceptualization for a Different Age

The remainder of this chapter will outline and explain one possible reconceptualization of a public recreation and park system that includes our current services as well as leisure education services. The suggested reconceptualization would also be beneficial in highlighting an expanded educational focus as well as simplifying the interpretation of an agency's services to its public. The proposed reconceptualization is primarily aimed at public recreation and park systems because therapeutic recreation has had a service conceptualization that includes leisure education as one of its components of service for a number of years. However, some of the implementation strategies may be applicable to any systems in their current or modified form.

Components of Service

A public recreation and park system could be reconceptualized to include three major components of service: an Education Component, a Resource Component, and a Community Organization and Development Component. Figure 4.3 portrays these three components of service.

Figure 4.3
The Recreation and Leisure Service Components

Education Component

Resource Component

Community Organization and
Development Component

The breakdown of these three components into subcomponents is depicted in Figures 4.4 to 4.6.

The Education Component of the service system (Figure 4.4) would focus upon educating clients regarding leisure, leisure skills, leisure resources, and developing client's self-awareness in relation to leisure. The objectives of this component would be the same as those outlined in the current model of leisure education or those developed by the staff of the service system.

Figure 4.4
The Education Component

Leisure Awareness	Self-awareness
Leisure Skills	Leisure Resources

The Leisure Resources Component of the system (Figure 4.5) would be the component that focuses on providing information on the leisure opportunities and resources available in the entire community, the surrounding areas, the state, the nation, and the world. The information base would include public, private, and quasi-public resources and opportunities, not simply the opportunities and resources provided by the community recreation, parks, or leisure service agencies. Further, this component would be the component that is involved in recreation and leisure programming as well as the development and maintenance of recreation and leisure areas and facilities. Lastly, the checkout and rental of recreation equipment for use by clients would be offered. The resources component would be responsible for information collection and dissemination as well as the actual provisions of programs, areas, and facilities for leisure participation opportunities.

Figure 4.5
The Leisure Resources Component

Community Leisure Information Public Private Quasi-Public	Leisure Programs for Participation Opportunities
Equipment Check-Out and Rental	Provision of Leisure Areas and Facilities

Community organization and development of public, private, and quasi-public leisure opportunities, areas, and facilities would be the emphasis of this system component (Figure 4.6). In this capacity the system would act as a community recreation and leisure coordinating, facilitating, and development body. It would seek to encourage the development and coordination of a rich, well-rounded, and balanced repertoire of leisure opportunities and resources for the entire community. It would also seek to develop partnerships and collaborations with other community agencies in order for the community to have the richest leisure resources possible. This component would also include aiding other systems, such as the school, adult education, and community schools; youth organizations; and health systems in including a focus on leisure education.

Figure 4.6
Community Organization and Development Component

Leisure Participation Opportunities	Leisure Areas and Facilities
Leisure Education	Partnerships and Collaborations
Community Development	

The next three figures (Figures 4.7 to 4.9) illustrate possible implementation strategies that could be used in each system component to accomplish its objectives. The education component strategies are divided into in-house (within the agency) and outreach strategies for both children and adults.

As is readily apparent in the Implementation Strategies figures (Figures 4.7 and 4.8), the Education Component of the system utilizes a variety of strategies to educate for leisure. Traditional recreation and leisure programs are used only for children to infuse a leisure education focus in activities and programs, to use teachable moments to develop skills such as decision making and problem solving, and to include activities developed specifically for leisure education as a part of the activity program. Other strategies utilize media, publications, presentations, classes and workshops, and computers specifically designed to educate adults and children regarding leisure. The focus of these strategies in the Education Component differ from those in the Leisure Resources Component in that, in the Education Component, the focus is upon developing an understanding of leisure and its relationship to one's personal life. The focus in the Leisure Resources Component, which uses some of the same techniques, is on providing information and education leisure and recreation sources and opportunities. The school-based outreach strategy for children is one where recreation and leisure personnel go into the schools and present leisure education sessions to classes or groups.

Figure 4.7
Implementation Strategies for the Education Component

In-House		**Outreach**	
Children	**Adults**	**Children**	**Adults**
Infusion	Classes	School-based	Presentation to Community Groups
Teachable Moments	Workshops	Media-based Education	Media-based Education
Leisure Education Activities	Leisure Assessments	Television Radio Cable Newspaper Column	Television Radio Cable Newspaper Column
Direct Leisure Skills Development	Direct Leisure Skills Development		
		Publications	Publications
Computer-assisted Learning	Computer-assisted Learning	Coloring Books Workbooks	Workbooks
	Leisure Counseling		

The use of existing and specially developed publications and media for both children and adults are central to the Leisure Resources Component strategies to educate people on community leisure resources. This component also includes the provision of recreation and leisure programs, the provision of areas and facilities, and the provision of equipment checkout and rental by the system. As was stated previously, the emphasis the strategies used in this component would have is on leisure resource opportunities for participation rather than on developing an understanding of leisure per se.

Figure 4.8
Implementation Strategies for the Leisure Resources Component

Publications
- Recreation Activities
- Community Resource Guides
- Leisure Experience Suggestions

Video Tapes
- Recreation Activities
- Community Resources
- Travel

Computer Programs & Internet Pages

Programs and Special Events

Areas and Facilities

Equipment Checkout and Rental

Telephone Leisure Hot Line

Newspaper Column & Calendar of Events

The established techniques for community organization and development would be the strategies used in the Community Organization and Development Component of the system. Again, its function is to coordinate and facilitate the development of leisure opportunities, community leisure resources, and leisure education, using all of the public, quasi-public, and private agencies and organizations in the community.

Figure 4.9
Implementation Strategies for the Community Organization and Development Component

Community Organization Planning Councils	Community Networking
Advocacy Groups and Individuals	

Using this different conceptualization of a recreation and leisure delivery system would have the advantage of expanding the service-base in a community. People who may not take advantage of the current programs offered by a public recreation and park system would have additional services, such as a leisure resource center, a telephone leisure hot-line, equipment checkout and rental, leisure assessments, leisure counseling, newspaper leisure columns, and Internet leisure resources and opportunities pages from which to select. Further, it would have the advantage of significantly expanding the system's visibility and the public's awareness of the system and its relevance. Most importantly, it is a conceptualization that could greatly enhance people's awareness of leisure as well as provide an increase in community leisure opportunities and resources.

Most managers' immediate reaction may be that such a system would require additional staff and resources that would be beyond their ability to attain in this time of downsizing and cutbacks. However, this different conceptualization could be attained by a *reallocation* of staff and resources during a period of gradual transition. Such a system would require personnel with a philosophy different from our traditional recreation philosophy as well as personnel with different skills and abilities. It does not mean that current personnel would not be useful in the programming and facilities areas just as they are now. Additionally, in-service education and reassignment of staff according to their interests and competencies could assist in a systems transition. Then the hiring of personnel, as positions become available, with competencies in leisure education, leisure counseling, media communication, community organization and development, and such, could complete the transition.

Whether or not the conceptualization presented here is what our service systems of the future will evolve into or whether another innovative model will emerge, remains to be seen. However, it is clear that if we, as a profession, are serious about making a difference in the lives of individuals and their communities, then we must design systems and employ techniques specifically to assist people in experiencing the benefits of leisure. The Chinese definition of insanity is to continue behaving in the same way while expecting different results. If we want different results from our professional efforts, we must engage in different professional behaviors. The Chinese definition of insanity can be our challenge or our epitaph.

Summary

The ideas and suggestions offered in this chapter are by no means inclusive of all the strategies and techniques that leisure systems can employ in educating for leisure. Many additional strategies need to be developed by creative personnel and then shared with the rest of us. The way these strategies have been devised is through people coming up with an idea of what may work, trying the idea out, and refining it. There is no one way or right way to implement leisure education. It is a matter of analyzing one's system, goals, and personnel, and then determining what is possible and feasible within that system.

Chapter 4 References

Kubey, R., & Csikszentmihalyi, M. (1990). *Television and the quality of life.* Hillsdale, NJ: Lawrence Erlbaum.

Robinson, J.P. (1990, November). The leisure pie. *American Demographics.*

Szalia, A. (Ed.). (1972). *The use of time: Daily activities of urban and suburban populations in twelve countries.* Moulton, the Hague.

Stumbo, N.J., & Thompson, S.R. (1986). *Leisure education: A manual of activities and resources.* State College, PA: Venture Publishing, Inc.

Leisure Education Program Planning

Chapter Overview

An overview of the program planning process as it applies to leisure education program development is the focus of this chapter. Comprehensive and specific programs are differentiated, and guidelines for developing both types of programs are provided. Since leisure education may be new to many students, particular attention is paid to planning implementation strategies and long range plans for leisure education implementation.

Introduction

Planning for leisure education can, and should, take place on two different levels. The first level of program planning is the agency level; this level is referred to as *comprehensive program planning*. A second level of program planning is developing *specific programs.* These levels are discussed in turn. Comprehensive program planning involves assessing client needs to determine the appropriateness of leisure education for an agency's mission and goals. Once this step has been taken, the agency needs to analyze its mission statement to be sure that it includes a declared intent to educate clients for leisure. A mission statement such as "*To provide a comprehensive system of leisure services that assist people in the development of leisure awareness, attitudes, and skills that promote personal leisure participation and satisfaction,*" clearly delineates the intent to educate for leisure.

Likewise, agencies need to reflect leisure education in their agency goal statements. This may require modifying a current goal statement or developing new leisure education goals to be included by the agency. The following examples outline some of these types of goals. This is by no means meant to be an exhaustive list but is offered as examples from which an agency can develop its own goals:

- to develop an awareness of leisure and its significance to one's life.
- to provide information related to leisure resources and opportunities.
- to develop an acceptance of personal responsibility for leisure and meeting leisure needs.
- to provide opportunities for exploring personal leisure attitudes and values.
- to develop leisure problem-solving and decision-making skills.

The second level of program planning consists of developing *specific programs*. A specific program is defined by Peterson and Gunn (1984) as a set of activities and its corresponding interactions that are designed to achieve predetermined objectives selected for a given group of clients. A specific program is implemented and evaluated independent of all other specific programs. The steps involved in developing specific programs for leisure education are the same as those involved in any other kind of recreation or leisure program. The program planning process is generic regardless of the type of program being developed. Planning specific programs generally includes the following steps:

1. Identifying target groups based upon priority needs.

2. Developing program goals and objectives.

3. Selecting or designing experiences (the content) to achieve the specified objectives.

4. Determining method(s) of presentation of the experiences.

5. Specifying an implementation description (Peterson & Gunn, 1984) that includes determining the
   a. number, length, and frequency of sessions,
   b. staffing requirements,
   c. facility, equipment, and supplies needed.

No attempt is made in this text to explain the step-by-step processes involved in comprehensive and specific program planning. For excellent descriptions of these processes, the reader is referred to Rossman's *Recreation Programming: Designing Leisure Experiences* and Peterson and Gunn's *Therapeutic Recreation Program Design.* Both of these texts offer comprehensive and detailed information on program planning.

However, since leisure education content and processes may be new to some practitioners, specific considerations and guidelines are given below to assist in the planning process.

Comprehensive Planning Level Considerations

Once leisure education has been included in the agency's mission statement and goals, the next consideration would be to identify target groups for leisure education based on priority needs. In public recreation and leisure settings, an agency may decide to target elementary and middle school age children, pre-retirees, and working adults in the community at large. In a therapeutic recreation department, it could be that the entire patient population is the target group since leisure education is one of three components of service in the therapeutic recreation continuum.

In either of the above cases, the next step would be to identify priority leisure education components and subcomponents for each of the target groups based on its identified needs. The components and subcomponents can be drawn from any of the models for leisure education outlined in Chapter 3. For example, it may be decided that for elementary school children the following components and subcomponents are priority needs:

Example 1. School age children
Component: Leisure awareness
Subcomponent: Knows what the term leisure means

Component: Self-awareness
Subcomponent: Leisure barriers or constraints

Component: Leisure Skills
Subcomponent: Decision making
Subcomponent: Leisure activity skills

Component: Leisure Resources
Subcomponent: Community leisure resources

The subcomponents identified for each target group can then be used as a basis for developing goals and objectives for specific program plans.

A second consideration that must be addressed at the agency level, as well as the specific program planning level, is what implementation strategies (infusion and direct strategies) the system could use, given its current staff and resources (a list of strategies can be found in Chapter 6). For example, a community agency may want to implement television "spots" to begin raising the leisure awareness of adults in the community. However, given the skills of the current staff and the limited fiscal resources of the agency, it may not be feasible to use any one particular strategy at this point in time. Additional related questions that can provide guidance in selecting implementation strategies are as follows:

1. **What strategies can be used in the agency with a reallocation of the staff or resources or with pulling together the resources that are already available?** For example, one community allocated 50% of the time of one of its staff to provide leisure education to elementary school classes in the city. Another assigned two staff members to be a part of their "outreach" speakers bureau. These staff responded to community organizations' request for speakers by providing mini leisure education presentations to community groups.

2. **What strategies could be used by modifying the implementation strategies suggested?** A therapeutic recreation department may not be able to use commercial television to aid in its leisure education program. However, it may be able

to use the agency's closed-circuit patient education network for leisure education.

3. **What strategies could be used with staff training or minor additional resources?** For example, current front line leaders may not know how to facilitate client decision-making, problem-solving, and planning skills as a part of their program. However, with staff training, leaders can be taught and can practice the skills needed to include this element as a part of the ongoing program. In relation to minor additional resources, one community agency used university field work students to develop a community leisure resource guide, while another added one dedicated phone line as a leisure hot-line to announce leisure opportunities in the community.

Table 5.1, an Implementation Strategies Worksheet, may be helpful in identifying possible strategies at the agency level. The worksheet breaks the strategies down into four categories: 1) strategies that can be used immediately with no modification required; 2) strategies that can be used but would need to be modified for the agency's particular setting; 3) strategies that would be used by reallocating selected agency resources; and 4) strategies that can be used but would require staff training.

Another consideration at the comprehensive planning level is developing long-range plans for leisure education implementation. Most systems may not be able to execute all of the strategies that are possible for their agency at the inception of the leisure education efforts. Developing long-range plans sets forth the agency's future goals. This step involves identifying future target groups, identifying implementation strategies the agency wants to phase in over time, determining the resources necessary for implementation, and setting target dates for the addition of each strategy. Using Table 5.2, a Long-Range Implementation Worksheet, can guide such future planning efforts.

Table 5.1
Implementation Strategies Worksheet

Strategies That Can Be Used Immediately Without Modification		
Target Group	**Infusion**	**Direct**
Strategies Needing Modification		
Strategies Needing a Reallocation of Resources		
Strategies Requiring Staff Training		

Table 5.2
Long-Range Implementation Worksheet

Target Group	Strategy	Staffing Requirements	Resources Needed	Target Date

Specific Program Planning Considerations

As was stated previously, the program planning process for specific programs is generic regardless of the type of program being developed. However, since planning leisure education programs may be unfamiliar to some practitioners, special considerations for designing specific programs are enumerated.

Once a target group has been identified and the priority leisure education components and subcomponents have been selected in the comprehensive planning stage, practitioners have many valuable resources that can be used to aid in developing specific programs. There are resources, such as Chapter 6 of this text, that contain already developed units that include program goals, program objectives, background information for the facilitator, and leisure education activities and experiences to accomplish the objectives. Stumbo and Thompson's *Leisure Education: A Manual of Activities and Resources I and II* also has goals and objectives for the leisure education activities included in the manuals. In therapeutic recreation, the following resources provide specific leisure education programs that can be used in designing specific leisure education programs:

- John Datillo and William D. Murphy, *Leisure Education Program Planning,*
- Colleen Hood and Carol Peterson, *Therapeutic Recreation Needs in Chemical Dependency Treatment,*
- Kenneth F. Joswiak, *Leisure Education Program Materials for Persons with Developmental Disabilities.*

While these resources are targeted for therapeutic recreation systems, many of the specific programs are equally applicable to other non-therapeutic, recreation, client groups. Once practitioners become familiar and comfortable with leisure education goals, objectives, activities, and implementation strategies, it will then be easy to develop their own specific leisure education programs using the generic specific program planning process previously outlined in the beginning of this chapter, as well as developing their own unique leisure education activities and experiences.

An example of four of the steps involved in specific program planning applied to leisure education follows:

1. Write goals and objectives for each identified priority subcomponent. Example:
   Component: Leisure Awareness
   Subcomponent: Know what leisure is
   Goal: The participant will develop an understanding of the concept of leisure.
   Objective(s):
   Participants will:
   a. define leisure;
   b. identify three primary components of leisure;

c. identify leisure experiences in their own lives.

2. Identify leisure education program activities or experiences from a variety of resources to meet the stated objectives. Example:
   Objective: Participants will identify the sense of freedom they feel in various life situations.
   Program Experience(s): "My Sense of Freedom" worksheet (Mundy)

3. Identify leisure education strategies to accomplish the objective. Example:
   Program Experience(s): "My Sense of Freedom" worksheet (Mundy)
   Strategies: The instructor will provide participants with a
   a. mini-presentation of the concept of freedom,
   b. worksheet,
   c. group discussion.

4. Implement the plan and evaluate the outcomes.

Planning to include leisure education as one of the components of an agency's service is critical to a successful outcome. Just as a special event or the development of a leisure skill requires careful and thoughtful planning, facilitating the development of an understanding of leisure that can lead to leisure satisfaction requires the same careful and thoughtful planning. The planning process is the same. Only the content, activities, and strategies may differ from traditional recreation and leisure programming. However, with the number and variety of resources that are available today to assist practitioners, the successful implementation of leisure education can be accomplished with greater ease than ever before.

Summary

Comprehensive and specific program planning for leisure education is one of the most critical tasks in translating the agency's commitment to educate its clientele for leisure into an operational reality. The process of planning for leisure education is the same process used for planning other recreation and leisure programs. The content and focus of the planning is the only difference in the process. However, since leisure education is new to many practitioners, the fundamental shift in the agency's philosophy, goals, facilitation techniques, and implementation strategies needed for leisure education may pose a major challenge to the agency and its staff.

Chapter 5 References

Datillo, J., & Murphy, W.D. (1991). *Leisure education program planning*. State College, PA: Venture Publishing, Inc.

Hood, C., & Peterson, C.A. (1990). *Therapeutic recreation needs in chemical dependency treatment.*Champaign, IL: Office of Recreation and Park Resources, University of Illinois.

Joswiak, K.F. (1989). *Leisure education program materials for persons with developmental disabilities.* State College, PA: Venture Publishing, Inc.

Peterson, C.A., & Gunn, S.C. (1984). *Therapeutic recreation program design.* Prentice-Hall: Englewood Cliffs, NJ.

Rossman, R. (1995). *Recreation programming: Designing leisure experinces.* Champaign, IL: Sagamore Publishing.

Stumbo, N.J., & Thompson, S.R. (1986). *Leisure education: A manual of activities and resources.* State College, PA: Venture Publishing, Inc.

Chapter 6

Leisure Education Units for Implementation

The focus of this chapter is to provide a series of units that have been designed based on the author's model of leisure education outlined in detail in the previous chapter. Each unit presented identifies the following: 1) the leisure education component (leisure awareness, self-awareness, leisure skills, and leisure resources; 2) the subcomponent; 3) a program goal; and 4) program objectives for the unit. These are followed by background information on the topic at hand, as well as learning experiences to assist the facilitator in implementing the units.

The units and their accompanying learning experiences can be used as presented or with additions or modifications. For example, leisure education activities designed by other authors or the facilitator can provide additional or alternate activities for the ones presented. These units have been developed to serve as illustrations or examples that can be used by facilitators in custom designing their own units for their specific populations.

It should also be pointed out that there are no age or setting differentiations in this chapter. Some special issues and considerations are presented in the remaining chapters of this book. However, the objectives and many of the program experiences are generically appropriate and would differ only in methods of presentation, levels of sophistication, and conceptual difficulty. Many simple program experiences have been utilized with elementary school children, college students, working adults, and retirees, with equal success when the session was carefully planned to meet the individual or group needs, interests, and levels of sophistication. The remaining chapters give specific suggestions for therapeutic recreation, corrections, and aging populations.

LEISURE AWARENESS

Component: Leisure awareness

Subcomponent: Definition of leisure

Program Goal: Participants will develop an understanding of the concept of leisure.

Program Objectives:
Participants will:

1. define leisure.

2. identify three primary components of leisure.

3. identify leisure experiences in their own lives.

Background Information:

While there are numerous definitions of leisure than can be utilized, this book uses the definition of leisure as a state characterized by a sense of freedom and internal motivation in self-selected experiences (Iso-Ahola, 1980). As was stated earlier, Iso-Ahola's work also points out that for most individuals, this state is achieved in nonemployment time (Iso-Ahola, 1980, p. 8). When working with very young children, the mentally retarded, and certain psychiatric patients, the term may need to be defined more simply, such as, when you are free to choose what you want to do.

Program Experiences:

1. The facilitator may begin by either having participants give their definitions of leisure or by providing a definition of leisure for the discussion. Another effective technique that can be used is to begin the session by having everyone close their eyes or pick a point of focus somewhere in the room. Then guide them verbally through the following scenario by asking the following:

   a. Where would you *really* rather be right now?
   b. Picture where you are.
   c. Tune in to what you are doing.

d. Who have you chosen to bring with you or leave behind?
e. Tune into what you are feeling.
f. Enjoy this nice respite for a moment. Then when you are ready, bring your focus back to the present.
g. During that experience, would you say you were working—involved in daily maintenance activities—or in leisure?
h. Why do you think that?

2. Whatever method is used to begin a discussion of leisure, it is important to point out that leisure is a state characterized by the following:

   a. a sense of freedom,
   b. internal motivation,
   c. self-selection or self-direction in the experience.

Component: Leisure awareness

Subcomponent: The concept of freedom

Program Goal: Participants will understand the concept of freedom.

Program Objectives:

Participants will:

1. identify the sense of freedom they feel in various life situations.

2. identify the factors that contribute to or detract from their sense of freedom.

3. categorize factors into internal or external influences.

4. clarify their beliefs regarding freedom in their own lives.

5. identify strategies that they believe will be able to help them increase their sense of freedom.

6. have the opportunity to utilize a strategy to increase their sense of freedom.

Background Information:

A perceived sense of freedom is a primary determinant of achieving leisure. It is, therefore, critical that participants understand that freedom is a feeling of being in control of one's own actions. It is where there is a minimum of perceived and real external control, external constraints, compulsory activities, and external rewards and punishments directing their behavior.

Program Experiences:

1. Have participants fill out Worksheet 1, "My Sense of Freedom," or generate a list of their own life situations that they can use to rate their sense of freedom.

2. After completing the worksheet discuss the following:

   a. What factors contribute to you feeling a sense of freedom?
   b. What factors detract from you feeling a sense of freedom?
   c. Which of these factors are internal? Which are external?

3. Pass around Worksheet 2, "Viewpoints," and have participants indicate whether they agree or disagree with the statement. Discuss their views, why they hold that view, and the way their views may, or do, influence their lives and their leisure.

4. Ask, "Are there some realistic ways you can increase your sense of freedom in your life? What are they?"

   You may want to suggest ways people have been able to increase their sense of freedom by strategies such as what follows:

   a. reevaluating the "have to" and "should" messages we learned early in life in relation to what is realistic today and what we believe at this point in our lives;
   b. fine-tuning our organization, planning, and time management skills;
   c. reevaluating the number and extent of obligations we voluntarily assume;
   d. expanding our awareness of the variety of options that are available to us;
   e. discussing issues with significant others rather than the following options:

      - *mind reading* —thinking we know what someone else is thinking or will think, rather than checking it out.
      - *fortune telling*—a negative prediction of results taken as fact, even though it is usually unrealistic.
      - *catastrophizing*—blowing the potential for negative results out of proportion.

   f. changing our thoughts on how we choose to view a situation and thereby changing our feelings about the situation. (See Chapter 1, "Internal Factors Influencing Perceptions of Freedom.")

5. Have each participant select a strategy they feel will help them increase their sense of freedom in their life to work on and then report back to the group on their experience.

WORKSHEET 1
My Sense of Freedom

Directions: Rate each of the following life situations (adding your own if you so choose) according to how free you feel in each situation. Mark only those applicable to your life.

Life Situations	My Feeling of Freedom				
	High				Low
	5	4	3	2	1
From the time I wake up in the morning until I get to work or school	5	4	3	2	1
At work/school	5	4	3	2	1
At lunch	5	4	3	2	1
Between the end of work/school and dinner	5	4	3	2	1
In the evenings	5	4	3	2	1
On Friday afternoon	5	4	3	2	1
On Saturday	5	4	3	2	1
On Sunday afternoon	5	4	3	2	1
Before a vacation	5	4	3	2	1
When asked to do something social by my boss	5	4	3	2	1
When asked to do something social by my child/children	5	4	3	2	1
When asked to do something social by my significant other	5	4	3	2	1
When asked for a favor by a friend	5	4	3	2	1
When asked to take on a responsibility by a professional, community, or religious organization	5	4	3	2	1

WORKSHEET 2
Viewpoints

Directions: Indicate whether you agree or disagree with the following statements.

	Agree	Disagree
1. As human beings we possess the freedom to choose among alternatives.	______	______
2. Because we are free to make choices, we can direct our lives.	______	______
3. We can influence our destinies through the choices and decisions we make.	______	______
4. Although our freedom may be partially limited by circumstances, we are still able to be self-determining through our freedom to make choices.	______	______
5. It is a mistake to assume we cannot become free until other give us permission to be free. We must retain final "permission rights" for ourselves.	______	______
6. If we wait for other to grant us the freedom we want or blame others for our lack of freedom, we diminish our power to take control of our lives.	______	______

(Paraphrased from Harry Browne, 1973)

Component: Leisure awareness

Subcomponent: Self-responsibility

Program Goal: Participants will develop a realistic sense of responsibility in relation to their own lives and leisure.

Program Objectives:

Participants will:

1. assess and clarify their personal responsibilities in relation to leisure.

2. identify how assuming too much or too little responsibility can affect their lives and other peoples' lives.

3. identify areas in which they feel they need to accept more or less responsibility.

4. identify strategies to accept more or less responsibility.

5. practice self-responsibility in relation to their leisure in the program and in their lives.

Background Information:

Scott Peck has stated, ". . . the problem of distinguishing what we are and what we are not responsible for in this life is one of the greatest problems of human existence" (Peck, 1978). He further affirms, ". . . we must continually assess and reassess where our responsibilities lie in the ever changing course of events" (Peck, 1978). As human beings, we begin this struggle early in our lives. As children, we vehemently disavow any responsibility for the fight we are in with our sibling. *He* "started it!" We were just sitting there when we began to be hit upon. We have selectively disregarded the fact that we tried to trip the passing sibling. We vacillate from this stance of no responsibility to other situations in which we feel total responsibility. We are outside playing and our brother falls off the swing. We feel responsible. Mother is crying and unhappy. We feel it is our fault and, therefore, it is our responsibility to make her feel better. Through experiences such as these we are attempting to learn what are and what are not our responsibilities in this world.

Unfortunately, many children are given mixed or incorrect messages about what responsibilities are theirs, what responsibilities are shared, and what responsibilities belong to other people. All too often, parents who are confused about what issues are theirs blame children for things that are really their responsibility. A comment such as, "*You* make me mad," says you are responsible for my anger. This is a very different message from, "When you behave in that way, *I* get angry." *You* statements shift the responsibility to another person. *I* statements communicate that I am responsible for my feelings, my behavior, my choices, and my actions.

In this life we are responsible for our own lives. We are responsible for our own feelings, choices, behaviors, actions, and perceptions of the world and the people in it because we are free to choose, feel, perceive, and behave. Ultimately, the only thing we can be responsible for is ourselves and our own lives because this is the only area in which we really have control through the choices and decisions we make. In many instances, we may have been erroneously made to believe we are responsible and, therefore, we have control over things we do not . . . cannot control. If we have been told, in essence, "you are responsible for my feelings or reactions," and we accept that assessment, then we feel it is in our power to control the outcome. We feel we can fix things we cannot fix. We believe we can make everything okay when we cannot. We assume the role of the caretaker or the rescuer. The great cosmic joke is that someone has shifted the responsibility to us but has maintained the control for themselves and, thereby, ends up controlling us.

At the other end of the spectrum are those who believe and, therefore, feel that how we feel, how we react, how we behave, and what our lives are like is the result of what other people in our lives and circumstances are throwing our way. It is like living with a loose cannon to which we must constantly respond. This can make us feel we cannot really live our lives as we wish because we must constantly duck, deflect, dodge, or hide in order for our lives not to be blown apart. This type of thinking also tends to lead us to believe that if good things are happening to other people, it is because someone, somewhere, is sprinkling the pixie dust on them, giving them the good things of life.

Most of us are still grappling with what we are and what we are not responsible for. We may also be trying to sort out the degree of our responsibility in certain instances, as well as when we need to let go of certain responsibilities that have been ours previously. This is not an easy task. It can also be more difficult when we try to change old patterns we have established out of this confusion. It can be extremely difficult to tell someone you love that you are going to play bridge once a week over his objections, and the fact that he doesn't want to be alone is his problem, not yours.

The confusions over responsibility can impact dramatically upon one's leisure. Because the essence of leisure is a perceived sense of freedom, feeling overcome by responsibilities that are not ours or assuming that our fun, joy, and happiness is another's responsibility can dissipate our sense of freedom.

Program Experiences:

1. Introduce this unit by using the Scott Peck statements in the Background information and by telling the group that the purpose of these experiences is to enable them to assess and clarify this personal responsibility in relation to leisure.

   Give each participant Worksheet 2, "Viewpoints," to complete by indicating with which statements they agree or disagree. Then have the group discuss their responses and the reasons for their answers.

2. Discuss the following statements with the group. Have them indicate whether they agree or disagree with the statements.

   > "Since we possess the freedom to choose among alternatives, we are also responsible for our decisions that shape our lives."
   >
   > "The more we accept responsibility for the choices we make, the more we can consciously determine the direction we want our lives to take."
   >
   > "The more we accept responsibility for our own leisure and leisure experiences, the more we can consciously determine having time for leisure and the quality of our leisure experiences."

3. If the issues of joint responsibility and assuming too much or not enough responsibility surface during the discussion, the following questions can be used to further the discussion. If these concepts have not surfaced, the questions can lead into an examination of these issues.

   a. How can assuming too much responsibility affect you and other people?

   b. How can *not* assuming enough responsibility affect you and other people?

4. Have the participants complete and discuss their answers on Worksheet 3, "Who's Responsible?"

   a. What, if any, area(s) of your life do you feel you need to accept more responsibility? less responsibility?
   b. How can one go about accepting more or less responsibility in life?

WORKSHEET 3
Who's Responsible?

Directions: For each of the following statements, indicate who you think is responsible for the situation.

Codes: 1 = an area of *joint* responsibility; 2 = I am responsible; 3 = the other person is responsible.

_____ My children say they are bored.

_____ My spouse/significant other/friend says if I don't go fishing with him/her (which I don't want to do), he/she won't have fun and enjoy it.

_____ I don't have time for leisure.

_____ I am bored.

_____ My spouse/significant other says he/she doesn't have time to do what he/she wants to do.

_____ There are so many demands on me, I am too tired to do what I want to do.

_____ I feel there is nothing to do on the weekends.

Component: Leisure awareness

Subcomponent: Internal motivation

Program Goal: Participants will develop an understanding of the difference between internal motivation and external motivation.

Program Objectives:

Participants will:

1. define motivation.

2. differentiate between internal and external motivation.

3. identify feelings associated with experiences that are internally and externally motivated.

4. describe how internal motivation contributes to attaining leisure.

Background Information:

Motivation can be defined as a driving force behind behavior. It is what causes us to behave the ways we do and it moves us to action. Motivation can be internal or external in nature. Internal motivations are those primarily arising from within the individual. External motivations are those that come from the external rewards one may receive or the punishment one may avoid as a result of their action. Internally motivated experiences are critical determinants to achieving leisure because they are associated with more enjoyment, involvement, and with a perceived sense of freedom.

Program Experiences:

1. Define or ask participants to define the following terms: motivation, internal motivation, and external motivation, and give an example of each from their daily lives.

2. Discuss the differences in feeling when we do something we are internally motivated to do versus externally motivated to do. Then ask participants to identify which form of motivation is more closely associated with leisure and why.

Component: Leisure awareness

Subcomponent: The relationship of leisure to time

Program Goal: Participants will demonstrate an understanding of time and its relationship to and influence on their leisure.

Program Objectives:
Participants will:

1. identify when they perceive they have time for leisure during a typical week.

2. identify how and when they could have larger blocks of time for leisure during their week.

3. assess and clarify their beliefs about time and leisure.

4. identify factors that influence their own free time.

5. identify the degree and direction in which each factor influences their free time.

Background Information:

While leisure can occur at any time and in many life experiences, research is tending to indicate that for most people leisure occurs during nonemployment hours. This means participants need to look at their time, their use of time, and the relationship of time to their leisure.

Program Experiences:

1. Using Worksheet 4, "A Week at a Glance," have all participants mark when they perceive that they have leisure. Add the total number of hours they have leisure or have available for leisure during the week, on the weekends, and during the week as a whole.

2. Discuss the following:

   a. Why are certain times considered leisure to you and not to others?
   b. Do you have more, less, or about the same number of hours for leisure that you thought?

3. Using the same worksheet, ask if there are other or larger time blocks that could be utilized for leisure with more efficient use of time. Identify what changes would need to be made to open more time.

4. Discuss how the amount of time we have available in a block influences our perception of the number and type of choices we have available.

5. Share and discuss the following "Critical Time Concepts." The discussion can be through an open discussion or by using an agree-disagree approach.

Critical Time Concepts

- Time is one resource that is equally distributed.
- Time and what we do with it is a matter of the choices we make.
- We can never get "more time". We can only change the decisions we make regarding how we choose to use our time.
- Time is neutral. Our feelings about time are influenced by the choices we make and the experiences we have.

6. Develop a group-generated list of societal factors and personal factors that can influence a person's free time. Societal factors are things such as role expectations, society's idea of "success," the state of the economy, technology, and work patterns. Personal factors are things such as obligations, responsibilities, personal finances, choices made in other areas of one's life, and the outcome or payoff one receives from choices.

   Have participants identify the societal and personal factors that they believe influence the amount of free time they have and the quality of their free time.

7. Further discussion of societal factors that can influence our time and our leisure can be pursued by having participants complete Worksheets 5 and 6, "Old Sayings and Leisure" and "Societal Expectations."

8. Participants can draw, paint, or make a collage that, to them, represents societal expectations for the following:

   a. their own role (i.e., student, housewife, retiree, etc.);
   b. success.

Making a collage often has meaning since sayings and pictures are taken from magazines; it appears to emphasize the role of advertisement in relation to the areas mentioned.

9. Using the following examples (or others you make up), have participants discuss ways national and personal affluence and poverty would affect their free time.

    - *EXAMPLE A.* Our nation has been hit with an extremely high rate of inflation. Food, clothing, shelter, heating, air-conditioning, electricity, and gasoline prices have soared. In what ways could our national economic condition affect people's free time? In what ways can one's free time affect national and personal economy?

    - *EXAMPLE B.* Let's say that, as of this minute, you (or your family) has only $6,000 a year to live on. How might this affect the amount of free time you may have? How might it affect what you do during your free time? Where do you believe your priorities would be? How do you think you would view leisure? How would it affect your feelings of self-worth?

    - *EXAMPLE C.* It has just been discovered that your home is sitting on one of the richest oil fields in the nation. You (or your family) are suddenly rich beyond your wildest imagination. You will never have to work unless you want to do so. Write down what would be the first things you would want to do. How would you plan for it to affect the amount of free time you have? What would you do during your free time that you could not do before? How do you think you would view leisure? How do you think you would view life in general?

WORKSHEET 4
Week at a Glance

Times	Mon	Tues	Wed	Thur	Fri	Sat	Sun
6 A.M.							
7 A.M.							
8 A.M.							
9 A.M.							
10 A.M.							
11 A.M.							
NOON							
1 P.M.							
2 P.M.							
3 P.M.							
4 P.M.							
5 P.M.							
6 P.M.							
7 P.M.							
8 P.M.							
9 P.M.							
10 P.M.							
11 P.M.							
12 A.M.							
1 A.M.							
2 A.M.							
3 A.M.							
4 A.M.							
5 A.M.							

WORKSHEET 5
Old Sayings and Leisure

Directions: Check which of the following old sayings and phrases you believe have a beneficial, neutral, or detrimental effect on children's, adults', and your own leisure. Place the code letter in the appropriate space that most closely reflects your feelings.

KEY: P = Positive NU = Neutral N = Negative

Children's Leisure	Adults' Leisure	My Own Leisure	
______	______	______	"Anything worth doing is worth doing well."
______	______	______	"There are no prizes given for second place."
______	______	______	"Idle hands are the devil's work-shop."
______	______	______	"Birds of a feather flock together."
______	______	______	"The early bird gets the worm."
______	______	______	"To the winner goes the spoils."
______	______	______	"All work and no play makes Jean a dull girl."
______	______	______	"Families that play together stay together."
______	______	______	"The grass is always greener on the other side."

WORKSHEET 6
Societal Expectations

Directions: Rate the degree of effect you believe the following have on people's leisure in general and on your leisure specifically. Enter the number in the appropriate blanks that most closely reflect your opinion.

KEY:

Positive		Neutral		Negative
5	4	3	2	1

	Effects on people's leisure in general	Effects on my own leisure
Society's role expectation of men	________	________
Society's role expectation of women	________	________
Society's work role expectations	________	________
Society's family role expectations	________	________
Society's criteria of a "successful" person	________	________
Society's criteria of a "productive" life	________	________

Component: Leisure awareness

Subcomponent: Leisure experiences

Program Goal: Participants will increase their awareness of their own current leisure experiences.

Program Objectives:
Participants will:

1. identify experiences or activities in which they participate as leisure experiences.

2. identify the factors or explain why their experiences could be considered leisure experiences.

3. express themselves based on representations of the experiences they believe are symbolic of their leisure/leisure experiences.

4. identify the structure/components that affect and are involved in their leisure experiences.

Background Information:

Any experience one has in leisure can be viewed as or called a leisure experience if it perceived as such by the individual. The individual's perceptions, in the final analysis, are the ultimate criteria of what is and what is not a leisure experience.

Since leisure is characterized as a perceived sense of freedom and internal motivation in self-selected experiences, any life experience can be engaged in during leisure, and thus can be a leisure experience *when individuals perceive it to be a leisure experience.* Therefore, the countless forms and types of experiences are too numerous to list. The purpose of this objective is to show the infinite variety of experiences that are potentially leisure experiences and, although the experiences could be classified in many different ways, they may also be perceived by some people as leisure experiences while not by others.

Program Experiences:

1. Participants should identify the experiences or activities in their lives that they feel are leisure experiences and list them on Worksheet 7, "My Leisure Experiences."

   Through discussion or creative writing, participants could tell why the experiences listed are leisure experiences to them.

2. Have all persons draw their "Leisure Coat of Arms." This would include representations of what experiences they believe are most symbolic of their leisure and leisure experiences. An outline of a coat of arms can be pre-drawn and given out to be filled in.

WORKSHEET 7
My Leisure Experiences

Directions: In the spaces provided, list experiences as activities in which you currently engage that are leisure experiences for you.

Leisure Experiences	With Whom	Frequency	Expense	65	Level of Enjoyment	Originally Learned

In the columns next to each experience, code the experience using the following codes. More than one can be utilized for an experience.

1) With whom: A = Alone; FM = Family; FR = Friends.
2) Frequency: D = Daily; W = Weekly; F = Frequently; S = Seldom.
3) E = Expensive; IE = Inexpensive (not including initial investment).
4) 65 = You think you will be doing this when you are 65 years old.
5) Level of enjoyment: TF = Time filler; F = Fun; E = Enjoyable; P = Peak experience.
6) Originally learned: S = Self-taught; FM = Family; FR = Friend; SH = School; R = Recreation department or group.

Component: Leisure awareness

Subcomponent: Leisure experience

Program Goal: Participants will become aware of their own leisure activity patterns.

Program Objectives:
Participants will:

1. identify the development of patterns formed throughout their leisure experiences.

2. discuss the advantages and disadvantages of balanced and unbalanced leisure experience patterns.

3. identify the factors that they believe influence their leisure experiences.

Background Information:

People have patterns of leisure experiences or activities. Patterns can develop for some of the following reasons:

- interests,
- natural abilities or developed skills,
- knowledge,
- opportunities,
- needs being met,
- satisfaction, enrichment, or enhancement.

General patterns can usually be detected through categorizing experiences or activities. The focus of this learning experience is to have participants begin to identify their own leisure experience patterns through the use of categorization. The following categories are by no means comprehensive or the only categories that could be utilized with the group. They are suggestions only and others can and should be utilized where appropriate.

Forms of Leisure Involvement
(NRPA Kangaroo Kit, 1976)

physical - mental
individual - social
participant - audience
structured - nonstructured
active - passive
momentary - long term
planned - spontaneous

Location of Leisure Experiences

at home
in the neighborhood
at sites or places set up for or needed for the experience
at the home of friends
indoors/out-of-doors
in the community

Human Involvement in Leisure Experiences

(With whom do you usually engage in leisure experiences? Actual names can be used in this category.)

alone
with family members
with friends

Resources Utilized in Leisure Experiences

public (municipal, county, state, etc.)
commercial (businesses, etc.)
personal
private (clubs)

Frequency

almost daily
weekly
monthly
seasonally

Subcategories for Recreation Activities Listed as Leisure Experiences

dance
drama
music
hobby
art
fitness
sports
games
crafts
mental/table games
aquatics
reading
nature
outings
travel
collecting
volunteering

Program Experiences:

1. Have the group discuss why they believe people (or themselves) develop patterns of leisure experiences. Also discuss the advantages and disadvantages of balanced and unbalanced leisure experience patterns if it has not been discussed previously.

2. An interesting, sometimes startling learning activity is to have everyone complete Worksheet 8, "Leisure Experience Questionnaire." When the questionnaire has been completed, have participants compare (with the help of the facilitator) their answers on the questionnaire with the list of activities they actually engage in during their leisure. A discussion could follow using questions below:

   a. What did you find out that surprised you or that you didn't expect?
   b. What did not surprise you? What would you have anticipated?
   c. What did you find out by comparing the questionnaire to your leisure experience code sheet?

3. Have the groups write down, answer to themselves, or discuss the following:

   a. I learned about my leisure experiences that ________________.
   b. I see in my activities ________________________________.
   c. My leisure experiences primarily involve __________________.
   d. My leisure experiences don't include ____________________.
   e. I would like for my leisure experiences to include (or include more) ____.
   f. I would like for my leisure experiences to include less (or not include) ______________________________________.
   g. The adjustments I would like to make in my leisure experiences are ____________________________________.

WORKSHEET 8
Leisure Experience Questionnaire

Directions: On this short questionnaire, indicate the categories you believe your leisure experiences fall under.

1. My leisure experiences are usually

a.	_________ physical	_________ mental
b.	_________ individual	_________ social
c.	_________ structured	_________ nonstructured
d.	_________ active	_________ passive
e.	_________ momentary	_________ long term
f.	_________ planned	_________ spontaneous
g.	_________ expensive	_________ inexpensive

2. My leisure experiences most often take place

a.	_________ at my home	_________ away from home
b.	_________ indoors	_________ out-of-doors
c.	_________ at special places or sites needed for the experience	_________ no special places or sites

3. With whom do you usually engage in leisure experiences? (Actual names can be used.)

_________ alone
_________ a friend(s) name(s)_________________
____
_________ family member(s) name(s) _________________
____

4. What resources do you generally utilize in your leisure?

a. _________ personal
b. _________ commercial (businesses)
c. _________ private (clubs)
d. _________ public (municipal, county, state)
e. I would like for my leisure experiences to include (or include more) _________________________.
f. I would like for my leisure experiences to include less (or not include) _________________________.
g. The adjustments I would like to make in my leisure experiences are _________________________.

Component: Leisure awareness

Subcomponent: Leisure experiences

Program Goal: Participants will identify conditions, knowledge, skills, equipment, supplies, or places needed for one's own leisure experiences.

Program Objectives:
Participants will:

1. focus upon their own leisure experiences in order to increase the awareness of the knowledge, skills, equipment, supplies, and places for participation in their own leisure pursuits.

2. identify their leisure experiences with personal needs, wants, and expectations.

3. identify the factors that influence their satisfaction and enjoyment level of their leisure experiences.

Background Information:

Some leisure experiences require knowledge, skills, equipment, supplies, and places for participation, while others do not.

Learning Experiences:

1. Instruct participants to use their own leisure experiences in completing Worksheet 9, "Rating My Leisure Experiences," in which they rate their leisure experiences as high, moderate, or low in necessary knowledge, skills, equipment, supplies, or places for participation.

2. A follow-up discussion could center around the following questions:

   a. How would the level of knowledge, skills, equipment, supplies, and places aid in enjoyment and satisfaction or take away from it?
   b. What difference do you see in what one may *want* and what one may *need* in relation to leisure experiences? How might this affect experiences?

3. An effective wrap-up activity is to have the individual complete the following sentences verbally or in writing:

   a. In my leisure experiences, I ____________________.
   b. Some of the things I may want but do not need for equipment are ____________________.
   c. I realize that I ____________________.

WORKSHEET 9
Rating My Leisure Experiences

Directions: Rate your leisure experiences as ***high*** (3), ***moderate*** (2), and *low* (1) in terms of what you perceive they require for participation.

My Leisure Experiences	Knowledge	Skills	Equipment	Supplies	Special Place(s)

Component: Leisure awareness

Subcomponent: Leisure experiences

Program Goal: Participants will identify leisure experiences that are of interest to themselves.

Program Objectives:
Participants will:

1. be introduced to a variety of experiences and options for their leisure.

2. identify and discuss leisure experiences that are new to them, as well as experiences that they may enjoy under different circumstances.

Background Information:

Although a person may have leisure experiences that are and will probably continue to be enjoyable and satisfying, one of the purposes of leisure education is to acquaint individuals with a variety of experiences in order for them to have a broad base of options in leisure. Also, it is possible that there are leisure experiences that one may not even know exist that would contribute significantly to the quality of one's life if pursued. This objective is included in order to have participants begin thinking in terms of exploring new and different experiences in which they may have or develop an interest.

Program Experiences:

1. Verbally, or in writing, have everyone identify and then discuss the following:

   a. leisure experiences I haven't tried but think I would enjoy.
   b. leisure experiences that I didn't like but may if the circumstances were different.

   An alternative means to accomplish the same ends would be to have participants make a collage of the activities they haven't tried and another collage of the activities they may enjoy under different circumstances. The game of "Charades" could also be used for the two topics as well as the game "Password." Art and creative improvisation are also mediums through which the topics could be dealt with.

Partner Activity. Let everyone get a partner and then have each partner in turn explain to the other, "How to *never* try an activity you think you may enjoy."

2. Have the group discuss how they think the following sayings could or would affect *their* leisure experiences.

   a. "Don't knock it until you've tried it."
   b. "You have to know what there is to want before you can want it."
   c. "When in doubt, do nothing."
   d. "Don't expect too much and you will never be disappointed."
   e. "You will never know until you try."

3. If there are experiences that people have identified as wanting to pursue but have not acted upon, have them determine the following:

   a. the perceived reason(s) for not pursuing the experience up until now; e.g., time, location, setting, cost ($), availability, as well as personal, social, or emotional blocks.
   b. possible alternatives - are there other times, locations, settings, costs, means, etc., that would make exploring the new experiences easier or more pleasant?
   c. which alternative or course of action seems most feasible at this particular time?
   d. the immediate, near-future, or far-future plan of action to reach their own goal regarding the new experience(s).
   e. in future contacts with the individuals, have them determine the progress they are making toward reaching the goal(s) they have set.

4. Have participants refer to their leisure motivation inventory or assessment and determine what needs they perceive they can meet through the experiences they are interested in pursuing.

Component: Leisure awareness

Subcomponent: Leisure experiences

Program Goal: Participants will become aware of personal outcomes of leisure experiences and their value to the individual.

Program Objectives:
Participants will:

1. identify leisure experiences that are the most meaningful and beneficial to them.

2. clarify the benefits and outcomes of their own leisure experiences, as well as their perceptions of various leisure experiences.

3. identify leisure outcomes in relation to their own needs, values, and goals.

Background Information:

The process of making choices and decisions in leisure and acting on those choices has resulting outcomes, effects, or consequences. The outcomes of leisure experiences can be as varied as human emotions. Therefore, while the positive outcomes of leisure may receive the primary emphasis, the range of possible outcomes should be considered. Attention should also be drawn to the fact that the same outcomes or similar outcomes can result from very different forms of leisure experiences for the same individual.

Program Experiences:

1. Have everyone list the five leisure experiences that have the most meaning for them and from which they derive the most benefit. Then divide the group into partners and ask them to assume that "Your partner has the power to take away from you forever the experiences you have listed. You have one minute of completely uninterrupted time to tell your partner what you get out of your experiences, how they are of benefit to you, and why you should be allowed to continue them." After the minute has passed, have the partner who was the listener tell the group what he "heard" the person saying about how they were of benefit.

2. The "Meet Your Match Game" is a takeoff on the television "Match Game." Leisure experiences are given, and the participants try and match the outcomes they get from the experience with those of another player. The game highlights the variety of outcomes that different people perceive they get from the same activity.

3. Each person should take a piece of paper and tear it into five (5) pieces. Then ask participants, "If you could only have five outcomes, benefits, and feelings from your leisure experiences, what would they be?" Write one of these on each slip of paper. Then instruct the group to eliminate one of these, one at a time, until they only have two remaining outcomes/benefits/feelings.

4. A "Leisure Auction" can then follow this experience. List on a chalkboard the outcomes people in the group included in the last activity. Divide the group into smaller groups of 4-8 people. Tell each group you are going to have an auction. Each group has $1,000 with which to bid on the outcomes listed on the chalkboard. They need to determine which of the outcomes they want to have for their group and designate one person to do the bidding for the group. Auction off each outcome. Circle and discuss the outcomes which brought the highest price.

Component: Leisure awareness

Subcomponent: Leisure experiences

Program Goal: Participants will identify factors that can influence outcomes of personal leisure experiences.

Programs Objectives:
Participants will:

1. distinguish between "external-environmental" and "internal-personal" factors that influence their leisure experiences.

2. clarify and discuss various changes they would consider when dealing with their positive or negative influences on their leisure experiences.

Background Information:

The outcomes of leisure choices and the resulting experiences are determined by a number of factors. In order for persons to receive the optimum benefits and positive outcomes they may desire from leisure, it is necessary that they be aware of the factors that can and do influence their own experiences. This objective is designed to develop such an awareness within the participants. There are external-environmental factors that can influence leisure outcomes as can internal-personal factors.

Program Experiences:

1. Have the group identify and discuss factors that influence the outcomes of their leisure experiences. List these under headings of "External-Environment" factors and "Internal-Personal" factors. After the discussion, have everyone place a plus (+) or a minus (-) beside those factors that most influence the outcomes of their leisure experiences. In front of each factor identified, ask participants to rate on a scale of 1-5 the degree to which they believe that factor influences their outcomes (5 = high degree of influence, 1 = low degree of influence).

2. Encourage participants to identify and discuss what changes they could make to minimize or eliminate negative influences and maximize positive influences.

Component: Leisure awareness

Subcomponent: Leisure experiences

Program Goal: Participants will determine their satisfaction with their currently desired leisure outcomes.

Program Objective:
Participants will:

1. identify current outcomes from their leisure experiences.

2. determine whether they are satisfied or not with the outcomes from their leisure experiences.

3. determine and make any changes in their leisure to attain the outcomes they desire.

Background Information:

Once participants are aware of their leisure outcomes and the factors that can influence those outcomes, it is important for them to assess their level of satisfaction with their current leisure outcomes and make changes in their leisure experiences if necessary.

Program Experiences:

- Use Worksheet 10, "Information Processing on Leisure Outcomes," to have participants determine this level of satisfaction with current leisure outcomes and identify and discuss any changes they may want to make.

WORKSHEET 10
Information Processing on Leisure Outcomes

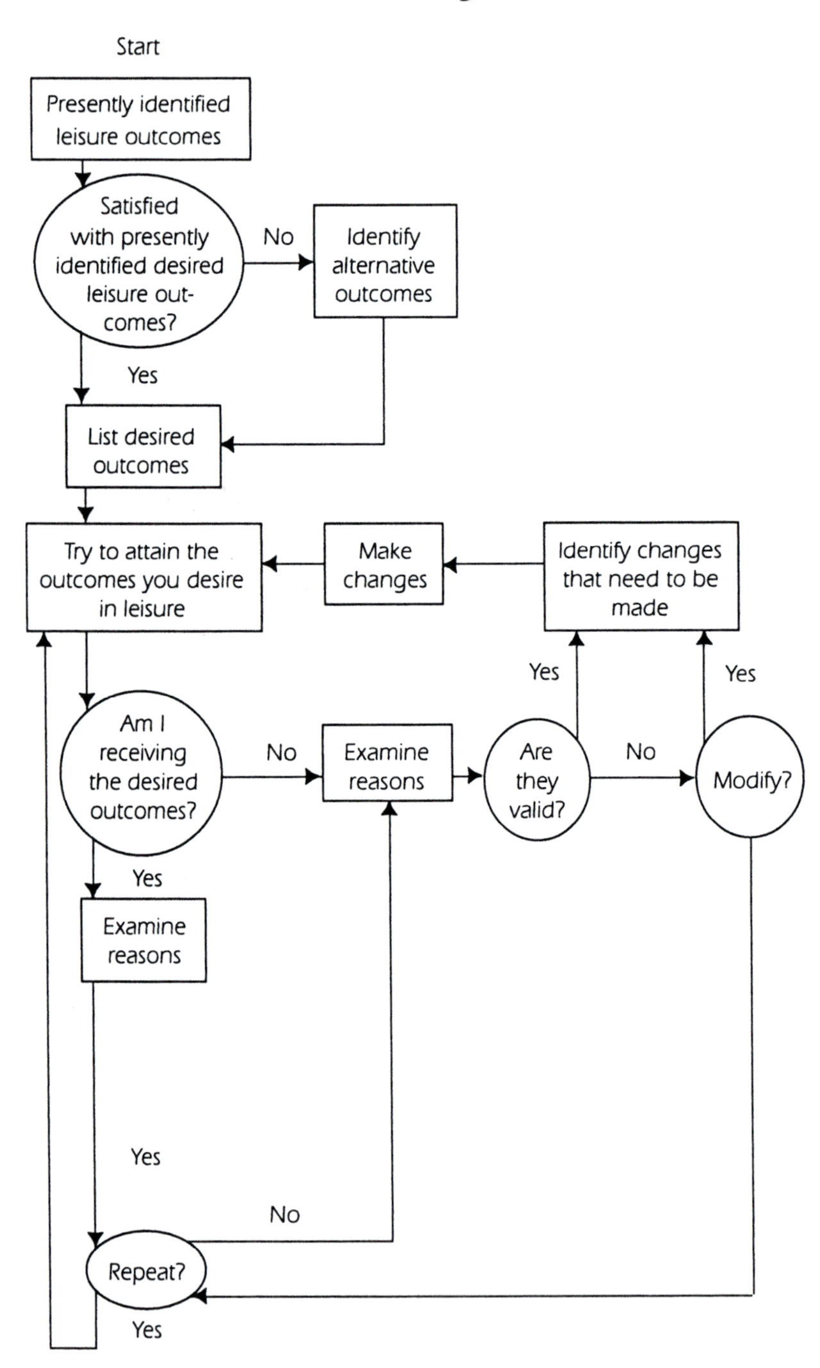

Component: Leisure awareness

Subcomponent: Relationship to one's life

Program Goals:

Part A: Participants will identify their own life activities.

Part B: Participants will categorize their daily life activities into self-perceived categories.

Program Objectives:
Participants will:

Part A:
1. identify their own daily leisure activities.

2. identify those activities that are satisfying and those that are not.

Part B:
1. determine if a balance exists in their daily life activities.

2. determine if they will make a change in those activities and how that change could be made.

Background Information:

Part A:
Persons engage in many different activities in their lives. This exercise provides participants with an opportunity to review, think through, and become consciously aware of some of their life activities.

Part B:
We know that an individual's perception of life and life experiences is of paramount importance. With this in mind, this exercise allows each participant the opportunity to discover how he perceives his daily activities.

PART A:

Program Experiences:

1. Have each person list or name some of the things he does during a day or week.

2. Have someone select one word that describes how he feels about his daily or weekly routine.

3. If the person is not satisfied or would prefer his life experiences to be more like what he has heard someone else describe, have him talk with that person and see what and how he is able to have that quality in his life.

Some Possible Means to Reach the Stated End

1. Each person could keep a daily log for a week and bring it in as a basis for further discussion or exploration.

2. List life activities spontaneously on a piece of paper. (The writing down of one's own answers is effective, revealing to the person, and has considerable impact. It is a technique that should be utilized extensively but without being overdone).

3. Utilize Worksheet 10, "Daily Life Activities."

4. Have group discussions of life activities for the total session.

Part B:

Program Experiences:

1. Each person places his daily life activities into varying categories or codes the activities listed on Worksheet 10 according to the suggested or self-determined categories.

2. Count the number of times each code has been utilized.

3. Reevaluate the one-word descriptor of these life activities to see if it is still applicable.

4. Discuss why one's own activities are in a particular category, why the same activities may be listed under different categories

for different people, what category most of their activities come under, whether there is a balance among the categories, and if the person would change the distribution among categories, how would they change it?

Note: Whatever means are selected or designed to reach the objectives, a follow-up discussion and sharing should ensue and be part of each session.

WORKSHEET 10
Daily Life Activities

Daily Life Activities	1	2	3

Relationships Perceived:

1 2 3

Codes:

WTD = Things I Want To Do	P = Pleasant	W = Work
HTD = Things I Have To Do	N = Neutral	L = Leisure
	U = Unpleasant	R = Recreation
		E = Education
		M = Maintenance
		C = Community Involvement
		Other:

Component: Leisure awareness

Subcomponent: Relationship of leisure to one's life

Program Goal: Participants will determine the relationship of leisure to their lives.

Program Objectives:
Participants will:

1. determine how leisure affects selected areas of their life.
2. determine how selected areas of their life impact their leisure.
3. determine how selected areas of their life impact their perceived sense of freedom, internal motivation, and free time.

Background Information:

Leisure does not exist as a separate, isolated part of one's life. There is a complex interaction and interrelationship with all areas of one's life. This unit helps participants explore and determine how leisure impacts areas of their lives and how other areas of their lives impact their leisure.

Program Experiences:

1. List the following areas of life on a chalkboard or hand them out to the participants on a piece of paper. Ask the group to discuss how each area affects their leisure and how their leisure may affect these areas of their lives:

   work
   family
   religion
   community involvement
   other
   school
   friends
   professional activities & affiliations
   maintenance activities

2. Following a discussion about leisure in general, have the group discuss how these areas of their life can influence their perceived sense of freedom, internal motivation, and free time.

Component: Leisure awareness

Subcomponent: Relationship of leisure to the quality of one's life

Program Goal: Participants will determine what relationship they perceive leisure has to the quality of their lives.

Program Objectives:
Participants will:

1. determine the factors that contribute to and detract from the quality of their lives.

2. determine how negative influences can be modified, moderated, or coped with more effectively.

3. determine how leisure contributes to the quality of their lives.

Background Information:

The quality of one's life is an individual perception. Two dimensions of the quality of life concept are the physical environment and the psychosocial factors and conditions (see Chapter 1 for more detail). The focus of this unit is to assist participants in identifying and examining factors that they perceive contribute to or detract from their quality of life.

Program Experiences:

1. Pass out Worksheet 11, "Influences on the Quality of My Life." Ask participants to list the things they feel that contribute to or detract from the quality of their lives. Discuss what things they have listed as contributing to or detracting from the quality of their lives.

2. Have persons rank the top five (5) things influencing their quality of life positively or negatively (1=most influence and 5= least influential).

3. Of the things that have a negative influence, brainstorm ways these influences can be changed, modified, moderated, or coped with more effectively.

4. Have participants determine which of the factors they have listed are leisure-related. Then have participants answer and discuss, "How does leisure influence the quality of my life?"

WORKSHEET 11
Influences on the Quality of My Life

Instructions: Under each category list the things you feel contribute to and the things that detract from the quality of your life.

Things that Contribute to the Quality of My Life

Environmental Factors (lakes, woods, green belts, cultural events)	***Psychosocial Factors*** (friends, family, health, work)

Things that Detract from the Quality of My Life

Environmental Factors	***Psychosocial Factors***

SELF-AWARENESS

Component: Self-awareness

Subcomponent: Leisure needs, motivations, and satisfaction

Information Background:

The ultimate goal of leisure education is to enable people to enhance the quality of their lives through leisure. For many individuals, this enhancement occurs frequently, automatically, predictably, and with little apparent thought or effort. For others, this is not the case. For individuals who seek more satisfaction in and from leisure, understanding the interaction of personal needs, motivation, and satisfaction as they relate to leisure can be productive.

According to Beard and Ragheb (1983), leisure motivation is the needs, drives, wishes, urges, and reasons that move individuals to seek and engage in leisure experiences. It is what causes and leads one to action. Therefore, needs and motivations are used synonymously herein. People experience leisure to attain satisfaction. Beard and Ragheb (1980) defines leisure satisfaction as

> the positive perception or feeling which an individual forms, elicits, or gains as a result of engaging in leisure activities and choices. It is the degree to which one is presently content or pleased with his/her general leisure experiences and situations. This positive feeling of contentment results from the satisfaction of felt or unfelt needs of the individual.

While it is recognized that 1) behavior is situational, that is, a person may choose the same experience at different times for different reasons and 2) as needs change, a person may seek a variety of experiences to meet their needs, there are general motivations and needs we seek to meet through leisure experiences. By helping participants identify their own motivations/needs in relation to leisure, they will be more knowledgeable in selecting experiences that have the greatest compatibility with their needs.

In educating for leisure, it is necessary to address the issue of satisfaction in two ways. One aspect of leisure satisfaction is to help individuals determine their current leisure satisfaction. This can be accomplished through using an instrument that measures leisure satisfaction, such as the one developed by Beard and Ragheb (1980) which can be found in Appendix A. A second aspect to address is assisting individuals in determining their current personal needs and how these can be satisfied in and through leisure. Attaining this end necessitates assisting individuals in identifying their current personal needs and then helping them develop a working knowledge of how to meet their own needs in and through leisure and leisure experiences. The following learning experiences are designed toward these ends.

Component: Self-awareness

Subcomponent: Motivation/Needs

Program Objectives:
Participants will:

1. identify their personal motivations/needs they seek to meet through leisure

2. identify the leisure experiences they tend to select to satisfy various needs.

3. identify personal needs they feel are not being met.

4. identify possible ways unmet needs can be met through leisure experiences.

Program Experiences:

1. Ask the group to generate a list of reasons, motivations, and/or needs they seek to meet through leisure. This can be an individual or group list. Then, using Beard and Ragheb's (1983) categories listed below, place the participant-generated motives/needs under the appropriate categories.

   Stimulus Seeking or Excitement Needs:

   These are needs in which people seek to elevate their arousal level of interest or stimulation. The arousal can be achieved through three components:

   Intellectual Component: This involves substantial mental activities such as learning, exploring, discovering, creating, or imagining.

   Social Component: This involves engagement for social reasons and includes the needs for friendship and interpersonal relationships as well as the need for the esteem of others.

   Competency-Mastery Component: This entails needs that individuals desire, such as achievement, mastery, challenge, and competence.

Stimulus-Avoidance Needs

These involve the drive to escape and get away from overstimulating life situations. Some individuals may seek to avoid social contacts—to seek solitude and calm conditions; for others, they may seek to rest—to relax and to unwind.

2. Administer the Beard-Ragheb Leisure Motivation Measurement (Appendix) to each participant to more accurately measure his leisure motivation.

   a. After completing the questionnaire, have participants add their scores for each category in order to identify their primary motives in leisure. The higher their score is in a component, the higher their motivation in that component.
   b. Discuss the following:

      1) Which motivations occur most frequently, less frequently, and why?
      2) Are some of the leisure experiences you tend to select to satisfy the needs under each category?
      3) Are the experiences you are currently selecting meeting the needs you have, or are alternatives or modifications needed in your activities?

3. Complete or answer the following:

   a. I am primarily motivated by ________________ in my leisure.
   b. I am least motivated by ____________________ in my leisure.
   c. I was aware that ____.
   d. I was surprised to see that _______________________________.

4. Ask each participant to write down three to five needs they feel they have that are not currently being me[illegible] to the items on the Leisure Motivation Measurement if they have difficulty. Have everyone identify which of their needs can possibly be met through leisure or leisure experiences. For each need identified, have each individual write down one need on a precut slip of paper to be turned in to the facilitator. Take one need at a time and have the group brainstorm how that need can be met through leisure. The same procedure can be used to identify and discuss needs that may be only partially met in their lives but they want more fully satisfied.

Component: Self-awareness

Subcomponent: Leisure satisfaction

Program Objectives:
Participants will:

1. examine the current level of satisfaction attained from leisure experiences.

2. compare their leisure motivation measurement with their leisure satisfaction measurement for compatibilities and/or discrepancies.

3. identify barriers or constraints to their leisure satisfaction.

4. identify factors that contribute to their leisure satisfaction.

5. identify alterations they want to make in order to attain a higher level of leisure satisfaction.

Program Experiences:

1. Administer the Beard-Ragheb Leisure Satisfaction Measurement (Appendix) to each participant. Have participants add their scores for each of the following six factors to determine their current leisure satisfaction. The factors are psychological, educational/intellectual, social, relaxational, physiological, and aesthetic-environmental.

2. Discuss the following:

   a. In what areas are you obtaining the highest level of satisfaction? least satisfaction?
   b. What are some of the experiences you tend to select that are providing satisfaction in the various areas?
   c. Are there possible barriers or constraints that affect your satisfaction in certain areas?

3. Have participants compare their leisure motivation measurement with their leisure satisfaction measurement and discuss compatibilities or discrepancies that may exist.

4. Ask participants to write down three to five of their most memorable, satisfying leisure experiences. (The emphasis needs to be

on "satisfying" rather than just memorable.) Explain that these experiences may include things like working in the garden on a spring morning, an evening at the ballet, a trip, or reading in front of a fire after a hectic day. Ask participants to share and discuss their experiences.

5. Follow up by having individuals write down what they think made these experiences satisfying. Was it who they were with? What they were doing? Where they happened to be? The feelings they experienced? (or other such factors).

6. Using a 1 to 10 scale (1=low, 10=high), have participants rate the level of satisfaction they are generally experiencing in their leisure right now.

7. Introduce the concept that there are elements of factors in our experiences that tend to lead to higher levels of satisfaction than others. For example, some people find that their most satisfying experiences occur when they are in the out of doors. For others, their greater satisfaction comes from being with a significant other. Therefore, if we can become aware of the things that make our experiences more satisfying in general and in specific situation or under specific conditions, we can enhance our satisfaction.

8. Have each person fill out and discuss Worksheet 12, "Things I Find Most Satisfying in My Leisure."

9. Introduce the idea that, in certain situations or under certain conditions, what we may need, and thus find satisfying, may differ. For example, when some people have had a stressful day, they may want to be at home, where it's quiet and they can try to relax. Other people may want to go out that evening and play tennis or run. In order to become more aware of individual's needs and satisfaction in certain situations, ask everyone to fill out Worksheet 13, "When . . . I . . . ."

10. At the end of the session, have participants complete the following sentences:

    a. I would like for my leisure experiences to include (or include more) ____________________.
    b. I would like for my leisure experiences to include less (or not include) ____________________.
    c. The adjustments I would like to make in my leisure experiences are ____________________.

WORKSHEET 12
Things I Find Most Satisfying in My Leisure

Directions: Check each of the following factors you generally find the most satisfying in your leisure. Some of these may depend on the time and circumstances that exist at a particular time. However, on the whole, what do you *generally* find most satisfying?

I. Generally, I am most satisfied or rewarded by leisure experiences that are as follows:

______	competitive	______	unstructured
______	structured	______	passive
______	active	______	unscheduled
______	scheduled	______	dual
______	individual	______	spontaneous
______	planned	______	social
______	physical	______	indoors
______	out-of-doors	______	away from home
______	at home	______	relaxing, quiet
______	stimulating	______	small group
______	cooperative	______	mental

II. Fill in the blanks regarding what you generally find the most satisfying in relation to your leisure experiences for each of the following categories. For example: What sex? <u>The opposite sex.</u>

With whom? ____.

What sex? ____.

What number of people? ____________________________________.

What environment/setting? __________________________________.

What time of day? ____.

WORKSHEET 13
When . . . I . . .

Directions: A great deal of what we find satisfying depends on what we may be experiencing at a particular time. Think of various situations in your life when you may experience certain needs and thus find more satisfaction in specific types of leisure experiences.

1. When I: — I tend to find more satisfaction in leisure experiences that:

Feel: ____________ ____________________
____________ ____________________
____________ ____________________
____________ ____________________
____________ ____________________

Am: ____________ ____________________
____________ ____________________
____________ ____________________
____________ ____________________

2. When I: — I tend to find more satisfaction in leisure experiences that:

Feel: ____________ ____________________
____________ ____________________
____________ ____________________
____________ ____________________
____________ ____________________

Am: ____________ ____________________
____________ ____________________
____________ ____________________
____________ ____________________

Component: Self-awareness

Subcomponent: Leisure goals

Program Goal: Participants will identify and prioritize their leisure goals.

Program Objectives:
Participants will:

1. identify their leisure goals.

2. evaluate each goal in relation to their assets and constraints.

3. identify factors that will help or hinder attaining each goal.

4. rate each goal according to the criteria of desirability, satisfaction, meaning, and enhancement of self.

Background Information:

In order to achieve one's goals, an individual needs to clearly identify those goals. Likewise, different goals may have different priorities in a person's life. The purpose of this objective is to facilitate the identification and prioritization of leisure goals.

Program Experiences:

1. Participants should do the following:

   a. Identify the leisure goals they wish to obtain in or from leisure and leisure experiences;
   b. Evaluate the goals as realistic or unrealistic, given their present assets and constraints;
   c. Taking each goal, identify the following:

      1) What will help you attain the desired goals?
      2) What will hinder you in reaching the desired goals?
      3) What experiences and behaviors will help assist or hinder your reaching the goals?
      4) What skills do you presently have or what skills will you need to develop or fine-tune to help you reach your goal?

   d. Rate the goals on a scale of one to five, according to the criteria of desirability, satisfaction, meaning, and enhancement of self.
   e. List the goals in order of importance: 1) at the present time and 2) in the future.

2. Participants can use the "Information Processing on Leisure Outcomes," Worksheet 10, on their own in the current session as well as individually when they feel the need of it in the future.

Component: Self-awareness

Subcomponent: Leisure interest

Program Goal: Participants will identify leisure experiences in which they are interested.

Program Objectives:
Participants will:

1. identify leisure experiences they have not tried but would like to try.

2. identify leisure experiences they have had in the past that they may enjoy now under different circumstances.

3. identify reasons for not pursuing leisure experiences they have wanted to try.

4. identify the needs they think these new activities will satisfy.

Background Information:

Although a person may have leisure experiences that are currently enjoyable and satisfying, one of the purposes of leisure education is to acquaint individuals with a variety of experiences in order for them to have a broad base of leisure options. There may be experiences that would contribute significantly to the quality of one's life if explored and pursued. These experiences are designed for participants who are interested in exploring new, different, and intriguing experiences.

Program Experiences:

1. Verbally or in writing, have everyone identify and then discuss the following:

   a. Leisure experiences I haven't tried but think I would enjoy.
   b. Leisure experiences I didn't like but may enjoy if the circumstances were different.

   An alternate means to accomplish these same ends would be to have each person make a drawing or collage of activities in each of these categories. Modified games of Charades or Password could also be used for the two topics.

2. Have the group discuss how they think the following sayings could or would affect their leisure:

    a. "Don't knock it until you've tried it."
    b. "You have to know what there is to want before you can want it."
    c. "When in doubt, do nothing. "
    d. "Don't expect too much and you will never be disappointed."
    e. "You will never know until you try."

3. If there are experiences that people have identified as wanting to pursue but have not acted upon, then have them determine the following:

    a. The perceived reason(s) for not pursuing the experience until now. *Example:* time, location, setting, cost ($), availability, as well as personal, social, or emotional blocks.
    b. Possible alternatives: Are there other times, locations, settings, costs, means, etc., that would make exploring the new experiences easier or more pleasant?
    c. Which alternative or course of action seems most feasible at this particular time?
    d. The immediate, near-future, or far-future plan of action to reach their own goal regarding the new experience(s).
    e. In future contacts with individuals, have them determine the progress they are making toward reaching the goal(s) they have set.

4. Have participants refer to their leisure motivation inventory to determine what needs they perceive they can meet through the experiences they are interested in pursuing.

5. A formalized interest inventory is also an excellent source of identifying leisure interests. A leisure interest measurement can be found in the Appendix.

Component: Self-awareness

Subcomponent: Leisure interest

Program Goal: Participants will explore a variety of new leisure experiences in which they have an interest.

Program Objectives:
Participants will:

1. engage in new leisure experiences they have not previously tried.
2. assess their own level of enjoyment and satisfaction in their new experiences.
3. identify reasons for their enjoyment and satisfaction or lack of it.

Background Information:

The central focus of this objective is to acquaint people with a wide variety of leisure experiences and to enable them to learn about, explore, and try these experiences. When the agency involved in educating for leisure provides opportunities to explore new experiences, particularly recreation activities, a "cafeteria style" approach is particularly appropriate and effective. In the cafeteria-style approach, people are not locked into a class or other instructional or experiential units for an extended period of time. The traditional system of service/delivery tends to be counterproductive to exploration on a wide scale. In the cafeteria-style approach a system would set up opportunities for mini-experiences that are designed strictly to create or detect new leisure interests that individuals could then pursue as their interests developed.

Another key to success in providing opportunities for leisure exploration is providing a wide variety of types of experiences that far exceed the bounds of any system's usual core-program parameters. Of special importance is the provision of mini- experiences that are probably not known or tried. For example, Timberlane Elementary School in Tallahassee, Florida, has set aside one afternoon a week for an "exposure-experience afternoon." Parents or volunteers from the community who have an expertise in various areas come into the school and offer, on a modified mini-experience basis, activities ranging from macrame to cake decorating. In order to generate further interest, each activity was given a nontraditional, kicky name.

Sewing was called "Rip and Stitch" and carpentry was entitled, "Bang and Build." The activities offered by Timberlane far exceeded the confines of what the school could offer as a part of its regular program. Additionally, by using nontraditional titles, the program area broke down the usual sex-linked activity participation. Girls were involved in "Bang and Build" and boys were making and decorating cakes for Valentine's Day.

In providing opportunities for leisure exploration, it is critical to structure and control as many of the external environmental conditions in and surrounding the experience as possible. This will allow the person involved to evaluate the experience rather than the leadership, instruction, setting, etc. As is well known, one's favorite, preferred leisure experiences can be ruined or highly facilitated depending upon the "leader" involved. There are also those unique individuals who could take the topic of why spiders don't stick to their own spider webs and make it into a stimulating, exciting phenomenon.

When enabling people to explore a variety of leisure experiences, remember that no one agency has to provide and offer all of the necessary activities within the confines of its own parameters. Such a task is physically and fiscally impossible for most agencies. The total community (city, county, state) should be utilized as a leisure resource bank comprised of public, private, and quasi-private resources that offer opportunities for leisure exploration and experiences.

Leisure Exploration Suggestions

1. One of the means that could be utilized to acquaint people with a wide range of leisure activities is through multimedia resources such as films, video tapes, slide tapes, books, and cassette tapes. These same media could be developed into self-instructional packages to provide alternative instructional means that people could pursue alone in the settings and times of their choice.

2. Through the use of educational television facilities, instruction in and exposure to varying leisure experiences could be brought into homes as readily as Julia Child brings French cooking into the kitchens throughout America.

3. Agencies could offer (sometimes even cooperatively) adventure weekends where individuals could experience one or more leisure pursuits where there may be an interest on a one-or two-

time basis. The range of activities that could be offered in such a program are limitless. Super Saturdays or Fantastic Fridays could be established to also offer mini-experiences.

4. Agencies could have a leisure counseling component within their service systems. The Milwaukee Leisure Counseling component has been computerized for community use. The non-computerized inventories, instruments, and information are available for the cost of the materials to any system for the ordering.

The above suggestions are not meant to imply in any way that an agency should replace their regular program or service-delivery system. These ideas are suggested to increase the public's options of how, when, and where they can learn about and explore leisure activities that may come to contribute to the quality of their lives. In order to truly educate for leisure, an agency or system must be able to make available alternative learning, service, and experience modalities that are compatible with the needs and interests of people. Systems need to have or develop the flexibility to fit people and their styles and patterns rather than having people fit into structures for the ease of administration. The administration of such flexibility and alternative programming and services requires a new set of skills and competencies still to be developed and utilized by leisure service personnel even though some other disciplines currently have this expertise.

Program Experiences:

1. Once participants have identified leisure experiences they want to explore, the facilitator and/or group members will help them with the following:

    a. identify resources to learn more about the experience,
    b. determine where and when the experience is being offered or where and when it is available,
    c. determine the resources needed for the experience; i.e., equipment to borrow, rent, buy; cost of class or participation; time; transportation, etc.

2. After participants have explored each activity, have them identify and discuss the following:

    a. their level of enjoyment and satisfaction,
    b. their reasons for enjoyment and satisfaction or lack of it.

Component: Self-awareness

Subcomponent: Leisure interests

Program Goal: Participants will determine their own preferences for the components and conditions surrounding their leisure experiences.

Program Objectives:
Participants will:

1. complete Worksheet 14, "Inventory of Preferred Leisure Factors and Conditions."

2. evaluate their leisure experiences in relation to the factors and conditions they prefer in leisure.

3. identify any discrepancies between their leisure experiences and the factors and conditions they prefer.

4. identify why they do or do not prefer certain factors and conditions in their leisure or leisure experiences; and how they affect their experiences as well as their feelings.

5. identify how their experiences may be modified to obtain more enjoyment and satisfaction.

Background Information:

It is possible to select, modify, or change leisure experiences to have more quality by controlling those facets of one's own leisure experiences that are modifiable and open to change because:

1. People have varying levels of leisure experiences in terms of satisfaction, enrichment, and enhancement.

2. The experiences or the activity itself, the factors in the experience, and the conditions surrounding the experience can increase or decrease the enrichment, satisfactions, or enjoyment.

The purpose of the present objectives are to help the participants focus upon their own preferences for the conditions and factors they prefer in their leisure experiences that are related to the quality of their experiences.

Program Experiences:

1. Have the participants relist their preferred leisure experiences and possible new interests.

   Administer Worksheet 14, "Inventory of Preferred Leisure Factors and Conditions" in order for each participant to identify his preference for or dislike of leisure factors and conditions. Each leisure list should then be cross-checked against the inventory for verification of the answers on the inventory. Any discrepancies should be noted and discussed in depth. The discussion will usually center around why would one be willing to participate in an experience where there are factors that one may actually dislike.

2. *Partner Activity.* Have each partner in turn have two minutes of uninterrupted time to tell the other why they do not like a particular factor or condition in their leisure, what it does to the experience, and how it makes them feel.

3. Have participants identify how they may be able to modify their experiences in order to gain more enjoyment and satisfaction.

WORKSHEET 14
Inventory of Preferred Leisure Factors and Conditions

Directions: Please rank, in order of general preference, your three (3) most preferred choices to each of the following questions. One indicates the most preferred, two the next most preferred, and so on.

1. How many people do you prefer being with during your leisure?

_____ alone
_____ with one person
_____ with a small group (3-5)
_____ with a medium-sized group (6-12)
_____ with a large group (13 or more)

2. What age-group do you prefer being with during your leisure?

_____ your same age
_____ younger than you
_____ older than you
_____ no preference

3. With which sex do you prefer to spend your leisure?

_____ male(s)
_____ female(s)
_____ both sexes

4. With people of what familiarity do you prefer to spend your leisure?

_____ spouse
_____ spouse and children
_____ friend(s)
_____ family (other than spouse and children)
_____ acquaintance(s)
_____ stranger(s)

5. With people of what marital status do you prefer to spend your leisure?

_____ single individuals
_____ married individuals
_____ both married and single individuals

______ single couples
______ married couples
______ both married and single couples

6. What nature do you prefer your leisure activity to involve?

______ physical
______ intellectual
______ social
______ emotional
______ creative

7. Which of the following do you prefer in your leisure?

______ mental stimulation
______ interaction with people
______ physical exertion
______ skill requirement
______ obvious results
______ involvement as a spectator
______ relation
______ other (specify)

8. What feelings do you prefer to receive from your leisure?

______ feeling of achievement
______ feeling of pleasure
______ feeling of satisfaction
______ feeling of relaxation
______ feeling of self-worth
______ feeling of recognition
______ other (specify)

9. In what environment do you prefer to spend your leisure?

______ indoors or around the home
______ in a city or town
______ by a body of water
______ in the mountains
______ in the forest

10. In what degree of familiarity do you prefer to spend your leisure?

______ in an unknown place
______ in a place similar to other places you've been
______ in a place you've been to before

11. What kind of climate do you prefer to spend your leisure?

______ hot
______ moderate
______ cold

12. During what time of day do you prefer your leisure?

______ morning
______ afternoon
______ evening

13. How do you prefer your leisure to be structured?

______ a lot of rules and regulations
______ some rules and regulations
______ no rules and regulations

14. On how many activities do you prefer to focus upon during your leisure?

______ one activity
______ a few activities (2-5)
______ many activities (6 or more)

15. In activities involving skills, you prefer to be with people of what level?

______ of greater skill level than you
______ of less skill level than you
______ of equal skill level

16. Which do you prefer in your leisure activities?

______ no competition
______ a little competition
______ lots of competition

17. What participation level do you prefer in your leisure?

______ to be a spectator
______ to be an occasional spectator
______ to be an active participant

18. What length of project do you prefer to do in your leisure?

_____ short term (can complete in a few hours)
_____ medium (can complete in a few days)
_____ long term (required a week or longer to complete)

19. Do you prefer activities that require a leader?

_____ no
_____ yes (if "yes," please continue with the last two questions.)

20. What age leader do you prefer in your leisure?

_____ near your age
_____ older
_____ younger

21. Would you prefer your leader to be?

_____ a friend
_____ an acquaintance
_____ a stranger

Now go back and look over your selections and circle the three (3) checked items you consider most important in your leisure.

This inventory is a compilation of selected questions from the study by Fandozzi (1976).

NOTE: In identifying preferences for and dislikes of factors and conditions, facilitators as well as participants often focus upon trying to analyze *why* the preference or dislike may exist. This line of inquiry is often a nonproductive, frustrating pursuit because of the multiplicity of conscious and unconscious motivations involved. Therefore, it is recommended that the discussion center around the identification of "what" one prefers or dislikes without becoming entangled in an analysis of why the attraction or avoidance may exist. For, regardless of why the situation is as it is, the important element is that it does exist.

Component: Self-awareness

Subcomponent: Constraints

Program Goal: Participants will increase their understanding of leisure constraints in their life.

Program Objectives:

Participants will:

1. identify general leisure constraints—constraints that limit access to leisure services and constraints that affect their level of leisure satisfaction

2. assess the degree of influence of each constraint on their leisure.

3. identify ways for overcoming or moderating selected constraints on their leisure.

Background Information:

Leisure researchers and practitioners have shown a growing interest in leisure barriers and constraints in the past decade. This interest has included investigating categories of constraints, the relationships existing among forms of constraints, and the part constraints play in relation to leisure opportunities, participation, and satisfaction (for in-depth information, see *Journal of Leisure Research, 23*(4) 1991 and *Constraints on Leisure* by M. G. Wade, 1985).

The original terminology in this area was referred to as barriers. The current terminology being used is leisure constraints because of its broader, more inclusive nature. Jackson (1988) views a leisure constraint as anything that inhibits a person's ability to participate in leisure activities, to have the time to do so, to access leisure services, or to achieve the desired level of satisfaction. Jackson (1990), as well as other researchers (Crawford & Godbey, 1987; Henderson, Stalnaker, & Taylor, 1988) refer to constraints as being of two types. One is antecedent constraints and the second is intervening constraints. Antecedent constraints are those that affect leisure preferences before or as they are forming. Intervening constraints are those that occur once leisure preference have been established. Jackson's (1990) model depicts the role of constraints on leisure as shown in Figure 1.

Figure 1
Jackson's (1990) Leisure Contraint Model

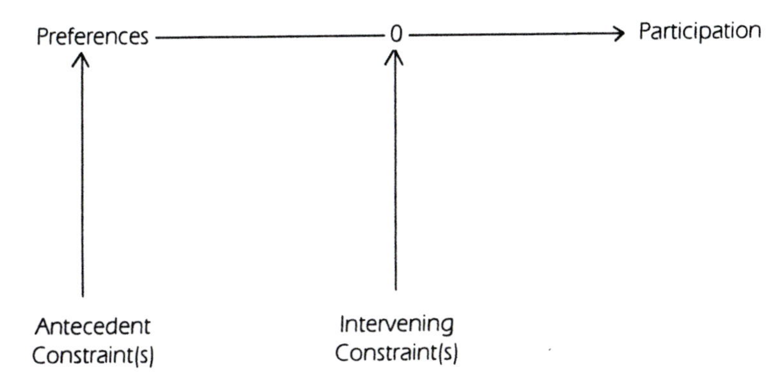

Antecedent constraints include both psychological and sociological aspects of the individual. Psychological states and attributes include, among many others, one's socialization, motivation, perceived sense of self, personal capabilities, personality, disability, and depression. Sociological aspects are those frequently associated with variables, such a family's economic and educational levels and social status, as well as race and gender.

Intervening constraints are those that impede a person from acting upon a leisure preference once it has been established and includes factors such as lack of time, money, opportunity, health, family obligations, as well as social conditions. Common social conditions—such as societal attitudes toward people with disabilities, ethnic backgrounds, gender, and race—can act as constraints on fulfilling leisure preferences.

The concern with leisure constraints over the years has centered around the assumption that there is a direct link between constraints and participation. That is, constraints that people perceive lead to less participation in preferred leisure experiences than they would like or in non-participation (Shaw, Bonen, & McCabe, 1991). However, empirical studies (Shaw et al., 1991; Kay & Jackson, 1991) suggest that reported constraints do not necessarily mean less leisure nor lower participation in leisure experiences. The work of Kay and Jackson (1991) further suggest that, by exerting effort to overcome constraints, individuals can succeed in maintaining their desired level of participation.

In educating for leisure, we need to keep in mind that our focus of attention is on individuals and individual behaviors as they relate to the participant's desired level of leisure, leisure participation, and satisfaction. While empirical studies help us to understand the overall phenomenon of constraints on leisure, as practitioners we may be working with individuals whose leisure, leisure participation, and leisure satisfaction may not be at as high a level as they desire because of constraints they have not yet learned to overcome. While these studies show that some constraints can be overcome and that constraints don't necessarily mean less leisure or less participation, it should be kept in mind that this is aggregate data from many people. In both of these studies, individual respondents felt constraints that prevented them from attaining their desired level of experience. The area of constraints is a particularly important area of attention for therapeutic recreation specialists and other professionals working with special groups that are particularly susceptible to personal and social conditions that can adversely influence leisure, participation, and satisfaction.

Program Experiences:

Identifying one's leisure constraints can be done one of two ways. One way is to have each participant spontaneously list his perceived leisure constraints. A second way is to give everyone a list of leisure constraints from which they identify the constraints that affect their lives. Experience with both methods has shown that spontaneously listing constraints seems to be a more reliable method than providing a list. With the provided list, people tend to mark more constraints simply because they are there and visible.

1. Begin with a discussion of what is meant by leisure constraints, according to Jackson's (1988) definition (p.216), and why it is important to identify one's personal leisure constraints. Also, state that research has suggested that by individuals exerting effort, constraints can be overcome or negotiated.

2. Have each participant spontaneously list perceived constraints on Worksheet 15, "Leisure Constraints" according to the following categories:

   a. general constraints,
   b. constraints that limit my access to leisure services,
   c. constraints that affect my level of desired satisfaction.

3. Once the constraints have been listed, have participants rank their degree of influence as a constraint on a scale of 1 to 3 (with 3=a major negative influence, 2=a moderate influence, and 1=a minor influence).

4. Next, have individuals review their lists and determine which constraints they most want to work on eliminating.

5. For each constraint that has been identified to be eliminated, ask the participants and/or the group to brainstorm ways of overcoming or compensating for the constraint.

WORKSHEET 15
Leisure Constraints

Directions: List constraints you feel prevent you from obtaining the level of leisure and/or leisure experiences you desire. Once the constraints have been listed, rank the degree of influence of each constraint on a sale of 1 to 3 (with 1=a major negative influence; 2=a moderate negative influence; and 3=a minor negative influence).

General Leisure Constraints	Constraints that Limit Access to Leisure Services	Constraints that Affect Level of Satisfaction
____________	____________	____________
____________	____________	____________
____________	____________	____________
____________	____________	____________
____________	____________	____________
____________	____________	____________

The constraints I want to work on are ____________________

____.

Ideas for overcoming moderating constraints:

Constraints 1.

Constraints 2.

Constraints 3.

LEISURE RESOURCES

Leisure resources are people, organizations, institutions, environments, commercial enterprises, communication structures, equipment, and materials available for leisure experiences. People need to know the leisure resources available to them in order to learn and access many leisure experiences. Additionally, knowing the resources that are available gives people multiple options from which to select.

The Leisure Education Advancement Project of the National Recreation and Park Association developed a comprehensive leisure resources section in the NRPA Kangaroo Kit (Zeyen, Odum, & Lancaster, 1977). The leisure resources section of the Kangaroo Kit is being used as the basis of the material presented for this component of leisure education.

Due to the potentially repetitive nature of the material and possible program experiences related to leisure resources, the format for this section will differ from the other components of leisure education. This component will include program objectives related to leisure resources in a comprehensive list that will then be followed by a list of suggested activities that could be used for any of the objectives.

Component: Leisure Resources

Program Goal: Participants will identify, understand, use, and evaluate leisure resources available for their leisure experiences.

Program Objectives:
Participants will:

1. identify resources where they can get information that can be used for planning and carrying out leisure experiences (local newspapers, telephone directory, TV, radio, travel agencies, internet).

2. identify people in their immediate environment who can help with personal leisure interests.

3. identify resources in the community for leisure experiences.

   a. noncommercial organizations and institutions,
   b. commercial resources,
   c. environments,
   d. public resources.

4. identify leisure resources that are of personal interest.

S. identify local places that offer leisure opportunities that can be reached my means of transportation available to them.

6. evaluate leisure resources in relation to their interests, economic and time constraints, transportation availability, and other self-selected criteria.

7. evaluate leisure resources after use on self-determined criteria.

Program Experiences:

1. Develop a personal or group Leisure Resources Card File.

2. Identify and gather together resources, such as books or pamphlets, that can be used in a leisure resources center that

   a. teach leisure experience skills;
   b. identify local, state, national, and international leisure opportunities.

3. Develop a leisure calendar of events for a month and/or year for personal or group use.

4. Use a local or state map to show sites of available leisure resources.

5. Develop a "Fun and Free" list of possible leisure opportunities.

6. Develop a collage or mural of community leisure resources.

7. Establish a Leisure Information Newsletter.

8. Develop a community Leisure Resources Guide organized by areas of leisure interests.

9. Develop a computer community leisure resources program linked to and accessed by areas of leisure interests.

10. Take field trips to local leisure resources.

11. Invite representative of local leisure programs and facilities to speak to your group.

12. Develop a card file of sources of renting, leasing, selling, and free use of leisure equipment and supplies.

LEISURE SKILLS

Component: Leisure Skills

Subcomponent: Decision making

Program Goal: Participants will increase their understanding of choices and decision making in their life.

Program Objectives:
Participants will:

1. clarify their thoughts and beliefs regarding the role of choices and decisions in their life and leisure.
2. examine the degree of choice available in various areas of their life.
3. identify how choices and decisions in life in general impact their leisure.

Background Information:

The choices we make through the decision making process is the one mechanism available to us as human beings for controlling and directing our lives as well as our leisure. They are the guidance system of our lives. They are the tool that makes us the agents of our experiences rather than the passive recipients of uncontrollable circumstances and external forces.

Choice implies options. Choice is the process of *selecting* from available options. Decision making is the process through which we go to help us select the most desirable option that is available to us. For us to have a choice, we must have options or alternatives available from which to choose.

Our perception of the degree, number, and type of choices we have in our lives colors our entire view of our lives. Some people believe that they do not have choices. They feel they were handicapped at the beginning of their lives with detrimental home lives, socioeconomic circumstances, poor health, or other severely limiting conditions from which they will never recover. Other people believe they had a number of choices early in their lives but made choices with which they are now "stuck" and which have severely limited their current and future choices. These types of choices tend to be decisions such as getting married, not attending college, and having children. There are also individuals who possess an external locus of control talked about earlier. They believe they have few choices because their lives are controlled by other people and circumstances in their lives. They feel life is not going the way they want it to but that it is not their fault. Life has just dealt them a bad hand about which they can do nothing.

These perceptions can be partly accurate. There are circumstances, situations, and past decisions that can limit or eliminate some of our current options. However, numerous philosophies and mental health theories do not agree with the *conclusions* drawn from these perceptions. Individuals may have suffered from dysfunctional home lives. They may have made earlier choices which now, if the ensuing responsibilities are honored, will limit some choices. There are life circumstances over which the individual has no control. However, while numerous factors impinge on and influence some of our choices, they do not *control and/or eliminate the choices in our lives.* We are not stuck with no other alternatives or degrees of freedom, unless we choose to be. We are not the helpless recipients of what life has dealt us, unless we choose to be. Our lives are not beyond our control because we "don't have a choice," unless we choose not to make choices.

When people say they "don't have a choice," one of several things can be operating. They include some of the following:

1. They really believe they have no choices and thus no sense of personal power to affect their lives.

2. They may not be aware of what their options are. For whatever reason, they are unaware or cannot think of other alternatives.

3. They don't like the options they perceive they have and thus feel that they don't *really* have a choice, since their choice is between almost equally undesirable alternatives.

4. They have already chosen. Given the options available and their perceived possible consequences, individuals have already chosen their courses of action and thus feel that they "have no other choice," given the available options. The same dynamics can occur in relation to one's values, priorities, or goals; the person

may feel he can make only one choice. However, it is generally expressed as "I don't have a choice," when in essence he has already chosen.

5. The number, type, and extent of alternatives are limited, for whatever reason, and the person cannot see the other options that are available.

6. The options they want to have in their lives so far outdistance what is realistically available to them that they experience a sense of frustration, hopelessness, and helplessness, thus feeling that no options are available since the ones they want are beyond their reach at the current time.

It is not accurate that we "don't have a choice." We may not have a choice we like. We may not have a choice without some painful or costly consequences. We may choose not to make a choice on an issue at this time. But we do constantly have choices.

One may ask, "Does it really matter whether I say, 'I don't have a choice' or 'I'm not willing to pay the price or risk the consequences of any decision other than the one I have made?'" The answer is an unequivocal "yes, it does matter." It matters greatly because what we tell ourselves and other people about our available choices will lead us to feel powerless or empowered; having control in our lives or other people and circumstances being in control; and knowing at a cognitive and emotional level that we have the freedom that comes with choice or that we are not free to choose for ourselves.

Program Experiences:

1. Have each participant fill out Worksheet 16, "My Choice."

2. Duplicate and give each person a copy of the preceding "Background Information" on choices and decision making to read *after* they have completed their worksheets.

3. Have the group discuss what they think and feel about the following statements in the text:

   a. "While numerous factors impinge on and influence our choices, they do not control or eliminate choices in our lives."
   b. "We are not stuck without alternatives or degrees of freedom—unless we choose to be."

4. Using the list of six (6) things that can be operating when we say,

"I don't have a choice," ask the participants to refer to Worksheet 12, "My Choice." For "1. Areas of my life or circumstances in which I have *no* choice," have them clarify for themselves what is really operating in each circumstance and have them list what they perceive to be operating under the section called "Perception Check." Use the same procedure for "2. Areas of my life or circumstances in which I have *few* choices," and "3. Areas of my life or circumstances in which I have the greatest choice."

5. Group discussions can be conducted on other areas of the text and the worksheet.

6. Discuss how choices and decisions in life in general relate to and impact our future.

7. Close with participants writing a brief statement that begins, "I realize that my choices are . . ." and/or "My choices in leisure are ______."

WORKSHEET 16
My Choice

Instructions: Fill in the following worksheet according to the current state of your choices.

1. Areas of my life or circumstances in which I have **no** choice:

Areas/Circumstances	Why I Have No Choice	Perception Check

2. Areas of my life or circumstances in which I have **few** choices:

Areas/Circumstances	Why My Choices are Limited	Perception Check

3. Areas of my life or circumstances in which I have the **greatest** choice:

Areas/Circumstances	Why My Choices are Greater	Perception Check

Component: Leisure Skills

Subcomponent: Decision making

Program Goal: Participants will increase their understanding of decision making.

Program Objectives:
Participants will:

1. understand the definition of decision making and types of decisions.
2. identify conscious reasons why decisions may be difficult to make.
3. identify how decision making is avoided by people.

Background Information:

Child A: "My mother says I have to learn to make decisions."
Child B: "I never make decisions."
Child A: "I've noticed that. Why not?"
Child B: "I'm no fool! They can affect the whole course of a person's life."

Decisions can and do affect the course of our lives. Decision making is the process through which we move from awareness and knowing to action. There is a proverb that states, "To know and not to act is not to know at all." Yalom views a decision as the bridge between wishing and action (Yalom, 1980, p. 314). He says, "To decide means to commit oneself to a course of action. If no action ensues, I believe that there has been no true decision but instead a flirting with decision, a type of failed resolve."

Yates (1990) has defined decision as "an action taken with the intention of producing favorable outcomes." Beyth-Marom, Novik and Sloan (1987) say, "In decision, it is knowledge of what to do that is sought." The decision-making process is the action through which we attempt to determine what we need to do to produce favorable or satisfying outcomes. Decision making is viewed by various authors as a multi-staged processing of information, through a linked sequence of steps, to produce a set of favorable outcomes.

In educating for leisure, there are two foci related to decision making. One is to help people in determining what they believe are favorable or desirable outcomes they want in their lives as they relate to leisure. The second focus is upon presenting and giving practice in the steps in decision making. This unit will deal with the decision-making process. The units on outcomes and satisfaction deal with the other focus.

We all have our own unique ways in which we make decisions. Likewise, the process we use may vary according to the type of decision we are making. Five types of decisions that have been widely referenced in decision-making literature. These types of decisions can be seen to differ in effort, rationality, degree of awareness or consciousness, and impulsiveness. They are as follows:

1. **Reasonable Decision.** Arguments for and against various options are weighted or balanced until one is selected. There is a sense of freedom and lack of coercion with this type of decision. It seems to occur calmly.

2. **Willful Decision.** This type of decision generally involves major life decisions. There is a feeling of strenuousness and effort accompanying these types of decisions. It is frequently accompanied by what James calls a "slow, dead heave of the will."

3. **Drifting Decision.** These decisions are made by just "drifting" in a direction. None of the alternatives seems to have a powerful reason for selection or rejection so the decision is made almost as if by accident or default.

4. **Impulsive Decision.** The impulsive decision is exactly what the name implies . . . a decision made suddenly or abruptly, frequently as a result of frustration at not being able to come to a decision.

5. **Decision Based Upon Change of Perspective.** This type of decision is usually a result of an inner or outer experience that changes one's perspective. This can come as a result of a near-death experience, loss, trauma, etc.

Decisions can be difficult and painful to make. As we work with people facilitating their leisure decision making, an understanding of some of the conscious reasons making them difficult will be helpful. Yalom (1980) summed up one of the main reasons decisions are difficult when he stated, "One must relinquish options, often options that will never come again. Decisions are painful because they signify the limitations of possibilities . . . ." Decisions can also be difficult because they express who we are. Once a decision is made, we are exposed. Decisions also force responsibility of assumption on us. If an individual wants to avoid responsibility, that person will also attempt to avoid making certain decisions. The elements of uncertainty and ambiguity make decisions difficult. We do not know what the end results will entail. This doubt, uncertainty, and obscurity hampers decision making.

Since decisions can be difficult, an individual may avoid them. Decisions can be avoided in a number of ways. One prevalent means is procrastination. By simply waiting and postponing a decision, it may be made for one. Another means is by delegating the decision to someone else. For example, a person may be a volunteer coach for a team but wants to quit coaching. Instead of making an overt decision to quit, the person begins piling up absences. The league supervisor eventually has to tell the volunteer that he must get someone to replace him since he has to be absent so much. There are two additional means of avoiding decisions that will be helpful to understand. One is inattention and a second is refusal. Inattention refers to ignoring or just not focusing on the decision to be made. If you have ever had the experience of offering a child or a friend a number of alternatives, all of which are rejected, you have seen refusal in operation. A decision can also be avoided by rejecting all of the alternatives available.

The Decision-making Process

In everyday life, we may use a variety of means and steps to make our decisions. However, knowing, practicing, and being able to call upon a legitimate process when we need it is important for effective decision making. The decision-making process, as we generally know it, is made up of a sequence of steps and subroutines within the steps. Research suggests that "Though normative studies recommend a sequenced progression through the stages and subroutines of decision making, evidence does not indicate that it is followed by individuals or organizations" (MacPhail-Wilcox & Bryant, 1988). Decision-making literature, however, does show three major stages involved in the decision-making process. These general stages are as follows: 1) perception and information gathering, 2) information manipulation and processing, and 3) choice strategies (MacPhail-Wilcox & Bryant). Barnes (1971) reminds us of a crucial fact: "Decisions or judgments are never made by thinking more; there are always feelings underlying or joined with our judgments."

Each professional must decide the approach that appears to best fit the decision-making needs and level of the individuals with whom they are working. The approach taken here will be to introduce a sequenced decision-making process but stress that regardless of the process used, it needs to include information gathering, information processing, and choice strategies when the decision is of importance to the decision maker.

Likewise, it is critical to actively facilitate decision making within the system and by all of the personnel involved in the process of leisure education. There is a tendency for personnel in leadership and power or authority positions to maintain the decision-making power for themselves. If problems or opportunities arise, particularly where children or the individuals with disabilities are involved, the leader tends to solve the problem, make the final decision, or come up with the "best answer." At most, some leaders will involve the group in decision making by listening to the group's thoughts and ideas on what should be done before the leaders make their final decision. In order to educate for self-directed, satisfying leisure living and functioning, the decision-making ability of participants—not the leader—must be emphasized and perfected. This is not a new concept to recreation and leisure professionals. It is one of the basic principles taught in most professional curricula. The difference is that some professionals who have attempted to operate from this perspective get frustrated by the fact that it takes more time than just making the decisions themselves. It will be more time consuming; that is reality. However, the payoff to participants alone justifies the time. Decision making is at the heart of educating for leisure. It could even be argued that decision-making skills are the underpinning to achieving the highest level of leisure living, which is the ability to enhance the quality of one's own life through leisure.

Program Experiences:

Open the session with a presentation and discussion of the following topics:

- decision making,
- types of decisions,
- conscious reasons why decisions are difficult to make,
- how decisions are avoided by people.

Component: Leisure Skills

Subcomponent: Decision making

Program Goal: Participants will improve their decision-making process.

Program Objective: Participants will practice, critique, and refine their decision-making processes.

Background Information:

Although people are currently making decisions in leisure and in relation to leisure, teaching the steps in a decision-making process that individuals then adapt to their own styles can facilitate decision making in terms of ease, efficiency, and effectiveness. Sloan (1987) emphasizes that people making an important decision are under stress. He sees that a decision-making process can "compensate for errors in judgment that arise because of 'unpleasant emotional states' accompanying life dilemmas." The focus of the present objective is to acquaint participants with the steps in a formal decision-making process, how to use it, and its possible benefits.

Step 1. Clearly define the matter to be decided.

Step 2. Determine what choices or alternatives exist.

Step 3. Gather pertinent information related to the alternatives.

Step 4. List the advantages and disadvantages of each option.

Step 5. Weigh the possible cost and risk of negative as well as positive consequences.

Step 6. Prioritize the alternatives.

Step 7. Select what, in your best judgment, with the information and options available, is the best course of action.

Step 8. Implement the chosen course of action.

Step 9. Evaluate the decision made.

Program Experiences:

1. Introduce the decision-making process outlined above. Have each participant take some matter, real or made up, that he wants to decide in relation to leisure and use the process to make his decision.

2. Facilitate a group decision-making exercise using this same process.

3. Structure opportunities for participants to practice, using the process, for a period of time; then have the group or individual evaluate and discuss the results of the process as well as feelings about its use.

Component: Leisure Skills

Subcomponent: Decision making

Program Goal: Participants will increase their awareness of factors that can influence leisure decisions.

Program Objectives:
Participants will:

1. identify the factors that influence their leisure.

2. determine perceived degrees to which each factor positively or negatively influences the quality of their leisure.

3. identify how leisure decisions affect other areas of life.

Background Information:

Leisure decisions are not made in isolation, separate from other areas of life. There are factors that influence all of our decisions, including our leisure ones. If we are aware of some of the major factors that influence our decisions, it will help us make more effective and satisfying decisions.

Some of the factors that exert influences are as follows:

1. time
2. money
3. significant other people
4. weather
5. geographical location
6. an individual's own
   a. values;
   b. perception of self, others, and reality in general;
   c. social, emotional, physical, and intellectual functioning, and current state;
   d. attitudes;
   e. interests;
   f. needs;
   g. economic state;
   h. wants;
   i. skills and abilities.
7. known, anticipated, and unknown outcomes, results, or consequences
8. knowledge of the options that are available
9. requirements of the activity or experience:
   a. equipment;
   b. clothing;
   c. facilities;
   d. other people;
   e. space.

10. available resources/opportunities

Program Experiences:

1. Have the group identify and develop a list of factors that can influence leisure choices and decisions. It may be necessary to give one or two examples to begin the discussion.

   From the list of factors identified, have everyone identify those that tend to most influence their own leisure decisions. Their personal list could then be rank-ordered or rated on a scale of one to five to show the degree to which they perceive how each factor influences their leisure decisions.

   After the degree of influences has been determined, have individuals rate whether they perceive the influence as positive, neutral, negative, or beneficial or nonbeneficial to the quality of their leisure.

2. Participants can also discuss how their decisions regarding leisure affect other areas and factors in their lives.

Component: Leisure Skills

Subcomponent: Decision making

Program Goal: Participants will increase their understanding of the decisions they are currently making in leisure.

Program Objectives:

Participants will:

1. clarify the areas in which they are making decisions in leisure.
2. evaluate the decisions they are currently making in leisure.
3. determine the decisions they want to continue and the decision they want to change.
4. develop a plan of action for the area(s) they want to change.

Program Experiences:

1. Using Worksheet 17, "Leisure Decisions," have the participants determine and then discuss the following:

   a. whether they agree or disagree that they make decisions in their leisure in the areas listed.
   b. the advantages or disadvantages of the decisions they are currently making in their leisure.
   c. whether they want to continue the types of decisions they are making or whether they want to change them.

2. If there are changes that participants want to make, discuss or have them write out the following:

   a. what they perceive the payoff would be to themselves and others in making the desired change,
   b. the "cost" of making the change to themselves and to others.

3. Work with each participant to develop a plan of action to make desired changes.

WORKSHEET 17
Leisure Decisions

Directions: In the columns below, code the following: 1) whether you agree or disagree that these are areas in which you make decisions in leisure; 2) whether the current decisions you are making in leisure are an advantage or disadvantage to you; and 3) whether you want to continue the current decisions you are making in an area or change them.

	Agree Disagree	Advantage Disadvantage	Continue Change
1. Whether or not I have leisure	______	__________	______
2. What I do or do not do for leisure	______	__________	______
3. Whether what I do is for myself, others, or both	______	__________	______
4. When I will have leisure	______	__________	______
5. My level of proficiency	______	__________	______
6. The effort or energy I will expend	______	__________	______
7. My degree of concentration and attention	______	__________	______
8. The degree of perseverance I exhibit	______	__________	______
9. My interaction and communication style (i.e., cooperative, competitive, leader-follower, etc.)	______	__________	______
10. The amount of interaction I have	______	__________	______
11. The number and type of people with whom I interact	______	__________	______
12. The quality of the interaction	______	__________	______
13. The depth of the interaction (i.e., self-disclosure, meaning, relevance)	______	__________	______
Other:	______	__________	______
	______	__________	______

Code:	A = Agree	Ad = Advantage	C = Continue
	D = Disagree	Da = Disadvantage	Ch = Change

Component: Leisure Skills

Subcomponent: Decision making

Program Goal: Participants will increase their understanding of their own decision-making style.

Program Objectives:
Participants will:

1. assess their decision-making style in relation to leisure.

2. evaluate the advantages and disadvantages of their decision-making style in relation to leisure situations and outcomes.

Background Information:

Characteristic methods, or styles of decision making, have been documented (Witkin, Goodenough, & Karp, 1967; Myers, 1985) for a number of years. Witkin's dualistic typology and the Myers-Briggs four-quadrant typology are two of the most popular and widely utilized methods. Most individuals possess mixed characteristics of the different style classifications. However, one style will tend to be predominant. It should be emphasized that there is no right or wrong, good or bad, style of making decisions. Each style has its advantages and disadvantages in various situations.

Becoming aware of your decision-making style, with its accompanying advantages and disadvantages in relation to leisure, can help lead to more satisfying decisions. The following quick, informal assessment can be used with participants for discussion purposes. If a more formal test is desired, the Witkin or the Myers-Briggs tests can be purchased.

Program Experiences:

1. Worksheet 18, "Inventory of Leisure Decision-making Style," can be used for each person to assess his own style. Discuss whether or not a person's style tends to be the same for all areas of life or different. Areas for discussion could be leisure, work, family relationships, friends, etc. Ask if some characteristics are more prevalent than others in certain situations.

2. After taking the inventory, have the group discuss the advantages and disadvantages of each style in relation to the possible outcomes in situations like below:

a. what to do on a beautiful Saturday,
b. going to a movie or to play tennis,
c. going to a party and deciding the following:
   1) whether or not to drink
   2) how much to drink
   3) whether or not to "do" drugs
d. pulling a prank on someone,
e. returning to school.

3. Participants may assess their decision-making style and/or specific characteristics through a couple of methods. One method would be to have all participants complete Worksheet 19, "Inventory of Leisure Decision-making Style" worksheet. Then have participants go through the "Information Processing on Decision-making Style," Worksheet 15 in order to determine whether or not their decision-making styles or specific characteristics are producing the leisure outcomes they desire. A rating of five (5) would indicate generally desirable results and a rating of one (1) would represent undesirable outcomes.

WORKSHEET 18

Inventory of Leisure Decision-making Style

Directions: Read over the following characteristics of decision making in Styles A and B. In the box at the end of each category, check the style that is *most* characteristic of your decision making in leisure.

Analytical Style

1. High level of conscious awareness of alternatives, goals, and possible outcomes.
2. Analytical—identifies and weighs alternatives.
3. Strong reliance on information, facts, and data for decision making.
4. Cautious, careful, deliberate.
5. Thinks through probable actions of and reactions to decisions.
6. Tends to make few spontaneous, quick decisions.
7. Dissects and views the parts of actions and decisions.

☐

Intuitive Style

1. Low level of conscious awareness of alternatives, goals, and possible outcomes.
2. Makes decisions primarily by "feelings" of the moment, whims, or gut-level reactions.
3. Tends to make spontaneous, quick decisions.
4. Has limited use of and attention to information, facts, or data.
5. Focuses upon the "whole" of the experience or action and doesn't tend to view the "parts."
6. Has limited thoughts to outcomes, results, or consequences beyond the temporarily perceived emotional benefits of the attraction or avoidance of the action.
7. Chance-oriented.

☐

WORKSHEET 19
Information Processing on Decision-making Style

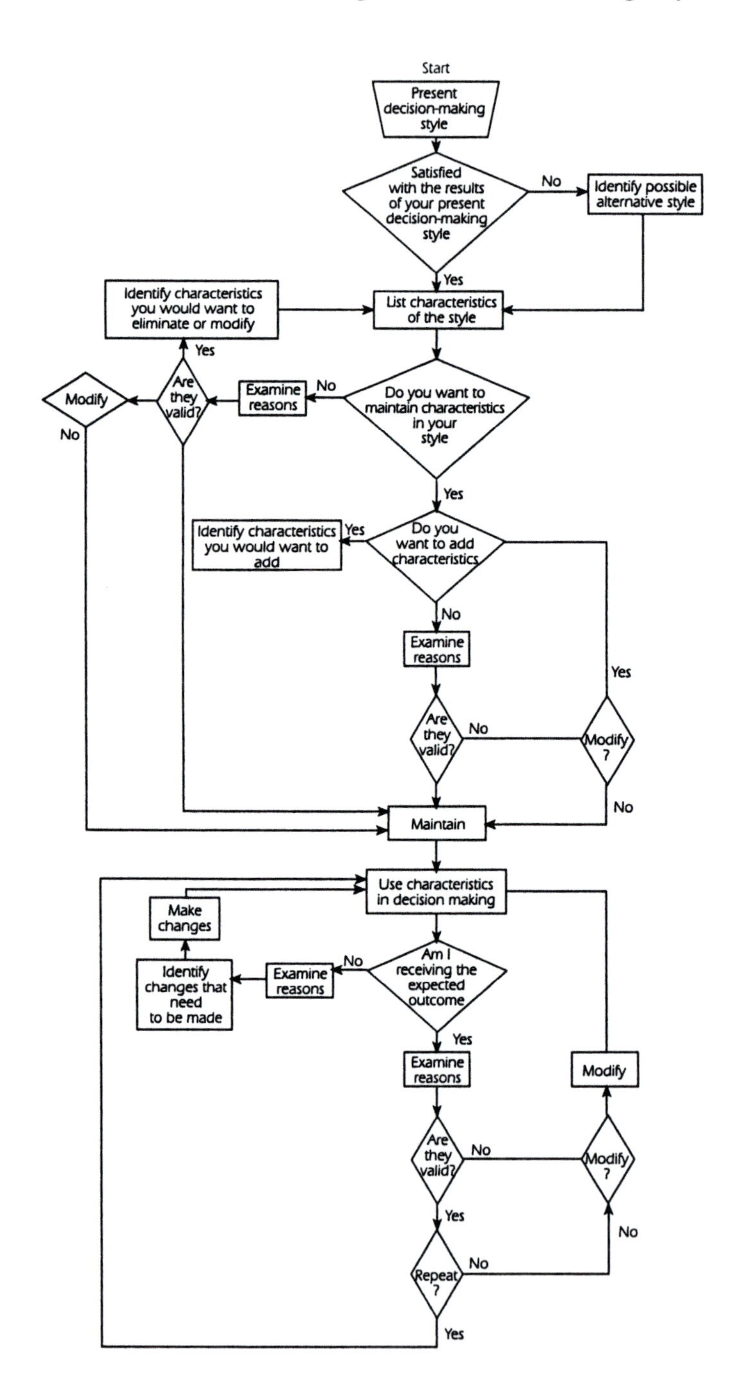

Component: Leisure Skills

Subcomponent: Values clarification

Program Goal: Participants will improve their ability to resolve conflicting personal values.

Program Objectives:
Participants will:

1. understand the concept and origin of values.

2. identify conflicting values related to their leisure and other areas of life.

3. demonstrate the ability to apply the process of resolving conflicting values to one area of their lives.

Background Information:

Values are learned. They are learned from our families, friends, teachers, religious guides, television, and other socializing agents who try to teach us how life should be lived. Our values basically are derived from what other people think. We eventually incorporate and own a certain number of values and claim them as our own. However, since our values are derived predominantly from other people, it means that

- our values are not necessarily "right" and people with differing values are automatically "wrong"; it simply means that we have learned different values.

- the values we were taught are frequently not clarified and critically evaluated by us to determine whether these are the values we want to guide our lives; often we mistakenly think that if a particular thing is what we were taught, it must be "right."

- as we mature and expand our experiences and consciousness, what we come to believe will conflict with what some other people believe.

- the values we hold will come into conflict with each other.

Values will clash, goals will clash, options will clash. This is a part of life. When we get into situations in life, and leisure in particular, where we are in conflict, having the ability to work through and clarify the conflicts in satisfactory ways can lead to more satisfying and enriching living.

The process hereby presented is one method to reconcile conflicting values. As with the other processes in this chapter, this process is just one of many that an individual can use. The suggested process is a modification of the work of Raths, Harmin, and Simon (1966) and Hawley and Hawley (1975).

Resolving Conflicting Values:

1. State as clearly and specifically as possible the values, choices, options, and/or decisions that are in conflict. For example, instead of saying, "I am in conflict between what I want to do and what my family wants me to do," state as specifically as possible what that conflict entails, "I need/want an hour of alone time during the day to do what I want to do. However, my children expect me to pick them up at school every afternoon, which is the only time I have for myself."

2. Determine the values that are involved in the situation, for example, freedom and self-determination versus wanting to be thought of as a good mother by family and other people.

3. Identify what influences are impacting upon the opposing identified values (what forces are compelling you in each direction), for example, feelings of pressure, stress, and that a person's life revolves around other peoples' needs and not that person's own needs, versus family and societal expectations regarding what being a good mother means.

4. List possible alternatives or options that exist to resolve the conflict.

5. Take each choice or option and list the following:

   a. positive personal benefits,
   b. positive benefit to others,
   c. negative personal effects,
   d. negative effects for others.

6. Rank each of the benefits in order of importance or influence.

7. Based upon the rank order, determine what is the best choice or option.

Learning Experiences:

1. Introduce the idea of values, what they are, where they come from, and how they will frequently conflict.

2. Have individuals or the group identify some of their values that may be in conflict regarding leisure and other areas of their lives.

3. Hand out and discuss the previous section, "Resolving Conflicting Values," as a process that can be utilized to help resolve conflicting values.

4. Take the participants through the process, using their personal conflict(s) related to leisure.

5. Discuss the helpfulness of the process in resolving the conflict, individuals' feelings and thoughts about the choices they made, and what questions or concerns may still exist or be unreconciled after making their choices. Assess whether or not the feelings, questions, or concerns are reconcilable. If so, determine how this can be accomplished. If not, what can be done to maximize one's comfort level?

Component: Leisure Skills

Subcomponent: Planning

Program Goal: Participants will improve their planning skills in relation to leisure.

Program Objectives:
Participants will:

1. clarify their feelings and perceptions regarding planning for leisure.

2. identify advantages and disadvantages of the planning process for leisure.

3. have the opportunity to utilize and refine the planning process in leisure-related ways.

Background Information:

The achievement of desired goals, outcomes, and quality experiences usually requires some type of planning. The planning may be informal, quickly processed, and so minimal that an individual may be totally unaware of the fact that he is planning at all.

For many people, planning is viewed as an unnecessary, burdensome process that takes the fun, enjoyment, and spontaneity away from any experience. Also, it is often viewed as "just not worth the effort for the return one gets." Conversely, there are people who would not act without extensive planning, which a non-planning onlooker might perceived as overkill in relation to the importance of the task at hand. In this objective, it is our intent to have all persons deal with their views and perceptions of planning—its advantages and disadvantages—in relation to various situations and to acquaint participants with a planning process that can be practiced and utilized in relation to leisure.

Practice in the use of planning skills is not built into the learning experiences that follow. Therefore, the facilitator will need to structure experiences and situations in order to give the individual participants an opportunity to practice and perfect the use of planning skills in relation to their own leisure.

There are many versions of the planning process that can be utilized. Although there are many commonalities in each version, it can be seen that the steps also vary. Therefore, the facilitator may want to experiment with several different versions in order to come up with one that is appropriate for use with the individuals or groups with whom he may commonly deal.

The Planning Process:

1. Determine what is to be done or accomplished (goal or outcomes).

2. If there is more than one goal, establish priorities for the following:

    a. now,
    b. in the near future,
    c. in the far future.

3. List the possible means or alternative means (how it can be done) to reach the goal.

4. Identify and list the resources that are currently available and those that are not available but are needed.

5. Determine the feasibility of each means identified.

6. Select the best means available.

Program Experiences:

1. Discuss with the group their feelings and perceptions of planning and amount of planning necessary in a variety of situations:

    a. going out to dinner,
    b. going on a camping trip,
    c. cruising to an island for a weekend,
    d. having a relaxed, nonstressful evening or weekend.

2. As a group, identify some possible outcomes or consequences of including or leaving out each step in relation to the above (and additional) situations.

3. Discuss the advantages and disadvantages of the following:

a. having someone else plan for them,
b. being involved in planning courses of action that will affect them,
c. planning totally alone,
d. planning with input from others,
e. planning jointly with others.

4. As participants use the planning process in leisure, provide opportunities for them to report and discuss the process as well as the results of the process.

Component: Leisure Skills

Subcomponent: Social interaction

Program Goal: Participants will improve their social skills.

Program Objectives:
Participants will:

1. assess their current social skills.

2. identify self-perceived problem areas they want to improve.

3. practice, critique, and refine social skills in progressively realistic social situations.

Background Information:

Social skills are probably one of the main influences upon the quality of our lives and leisure. Effective social skills involve basic communication with people, which in turn influences their association with us. People have problems with social interactions for several reasons. One is that they may have never learned certain social skills because of poor role models and/or significant adults have not given the necessary attention to the development of social skills. Another is that, although they have social skills, they don't perform them for emotional reasons (shyness, negative self-statements). However, social skills, like other skills, can be broken down into basic components that can be taught, practiced, and developed.

Program Experiences:

1. The "Social Skills Checklist" that follows, Worksheet 20, can be used for self-analysis by each participant. Have individuals fill out the checklist in relation to what they perceive to be current problem(s) that cause concern.

2. Once the self-perceived problem area(s) have been identified and rated regarding the most problematic areas, have each participant select the area(s) in which he wants to begin skill development.

3. For each of the areas identified, except the emotional antecedents area, have the group describe the verbal and nonverbal behaviors of people they have observed performing the skill(s) well

and people who do not perform these skills well. Since modeling and practice are important steps in social interaction skills development, this is a critical step in the process. The facilitator should be sure to add any successful behaviors the group may not identify.

4. An additional task of validating the list of successful behaviors could be done by having the participants observe the behaviors of people they think perform the skills successfully. This could also aid them in rounding out their list if it is not as complete as it could be.

S. Once the basic positive behaviors have been identified, the next step is practice and more practice. Begin with actual practice by first role playing within the group. Using a videotape of the practice sessions is extremely helpful. The nonverbal aspects of behavior are much easier to see and relate to, making change much easier.

6. Have group members then practice the behaviors with people within their support system, critique their performances, report back, and practice and refine the skill(s). The last step should be to practice these behaviors in the situation(s) the members feel are most problematic, critique their performances, report back, and continue to refine their skills if necessary.

7. Difficulties in the emotional antecedent area are more difficult to correct. For some people in the group, psychotherapy may be necessary. For others, learning to use affective techniques of behavioral change may be sufficient if the facilitator is or becomes skilled in the teaching of these techniques. Affective techniques include things such as attention manipulation, erasing, thought stopping, escaping, focusing, compartmentalization, transformation of thoughts, self-construct modification, and physiological self-management such as relaxation and meditation (Yates, 1985).

WORKSHEET 20
Social Skills Checklist

Directions: Circle the number of the items that you feel are currently of concern to you in your social interactions. Once these areas have been circled, go back over the list and underline the area(s) you feel are of the **most** concern to you.

Antecedent Feelings

A. I experience the following feelings regarding interacting with people:

1. shy/timid
2. awkward
3. anxious
4. sad
5. nervous
6. depressed
7. bored
8. aggressive
9. superior
10. fearful of the following:
    a. I will do something wrong,
    b. I will not be accepted,
    c. I will look bad.
11. distracted
12. worried
13. preoccupied
14. inferior
15. angry
16. impatient
17. tense
18. argumentative

B. The social skills I feel need further development or refinement are as follows:

1. initiating social interactions
2. greeting skills:

   VERBAL:
   a. saying "Hello" - "Hi,"
   b. matching greeting to person and situation.

   NONVERBAL:
   a. physical location,
   b. appearance,
   c. eye contact,
   d. tone of voice,
   e. facial expression,
   f. posture.

3. listening/understanding
4. responding skills
   a. comebacks,
   b. verbal reinforcement of others,
   c. nonverbal reinforcement of others,
   d. self-disclosure,
   e. disclosure of other things,
   f. sharing the interaction; reciprocity.
5. keeping a conversation going
6. accepting and giving compliments
7. declining requests and invitations
8. being assertive
9. making requests
10. issuing invitations
11. closing interactions
12. expanding and deepening relationships
13. preventing relationships from deteriorating

Component: Leisure Skills

Subcomponent: Problem solving

Program Goal: Participants will improve their problem-solving skills in relation to leisure.

Program Objectives:
Participants will:

1. understand the steps in the problem-solving process.

2. be able to apply the problem-solving process to their leisure related problems.

Background Information:

Solving problems is a constant in life. Problems are those unsettled questions, perplexities, or difficult human and situational circumstances that cause us a sense of discomfort. Problems can be major or minor, simple or complex, and easy or difficult to solve. The perception of how simple, easy, or major a problem is is determined by the individual experiencing the problem.

The focus of this unit is to teach participants a systematic problem-solving process that they can apply in their daily lives. While all of us must solve problems, few individuals have been exposed to or assisted in solving problems in a systematic, effective manner.

Like most leisure skills, enabling participants to improve their problem-solving skills is not accomplished in a onetime, isolated presentation and practice session using the problem-solving process. Such a presentation and practice may be necessary and appropriate as a starting point. However, facilitators then need to move participants along the continuum from leader-based problem solving to participant-based problem solving as a planned goal of the program.

In many human service fields, professionals get hooked into solving problems for participants. It can be a boost to the ego and it can give the leader a sense of accomplishment and control. However, solving problems for participants presents three difficulties: 1) participants have not learned or practiced problem solving for themselves and are thus no better equipped to handle future problems, 2) the feelings of self-esteem, accomplishment, power, and control are being experienced by the leader, not the clients, and 3) long-term dependence.

The Problem-solving Process:

Step 1. Identify the problem.

Differentiating between the problem and the symptoms of the problem is one of the first steps in the problem-solving process. Identifying the problem is a matter of judgment. Therefore, it is necessary to identify as specifically as possible what the perceived problem is. This can be done by describing the situation that requires a problem solution.

Step 2. Understand the problem.

Understanding the problem requires gathering information on the problem and how it affects people involved. Participants should answer the following questions:

a. Do I know all I need to know about the problem?
b. What information do I need that I don't have?
c. Where can I obtain the information I need?
d. How do others involved perceive the problem?
e. How is the problem impacting other people?

Step 3. Define the goal(s).

Once the problem has been identified and understood, defining the goal(s) that one hopes to accomplish through a solution to the problems provides guidance and direction when seeking solutions. Specifically defined goals aid in selecting an alternative that may exist and be available. For example, if a goal is to have evenings and weekends free, the choices will be different than if the goal is to have a half of each day free. Another factor to consider is that some goals may have to be reached in stages. For example, it may be necessary to first have weekends free for the first two months and then free up evenings.

Step 4. Identify options, alternatives, or solutions.

Identify and list the possible options or choices. It is also helpful to get ideas and suggestions from other people because of the tendency to not "see" all of the possibilities and select one of the first few choices, not realizing other options may be available. It should be remembered that as stress and tension increase in one's life, the ability to generate options for solving the problem tend to decrease As options are identified, ask the question: "Will this choice or option achieve the desired goal?"

Step 5. Identify the advantages and disadvantages of each choice.

This step involves identifying and examining the advantages and disadvantages of each option and the possible consequences of this option to those affected by it.

Step 6. Select a course of action or solution.

At this point, a decision is made regarding what option or solution will be selected. Review the choice, keeping the following questions in mind:

a. Is the choice compatible with my goals, values, needs, and interests?
b. Is it realistic?
c. Is it a choice that is best for me at this point in time?

Step 7. Implement the chosen course of action or solution.

Step 8. Evaluate the chosen solution and its results.

Step 9. Modify the course of action if necessary and implement it with modifications.

Program Experiences:

- Present and discuss the problem-solving process as outlined. Then have each participant select a leisure-related problem they feel they have and apply the problem-solving process to that problem. Participants can use one or both of the following worksheets to help process their problem: Worksheets 21 and 22, "Positive Problem Solving - Let's Brainstorm" and "Your Decision."

  During your work with participants, as they encounter problems, refer back to the problem-solving process and have them work through their problems using the same model.

WORKSHEET 21
Positive Problem Solving—Let's Brainstorm

I. Identify the problem: (specific) ______________________________

II. Be creative and list options and possible solutions.

☐ ______________________	☐ ______________________
☐ ______________________	☐ ______________________
☐ ______________________	☐ ______________________
☐ ______________________	☐ ______________________
☐ ______________________	☐ ______________________
☐ ______________________	☐ ______________________
☐ ______________________	☐ ______________________
☐ ______________________	☐ ______________________
☐ ______________________	☐ ______________________
☐ ______________________	☐ ______________________

III. √ the boxes for those that sound reasonable to you.

IV. Write in the three (3) "best" and why you chose them.

1) ____

____

2) ____

____

3) ____

____

V. Review steps I, II, III, and IV once again and now decide on your solution.

____

____

____

WORKSHEET 22
Your Decision

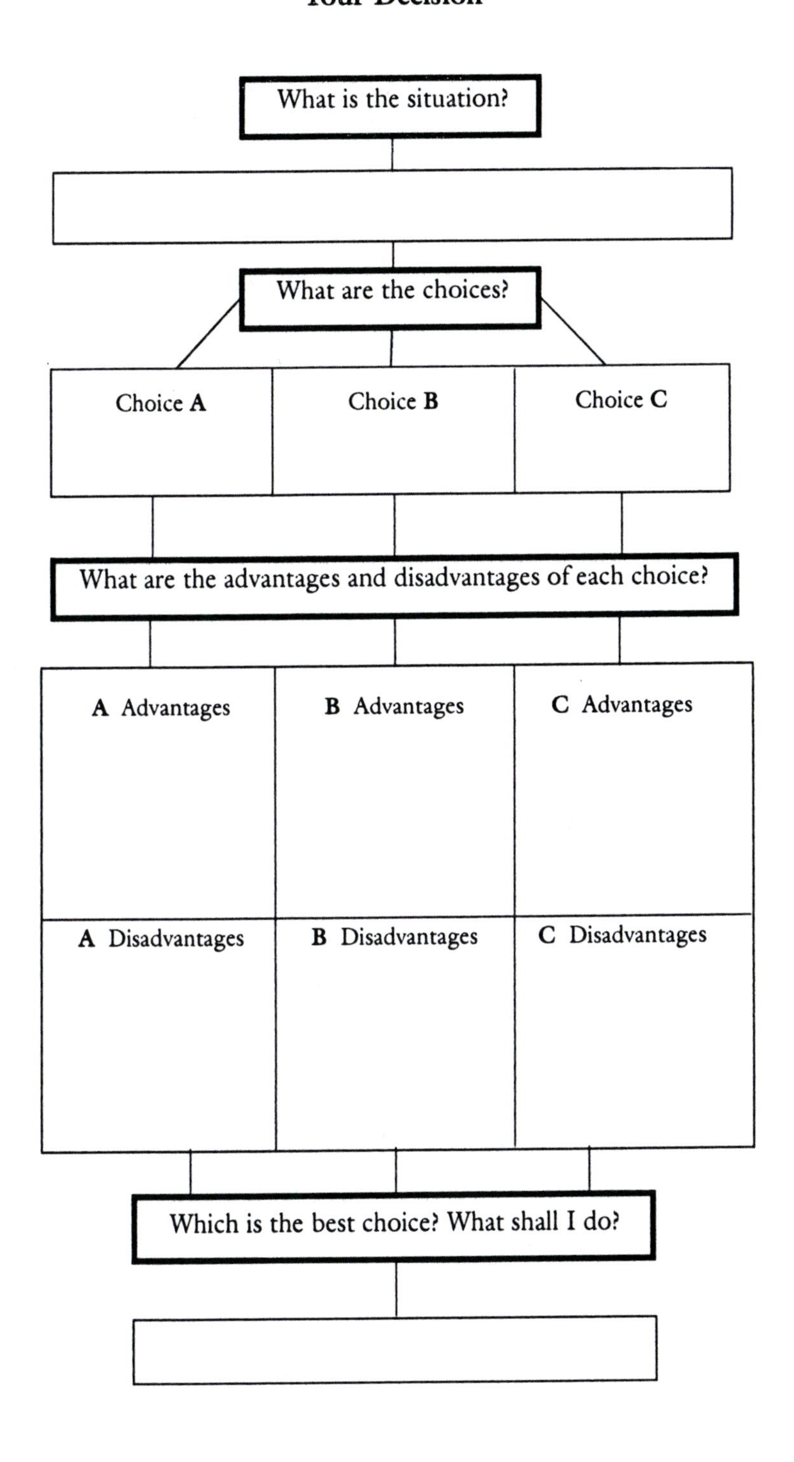

Component: Leisure Skills

Subcomponent: Behavioral change

Program Goal: Participants will be able to apply the process of behavioral change in an area of their life.

Program Objectives:
Participants will:

1. understand the steps in the process of behavioral change.

2. identify an area of their life in which they want to make a change.

3. demonstrate the ability to apply the process of behavioral change to one area of their life.

Background Information:

Years of working with the general public in leisure education has shown that, as a result of becoming more aware of leisure in their personal lives, people develop goals that necessitate some form of change in their behavior. Likewise, it was apparent that while leisure education experiences often provided the motivation for change, actual strategies and techniques on the process of behavioral change were missing subcomponents of the leisure education model. In keeping with the philosophy of personal leisure development used in this book, a focus on helping people to develop skills to change their own behavior when they feel the need has been included. The emphasis of this unit, as with the other leisure skill units, is upon the development of the individual participant's skill in behavior change so that, again, the person has the ability to direct his own behavior beyond the parameters of any program.

Whenever in the leisure education process a participant wants to change his behavior, the "teachable moment" is at hand to present the processes and techniques of behavioral change. It is critical that a person gains experiences in planning, monitoring, altering, and evaluating self-change efforts. Behavioral change does work and the more developed and skilled one is in the process, the more success he will enjoy.

The first step in any behavioral change process is the motivation to change one's behavior. This unit assumes motivation on the part of the participant and will focus on helping develop the skills in the process of behavioral change.

There are three excellent resources that provide detailed explanations and experiences in developing behavioral changes. These books are recommended for further in-depth reading for the facilitator prior to implementing this unit. Any one of these books could also be used as a supplemental resource for participants on this topic. The best of the three is *Self-Directed Behavior (4th ed.),* by David Watson and Roland Tharpe, 1985, Monterey, CA: Brooks/Cole Publishing Company. The other two resources are *Help Yourself: A Guide to Self-Change*, by Jerry A. Schmidt, 1976, Champaign, IL: Research Press; and *Self-Management: The Science and Art of Helping Yourself,* by Brian T. Yates, 1985, Belmont, CA: Wadsworth Publishing Company.

Steps in Behavioral Change:

Step 1. Set a goal(s).

a. Write down the goal(s). It will typically be vague and abstract. For example,

- I want more time for myself,
- I want to feel more comfortable in groups,
- I want more fun in my life.

b. Break a goal into smaller, more concrete steps by identifying what "wanting more time" may mean in terms of behavior. One of the difficulties in changing behavior is that the goals are generally too large and, thus, vague. Attach numbers to the smaller goal or target behavior. This makes the goal clearer and allows anyone to judge whether or not the goal has been accomplished:

- I will spend one hour a day reading for pleasure.

Other options for goals or target behavior:

- I will allow myself one evening a week to be with my friends,
- I will spend three weekends at the beach during the summer.

Once various options are listed, the individual selects one based upon his own priority of factors, such as importance, ease of accomplishment, or least disruption.

Step 2. Observe your own behavior.

Self-knowledge is the key to self-modification. Your actions, behaviors, thoughts, and feelings are embedded in situations, and each of these elements must be carefully observed. Self-observation is the first step on the road to self-directed behavior and it is the step most often omitted in our daily lives . . . . In order to change yourself, you have to know what you are doing." (Watson & Tharpe, 1985, p. 55)

a. There are two easy and helpful techniques for recording behavior. One by Watson and Tharpe (1985) recommends keeping a diary of some sort regarding the behaviors you want to change. Describe or count the frequency of the behaviors, determine what events trigger the behaviors, and the things that reward the behavior. The authors explain the use of several types of diaries in their book. One type is a structured diary where one records his behavior along with the antecedent events and consequences of those behaviors (an A-B-C approach).

Using the A-B-C structured diary, one first records the actions, thoughts, or feelings that are the focus of the change. Then enter under "Antecedents" the event(s) that proceeded it and under "Consequences" what followed it. For example,

Antecedents (A)	**Behaviors (B)**	**Consequences (C)**
What were you doing?	Actions	What happened as a result?
When did it happen?	Thoughts	Pleasant?
Who were you with?	Feelings	Unpleasant?
Where were you?		
What were you saying to yourself?		

Antecedents (A)	Behaviors (B)	Consequences (C)
Monday		
Kids nagging me to go to the movie with them.	I give in to kids' nagging and go to movie with them. Didn't take my hour for reading.	Kids happy and quiet. I was miserable. Movie was boring. I felt mad at myself and the kids.
Thursday		
Fran called for me play tennis.	Played tennis. Didn't take my hour for reading.	Had great fun. Usedto my hour for myself to do something as enjoyable as reading, only with a friend.

After seeing that playing tennis rather than reading was just as important and satisfying, a person may want to change her goal from "reading for pleasure for one hour a day" to something like "I will take one hour each day to do whatever I want to do."

A second technique for recording behavioral observations is one that records frequency or duration. Simple charts like the ones that follow could be used to record how frequently negative behavior occurs.

Frequency and Duration Charts

	Week 1	Week 2	Week 3	Week 4
Monday	√	√	√	
Tuesday				
Wednesday	√		√	
Thursday		√	√	
Friday	√	√	√	
Saturday				
Sunday				

Date	Occurrence of negative behavior
October 8	𝍸 𝍸 𝍸
October 9	𝍸 𝍸
October 10	𝍸 𝍷𝍷𝍷
October 11	𝍸 𝍸
October 12	𝍸 𝍷
October 13	𝍷𝍷𝍷𝍷
October 14	𝍷𝍷𝍷𝍷

b. After reviewing his behavioral charting, the person desiring to make the stated change should evaluate his progress over a predetermined time period to determine if adjustments are warranted. The goal or target behavior ("I will spend one hour each day reading for pleasure") could be kept as it is and other life adjustments made; it could be modified to specify only weekdays and not weekends; or it could be modified to have only a half hour per day. The only way to determine what is a logical and attainable goal is to state one, try it out, and then make adjustments as needed.

	One Hour of Reading Per Day - Attained				
Day	Week 1	Week 2	Week 3	Week 4	Week 5
Monday	X	X	X		X
Tuesday	X		X	X	X
Wednesday		X	X	X	
Thursday	X	X		X	X
Friday		X	X		X
Saturday					
Sunday	X		X	X	X

c. This review period is also a good time to determine whether there are small, specific acts that are chained together that interfere with the achievement of the target behavior. Self-observation can often make us aware that the target behaviors occur or fail to occur because of specific circumstances. For example, it may become apparent that if a salesperson does not take time at the end of the day to organize his work for the next day at the office, it must be done at home that evening. Whenever this occurs, the salesperson chooses to give up his hour of pleasure reading. Identifying this chain of events allows an opportunity for planning and changes in work life patterns that affect the target behavior.

Step 3. Work out a plan for change.

Developing an effective plan for change needs to involve an analysis of the type(s) of problem(s) one wants to change. The following questions developed by Watson and Tharpe (1985) are valuable in determining what types of problems exist so that a person may select strategies for a plan of change that works best in certain situations.

Antecedents of Behavior:

1. What stimuli seem to trigger the behavior? In what situations does the behavior occur?

2. Do you react automatically to some cue with undesirable behavior?

3. Do you react to some cue with an unwanted emotion? What is the conditioned stimulus for it?

4. What are you saying to yourself before the behavior?

Behavior:

5. Is it strong and quite frequent, or is it weak and not very frequent? What does this tell you about what you can do to change it?

6. Is any element of your problem due to something you are avoiding, perhaps unnecessarily?

7. Are you aware of models in your past whose behavior (or perhaps some aspect of it) you may have copied?
8. Does any part of your goal involve changing behaviors that are

resistant to extinction either because they are intermittently reinforced or because they are avoidance behaviors?

Consequences

9. Are your desired behaviors positively reinforced?

10. What about actions that make the desired behavior difficult? Are they reinforced?

11. Is it possible that the desired behavior is being punished?

12. Is your own self-speech rewarding or punishing your behavior?

If the problem is primarily in the antecedent area, the self-change plan will need to include strategies that modify the antecedents and/or initiate new antecedents. For problems in the behavioral area, substituting new thoughts and behavior, initiating incompatible behaviors, developing successive approximations toward the desired behavior, and developing and practicing new behaviors in the actual situations in which you want them to occur can be used. Regarding problems in the consequences area, an effective behavioral change plan needs to build in positive reinforcers or rewards following the attainment of the desired behavior. (A highly detailed explanation of these specific strategies can be found in Watson and Tharpe, 1985.)

Step 4. Continue self-observation and adjust the plan as it is put into practice and as you get more information on your behavior.

Anyone should expect relapses when attempting behavior change. It will not go perfectly. The important thing is getting to know one's own behavior, developing a workable plan, modifying the plan as needed, and persevering.

Program Experiences:

1. Outline and give examples of the steps in the process of behavioral change.

2. Have participants identify one area of their life in which a change is desired.

3. Using the change the participants want to make, have them begin by writing down the goal or target behavior in specific terms with numbers attached (Step 1).

4. Have participants select one of the techniques they will use to observe their own behavior for at least one week (Step 2).

5. After one week, have individuals review, report, and evaluate their progress. Based on their review, have each person identify the adjustments or modifications needed to attain each person's goals or target behaviors.

6. It is recommended at this point in the process that the facilitator work one-on-one with each person to work out each plan for change (Step 3). For some people, this will not be necessary because once they have specifically identified their target behaviors they are able to accomplish their goals. For others, change may be more complicated and the person may need assistance in learning and practicing strategies to modify antecedents, behaviors, or consequences.

Chapter 6 References

Barnes, K.E. (1971). Preschool play norms: A replication. *Developmental Psychology, 5*(1), 99-103.

Beard, J.G., & Ragheb, M.G. (1980). Leisure satisfaction: Concept, theory, and measurement. In S. Iso-Ahola (Ed.), *Social psychological perspectives of leisure and recreation* (pp. 329-353). Springfield, IL: C.C. Thomas.

Beard, J.G., & Ragheb, M.G. (1983). Measuring leisure satisfaction. *Journal of Leisure Research, 12*(1), 20-33.

Beyth-Marom, R., Novik, R., & Sloan, M. (1987). Enhancing children's thinking skills: An instructional model for decision-making under certainty. *Instructional Science, 16*(3), 2115-2231.

Browne, H. (1973). *How I found freedom in an unfree world.* New York, NY: MacMillan.

Crawford, D.W., & Godbey, G. (1987). Reconceptualizing barriers to family leisure. *Leisure Sciences, 9,* 119-127.

Fandozzi, R. (1976). *A study of individual affinity for activity components.* Tallahassee, FL: Author.

Hawley, R.C., & Hawley, I.L. (1975). *Developing human potential.* Amherst, MA: ERA Press.

Henderson, K.A., Stalnaker, D., & Taylor, G. (1988). The relationship between barriers to recreation and gender-role personality traits for women. *Journal of Leisure Research, 20,* 69-80.

Iso-Ahola, S. (1980). *Social psychological perspectives on leisure and recreation.* Springfield, IL: C.C. Thomas.

Jackson, E.L. (1988). Leisure constraints: A survey of past research. *Leisure Sciences, 10,* 203-205.

Jackson, E.L. (1990). Variations in the desire to begin a leisure activity: Evidence of antecedent constraints? *Journal of Leisure Research, 22*, 55-70.

Kay, T., & Jackson, G. (1991). Leisure despite constraint: The impact of leisure constraints on leisure participation. *Journal of Leisure Research, 23*(4), 301-313.

MacPhail-Wilcox, B., & Bryant, H.D. (1988). A descriptive model of decision making: Review of idiographic influences. *Journal of Research and Development in Education, 22*(1), 7-22.

Myers, I.B. (1985). *Manual, a guide to the development and use of the Myers-Briggs type indicator.* Palo Alto, CA: Consulting Psychologist Press.

Peck, S. (1978). *The road less traveled.* Simon and Schuster.

Raths, L.E., Harmn, M., & Simon, S.B. (1966). *Values and teaching: Working with values in the classroom.* Columbus, OH: Charles E. Merrill.

Schmidt, J.A. (1976). *Help yourself: A guide to self-change.* Champaign, IL: Research Press.

Shaw, S.M., Bonen, A., & McCabe, J.F. (1991). Do more constraints mean less leisure? Examining the relationship between constraints and participation. *Journal of Leisure Research,* 23(4), 286-300.

Wade, M.G. (1985). *Constraints on leisure.* Springfield, IL: C.C. Thomas.

Witkin, Goodenough, & Karp. (1967). Stability of cognitive style from childhood to young adulthood. *Journal of Personality and Social Psychology, 7*, 291-300.

Watson, D.L., & Tharpe, R. (1985). *Self-directed behavior.* Monterey, CA: Brooks/Cole Publishing Company.

Yalom, I. (1980). *Existential psychotherapy.* New York: Basic Books.

Yates, J.F. (1990). *Judgment and decision making.* Englewood Cliffs, NJ: Prentice Hall.

Yates, B.T. (1985). *Self-management: The science and art of helping yourself.* Belmont, CA: Wadsworth Publishing Co.

Zeyen, D., Odum, L., & Lancaster, R. (1977). *Kangaroo Kit: Leisure Education Curriculum.* Washington, D.C.: National Recreation and Park Association.

Leisure Education Facilitation Techniques

Chapter Overview

This chapter begins with a differentiation between the terms and concepts of facilitator and facilitation techniques and leader and leadership techniques. General facilitation guidelines are presented as well as guidelines for facilitating group discussions, value clarification exercises, and mini-lecture presentation skills.

Introduction

Recreation, parks and leisure services have historically focused on developing recreation and leisure activity skills. The principle skills needed by practitioners to accomplish this end were instructional and leadership skills to teach and lead recreation and leisure activities. Since many programs dealt with groups of people, group leadership skills were often also needed. These skills are still needed in certain areas of leisure education. However, since the individual developmental model of leisure education approaches leisure education as facilitating each person's ability to think through, determine, and evaluate her own leisure attitudes, values, behaviors, and decisions, as well as to understand the impact of these choices, additional leadership skills are needed to accomplish these new ends. The professional's role in the leisure education process is to enable people to determine, clarify, and evaluate their own answers to leisure-related questions, rather than providing answers for people. In the individual developmental approach it is the role of the professional to enable people to become their own "leaders" and the architects of their leisure. This necessitates developing skills that 1) ask questions rather than only provide "instruction" in the form of answers; 2) provide opportunities for personal awareness and clarification of leisure issues, problems, and values rather than imparting one's own ideas in the form of should's and ought-to's; and 3) enable people to utilize and expand their own capacities for self-determination rather than being leader dominated.

In this chapter the terms *facilitation techniques* and *facilitators* are used in place of the terms leadership techniques and leaders. This change in terms is used to denote a philosophical shift in the primary role, function, and skills professional personnel may have used in the past and may be using currently. The term leadership connotes there is a "leader" and a "follower." It further implies that the "leader" is the most active in any process and the "follower" is more passive to the directions of the "leader."

The term *facilitator* is used to signify a person who is skilled in helping clients to attain their own goals, to accomplish tasks themselves, and to develop their own skills. Facilitators assist, guide, question, and provide information where it is needed. The term *facilitation* is used to refer to the process of helping clients.

The remainder of this chapter outlines and discusses a variety of facilitation techniques that are compatible with and effective in facilitating the goals and objectives of leisure education. These techniques include general facilitation guidelines, values clarification, group discussion, counseling, instruction, and information processing. While it could be argued that areas such as values clarification and information processing could be classified as content areas or methods, they will be dealt with here as ways of facilitating the leisure development of people.

General Facilitation Guidelines

The following suggestions are offered as general facilitation guidelines to assist the facilitator in fostering participant self-leisure exploration. They will provide the facilitator with a client-centered approach to interactions and a repertoire of basic facilitation skills. These general guidelines can be used in facilitating leisure education activities as well as in personal, informal interactions with clients.

Facilitation Guidelines

1. **Be non-judgmental.** Many facilitators have difficulty in not judging people. We view beliefs, values, and actions through our own value filters, which we tend to view as "right" and "good." It requires a conscious effort not to judge people who hold views different from our own. However, effective facilitators convey that they want individuals to express themselves freely, without fear of approval or disapproval.

   The principle of being non-judgmental is one of the key elements in fostering open communication and expression of beliefs, ideas, and values. Thwarting statements like "Surely you can't believe that," "You have got to be kidding," or "I can't believe you think that after all we have talked about," kill open communication. Communication is also thwarted when participants feel the facilitator is not open to ideas and positions other than the ones the facilitator holds.

2. **Be aware of using interjectory statements.** Statements such as "Everyone knows . . ." or "Don't you agree that . . ." are subtle ways of interjecting our views on someone else. The facilitator needs to be aware of using such expressions and understand that they block communication and discussion. Participants pick up on these subtleties and recognize them for what they are, often even before the facilitator is aware of having said them.

3. **Avoid the should's, have to's, ought to's.** Facilitators who use phrases like "You should . . ." or "Everyone ought to . . ." are giving their own answers to participant problems. Again, this is a not-so-subtle mechanism of imposing one's own beliefs, values, and standards on someone else. Phrases such as "You may want to consider or think about . . . " or "Do you feel . . . may be an option or beneficial?" provide ideas the participant may not have considered, but do so in a non-directive, non-judgmental way.

4. **Use "I" statements when expressing opinions.** It is appropriate and helpful for facilitators to share their own opinions, thoughts, and values with participants if they are "owned" and identified as such. "I think . . ." or "I believe . . ." statements flag the communication from facilitators as simply their own opinions or views, to be assessed and responded to like all other opinions being expressed by group members.

5. **Use active listening skills.** Listening skills are one of the most basic communication and human relation skills upon which other more complex skills are built. Beginning facilitators often perceive listening to mean a laid-back, passive process. However, this is not the case. Listening, or active listening as it will be called here, is an active process in which the facilitator is intently involved in taking in and responding to the total communication. Active listening skills are comprised of four components: 1) attending, 2) paraphrasing, 3) clarifying, and 4) perception checking.

Attending

Attending means to focus our mind and attention on the person and his communication. Using attending behavior encourages the person to continue expressing himself freely. Individual perception that one is really being listened to has a powerful effect on reinforcing the open expression of thoughts and feelings. Brammer (1973) offers the following summary of guidelines for effective attending behavior:

1. Establish *contact* through looking at the client when she talks.

2. Maintain a *natural, relaxed posture* that indicates your interest.

3. Use *natural gestures* to communicate your intended messages.

4. Use *verbal statements* to relate statements without interruptions, questions, or new topics (pp. 83-84).

Paraphrasing

Paraphrasing occurs when the facilitator restates the participant's basic message in the facilitator's own words. The restatement is generally in fewer, simpler, and more concise words. An example of paraphrasing follows:

> ***Participant:*** My mother really drives me crazy. First she tells me she wants me to put my time and energy into my studies. Then she constantly bugs me to go out and do things with my friends.
> ***Facilitator:*** She really confuses you.
> ***Participant:*** That's the truth!

Paraphrasing lets the speaker know you are actively listening and trying to understand the message. It also checks your perception of the message to see if you really are understanding what the speaker is communicating. This type of interchange also encourages further verbalization.

Brammer's (1973) guidelines for paraphrasing follow:

1. *Listen for the basic message* of the client.

2. *Restate* to the client *a concise and simple summary* of the client's basic message.

3. *Observe a cue* or *ask for a response* from the client to confirm or deny the client's accuracy and helpfulness of the paraphrase for promoting the client's understanding.

Clarifying

Clarifying is used to help bring rambling or unclear communication into sharper, clearer focus. Phrases such as the following can serve a clarifying function: "You lost me there. Could you give me an example or put it a different way?" "I'm not sure I understand. Could you elaborate on that some more for me?" "Are you saying . . .?"

Guidelines suggested by Brammer (1973) for clarifying follow:

1. *Admit confusion* about the client's meaning.

2. *Try a restatement* or *ask for clarification*, repetition, or illustration.

Perception Checking

In perception checking, the facilitator checks out his perception of what the participant is communicating directly with the participant. Examples of statements for perception checks are "You seem to be expressing doubt about your decision;" "I am detecting that you feel taking time for yourself is selfish; is that accurate?" and "It seems to me that you are feeling you don't have any options; is that an accurate perception?"

Brammer's (1973) guidelines for perception checking follow:

1. *Paraphrase* what you think you heard.

2. *Ask for confirmation* directly from the client about the accuracy of your perception of what she said.

3. Allow the client to *correct your perception* if it was inaccurate.

The "Person" of the Facilitator

In discussing general facilitation guidelines, it is important to give attention to the fact that the *person* of the facilitator is critically important in fostering human growth and development. Often, facilitators do not think that who they are as people, what they value, what they believe, the personal characteristics they possess, and the way they interact with people have a significant effect upon the personal growth and development of their clients. They tend to believe that the most important elements in a helping relationship are the strategies, techniques, and processes they employ. However, there is growing evidence that indicates the *person* of the facilitator is as important and significant in the development of people as the methods used (Combs, 1969). Frances Cannon, in her classes at Florida State University, has advocated the need to develop the "conscious use of self" as one of the most important tools in facilitating human development. The conscious use of self refers to knowing and using those traits one possesses, as well as developing within one's self "ways of being" that have been found to be effective in helping relationships.

For further information and skill development on additional facilitation techniques, Brammer's book, *The Helping Relationship: Process and Skills,* is a helpful resource.

Leading Group Discussions

Leading group discussions is probably one of the most widely used facilitation techniques in leisure education. Group discussions are highly participatory, are participant driven, allow for the expression of varying values and opinions, allow group members to bring their individual life experiences into the group, and allow participants to learn from each other as well as the facilitator. It is a highly effective tool for expression, clarification, exploration, and change.

Guidelines for Facilitating a Discussion

To facilitate an effective discussion, follow some established guidelines:

I. Before beginning to use discussion in a leisure education session, the facilitator needs to think through several things.

  A. What do you, as the facilitator, hope and plan to gain from the discussion time?
    1. Is it knowledge and facts?
    2. Is it an effort to take the group beyond fact to insights or drawing conclusions?
    3. Is it to introduce the next topic?

  B. Once these questions have been answered, consider questions and statements such as the following:
    1. How to set the stage for discussion.
    2. How to enhance participation.
    3. What techniques can be used to prevent questioning from stalling or frustrating discussion?
    4. What to do if the group is not responsive.

Most immediately, be aware that questions and answers are not discussion. Questions and answers have their place, particularly in setting the stage for discussion, but there is more to discussion than questions and answers alone.

II. How to get the discussion started.

A. It may be hard to get started; people have a tendency to do the following:
   1. Being in the habit of sitting back and letting others talk.
   2. Feeling insecure.
   3. Fearing saying the wrong thing.
   4. Feeling a lack of group acceptance.

B. Create an informal, comfortable atmosphere. Get to know names through the use of name tags or by placing names on paper in front of each person.

C. Move people into the discussion as soon as possible:
   1. Start the discussion on an easy question so that people will hear their voices in the group.
   2. Sharing names and telling something about themselves can get people involved.

D. Plan an easy takeoff:
   1. Plan a general, nonthreatening topic and questions to start the group.
   2. Do ***not*** call on people. There are many more reasons not to use this method, particularly with adults, than reasons justifying its use. The reasons are numerous:
      a. the question may threaten the individual,
      b. the individual really may not have anything to contribute at the moment,
      c. others will wonder why this individual was picked out for special treatment,
      d. the behavior may suggest to the group that spontaneous contributions are not in order,
      e. the technique causes group members to be ready with a response in case called upon, rather than thinking about the problem under discussion.

III. How to incur participation:

A. The physical setup:

1. A comfortable room:
   a. ventilation,
   b. no glare in eyes.
2. A seating arrangement that promotes interaction:
   a. around a table is best,
   b. in circle if no table,
   c. in lines if circle is not possible.
3. Avoid a "leader spot."
4. Have available a large piece of paper or chalkboard on which to write main ideas.

B. The skills of the facilitator:

1. Be quiet—don't be afraid of silence:
   a. Deliberate silence is the most intriguing alternative to questions and one of the most effective. It is the simplest, yet the hardest to practice. Say nothing at all. When a person pauses, falters, or has ostensibly finished speaking (and yet the facilitator knows the matter is not clear or not finished), maintain a deliberate, relaxed, attentive, and appreciative silence lasting three to five seconds. Chances are the person will resume or another individual will enter into the discussion;
   b. Time is needed for sustained expression of thought. The act of expressing complex thought or interpretation requires more time than the act of expressing facts, giving descriptions, and the like. The very expression of complex thought is characterized by pauses, false starts, and other hesitations that occur both more frequently and for longer periods than they do during the expression of factual knowledge. The use of deliberate silence allows for greater participation and for more complex thought.
2. Act and think as a member of the group. Use of the term *we* can help accomplish this.
3. Listen to and accept every person's contribution:

a. respond to the person, not the idea;
b. let the group accept, reject, or respond to the idea;
c. be concerned with the ideas of the group members rather than with expressing your own ideas.

4. Seek to have members talk to each other rather than to you. Some techniques to help accomplish this:
   a. break eye contact with the person talking,
   b. use statements instead of questions during the course of the discussion.
5. Use declarative statements that allow participants to pick up on other peoples' comments. Interjecting a statement to redirect the topic will help discussion flow among the group. Below are several alternatives to the question and answer approach that should lead to stimulating thought, encouraging participation, and affecting discussion:
   a. ***Declarative Statement.*** The declarative statement is used in place of a question to express a thought that occurs to the facilitator in relation to something a group member may have just said (e.g., "It *is* important to . . ."). Sometimes a point needs to be made, and it can be made by declaring it instead of using a question.
   b. ***Reflective Restatement.*** Instead of "What do you mean?" state your understanding of what the participant said. Try "I get from what you say that . . ." or "So you think that . . ." This technique confirms that you are listening, that what the person has said has been a contribution, and that you are waiting for him or her to elaborate.
   c. ***State of Mind.*** When a group member has said something that is not clear to you or you feel that you have missed the point, truthfully describe your state of mind. This can be done by statements such as "I'm confused about what you're saying" or "I'm sorry, but I'm not getting it." A related state of mind situation could be where the facilitator might be wondering about something that is brought up in the discussion. That state of mind can be expressed by using a mixed

declarative-interrogative sentence: "I am just thinking about whether that would make any difference" or "I'm trying to remember what happens under these conditions." Frequently, another group member will step in and rephrase or elaborate.

   d. ***Invitation to Elaborate.*** This alternative is simple. Some useful phrases are as follows: "I'd like to hear more of your views on that;" "I'd be interested in your definition of (or your experience about) that;" "Perhaps you can give us an example to help us understand."

6. Encourage group members to raise questions regarding other members' contributions and comment on them to the speaker directly. This will help begin to facilitate discussion between group members rather than comments always flowing through the facilitator.
7. Turn questions back to the group. Try not to give answers unless the question is directed specifically to you.
8. Recognize "hidden agendas" that may be in operation in the group. Hidden agendas could be things such as the following:
   a. desire for recognition,
   b. competition between members,
   c. hostility to the leader,
   d. striving for a goal that is not the goal of this group.
9. Keep the discussion moving constructively. Use aids to move ahead:
   a. a chalkboard can be used to show the following:
      1) main points,
      2) goals.
   b. a timekeeper can report the following:
      1) time available,
      2) time passage,
      3) time remaining,
      4) speaking time limit of members when a ground rule has been established ahead of time.
   c. an observer can report to the group when the observer believes it has strayed from the subject:

- assist group by organizing and summarizing the ideas expressed and by doing so again at the end of the discussion.

10. Use different types of questions to facilitate discussion. Below are several different forms that questions can take to encourage discussion:
    a. to *open discussion*—
    "What do you think about the problem as stated?"
    b. to *broaden participation*—
    "Now that we've heard from a number of people, would others like to add their ideas?"
    c. to *limit participation*—
    "You have made several good statements, and I am wondering if someone else might like to make some remarks?"
    d. to *focus attention*—
    "Where are we now in relation to our goal for this discussion?"
    e. to *help the group move along*—
    "I wonder if we haven't spent enough time on this phase of the problem? Should we move to another aspect of it?"
    f. to *help the group evaluate itself*—
    "Let's take a look at our original objective for this discussion and see where we are in relation to it."
    g. to *help the group reach a decision*—
    "Am I right in sensing agreement at these points?" (Leader then gives brief summary of points.)
    h. to *lend continuity to the discussion*—
    "Since we can't reach a decision at this meeting, what are some of the points we should take up at the next meeting?"

Value Clarification

Value clarification experiences are planned learning activities or experiences designed to help people proceed through their process of valuing. When implementing value clarification experiences in leisure education, the facilitators will usually need to supplement these experiences with group discussion and interaction suggestions found in the general facilitation guidelines.

Harmin, Kirschenbaum, and Simon (1973) state that people do not need more values imposed upon them. Individuals do need to learn skills that will help them develop their own values in order to be able to deal with the multiplicity of problems and alternatives in today's complex society. "For this reason, it is more effective to teach the process of valuing than it is to teach one set of values" (p. 32).

Raths (1966) presented an outline of the valuing process composed of seven subprocesses to help people make satisfying and responsible choices in their lives rather than having to be told what to do. A helpful adaptation of Raths' subprocesses was presented in Harmin et al. (1973). The following include these two works.

The Valuing Process

Choosing One's Beliefs

A. Choosing freely.

If we are to live by our own value system, we must learn how to make independent choices. If we are able only to follow authority, we will be ineffectual when authority is silent or absent, when it gives us conflicting directions, or when our emotions impel us in contrary directions (Harmin et al., 1973, p. 32).

1. ***Preferences:*** What do I really like?
2. ***Influences:*** What influences have led me to this decision? How freely am I making my choice? (Hawley & Hawley, 1975, p. 146)

B. Choosing from alternatives.

For choice-making to have meaning, there have to be alternatives from which to choose. If there are no alternatives, there are no choices. The more alternatives available, the more likely we are to value our choices. Generating and considering alternative choices is necessary for clarifying and refining values (Harmin et al., 1973, pp. 32-33).

- ***Alternatives:*** What are the possible alternatives to this choice? Have I sufficiently considered the alternatives? (Hawley & Hawley, 1975, p. 146)

C. **Choosing, after thoughtful consideration of consequences.**
We need to learn to examine alternatives in terms of their expected consequences. If we don't, our choices are likely to be whimsical, impulsive, or conforming. By considering consequences, we lessen the chance of those consequences being unexpected or unpleasant (Harmin et al., 1973, p. 33).

- ***Consequences:*** What are the probable and possible consequences of my choice? Am I willing to risk the consequences? Are the consequences beneficial or harmful to me and others? (Hawley & Hawley, 1975)

Prizing One's Beliefs and Behaviors

D. **Prizing and cherishing.**
Values inevitably include not only our rational choices, but our feelings as well. In developing values, we become aware of what we prize and cherish. Our feelings help us determine what we think is worthy and important—what our priorities are (Harmin et al., 1973, p. 33).

E. **Publicly affirming.**
When we share our choices with others—what we prize and what we do—we not only continue to clarify our own values, but we help others to clarify their values as well. It is important to encourage participants to speak out about their beliefs and their actions in appropriate ways and circumstances (Harmin et al., 1973, p. 33).

Acting On One's Beliefs

F. **Acting.**
Often people have difficulty in acting on what they come to believe and to prize. Yet, if they are to realize their values, it is vital that they learn how to connect choices and prizing to their own behavior (Harmin et al., 1973, pp. 33-34).

- *Acting:* Am I able to act on this choice? Do my actions reflect the choices I have made? (Hawley & Hawley, 1975, p. 147)

G. **Acting with some pattern.**
A single act does not make a value. We need to examine the patterns of our lives. What do we do with consistency and regularity? Do these patterns incorporate our choices and prizings? If our life patterns do not reflect our choices and prizings, we then must reconsider our priorities or change our behavior in order to actualize those priorities (Raths, 1966).

- *Patterning:* Does this choice represent a continuing commitment through action? How can I change the pattern of my life so that this choice continually reflects my actions, values, and priorities? (Harmin et al., 1973).

Value Clarification Learning Experiences

Casteel and Stahl (1975) identify six formats for learning experiences useful to identify and clarify personal values. All six of these formats include a minimum of a learning resource and a set of questions to process the information or situation through decision making based upon one's values and feelings. A learning resource, which may be a new term for leisure professionals, is simply a "kickoff" or "takeoff" point for discussion and decision making. It can be things like poems, pictures, written statements of fact or opinion from newspapers, TV, books, cartoons, real or contrived problems or situations, old sayings, and pictures, to name a few. The learning resource is used to set the stage and to provide the direction and focus of the topic(s) to be discussed. The sets of questions are designed to make sure that understanding and comprehension of the problem or situation exist and to stimulate eventual decision making based upon personal values and feelings.

One of the advantages of learning value clarification formats is that once professionals understand the basic formats available, they can design their own value clarifications' experiences related to leisure.

The Basic Format

The most basic and simple format of the value clarification learning experience is one that includes both a learning resource and a set of questions related to the topic or focus of the discussion. The following is an example of this basic format:

Title: "Old Sayings"

Learning Resource: "Idle hands are the devil's workshop."

Discussion Questions:

1. What do you think this old saying means?
2. What does it mean to you?
3. What do you think it is saying about free time? What do you think it is saying about staying busy?
4. Do you agree or disagree with this old saying?
5. Why do you agree or disagree with the statement?
6. What are the advantages and disadvantages of agreeing with the statement? Of disagreeing with the statement?

Forced-choice Format

The forced-choice format is designed to have individuals determine what they think is the "best" choice among a number of attractive or unattractive alternatives. If the choices are among unattractive alternatives, then the individual must decide which one is the "least unattractive." For this technique to be effective, the alternatives need to be relatively equal in their attractiveness or unattractiveness. The following illustration, "Family Feud," is stereotypical in nature by design to show how value clarification experiences can be valuable in dealing with controversial issues:

Title: "Family Feud"

Learning Resource: The Nelson family is a closely knit family. The Nelsons have two children: a girl age 12 and a nine-year-old boy. Mr. Nelson is an accountant with an income that puts the family in an upper-middle income category. Mrs. Nelson quit teaching school after the arrival of the first child. She has been primarily a mother and a homemaker while the children have been growing up. Lately, she has realized she is feeling bored, confined, and lacking intellectual stimulation and satisfying social contacts. To help remedy the situation, Mrs. Nelson decides to join a literary discussion group that meets one night a week at the home of a friend of the Nelsons. Upon hearing Mrs. Nelson's decision, Mr. Nelson demands she drop out of the group in order to be at home in the evenings with him and the children. Faced with her husband's demand, Mrs. Nelson sees only three choices available:

1. Ignore her husband's demands and attend the literary discussion group over his objections.
2. Give up participation in the discussion group because her husband objects.
3. Demand that her husband give up his Thursday night bowling with his co-workers if she gives up her literary group.

Given only these three choices, Mrs. Nelson should . . . . Of these three choices, this is the best because . . . .

Discussion Questions:
1. What concerns you most about the decision you made?
2. On what values did you base your decision?
3. What do you think would be the consequences of the decision you made?
4. What do you think would have been the worst choice? Why?

Other Types of Questions:
1. What do you perceive Mrs. Nelson was being asked to give up?
2. Was Mr. Nelson right to demand his wife give up her group?
3. Would you refer to Mrs. Nelson as selfish? Irresponsible? Explain your answer.

Rank-order Format

Rank-ordering focuses upon a hierarchical internal belief system in terms of preferences, feelings, and priorities. It allows a wide perspective of a topic at hand and helps individuals sort and make decisions in relation to their priorities. Rank-ordering includes a learning resource, a list of options to be ordered, directions on how the options are to be ordered, and discussion questions.

Title: "Leisure Outcomes"

Learning Resource: Assume for a moment that for the rest of your life you could have only five outcomes, or benefits, from your leisure. All other benefits would be forever removed from your life. What are the five most important and valuable outcomes from leisure that you would most want to preserve? Tear a piece of paper into five pieces and write down one benefit or outcome you want to preserve on each sheet of paper. Once you have made your five choices, look at what you have written and determine if these are really the ones that are most important to you. If not, you may substitute another outcome for one you already have, but you cannot add more. Now look at your leisure benefits or outcomes. You must discard one of your five. Now, eliminate another of these from your life. Finally, eliminate one last outcome from your life.

Discussion Questions:

1. What were the five outcomes or benefits you choose as most important in your life? In what order did you eliminate them from your life?
2. What two were the most important to you? What was the basis of your decision?
3. What were the three least important to you? What was the basis of your decision?
4. What do you believe you would gain and lose by what you kept and what you eliminated?

Consequential Analysis Formats

The following consequential analysis formats can be added to value clarification experiences to help participants identify and process possible results of choices and decisions. There are three different consequential analysis formats that can be used. In each of the formats, participants can 1) make any decision they need to make, 2) identify possible choices in the situation,

3) narrow the choices or options to the most desirable, and then 4) use one of the consequential analysis formats to further process their options.

Format 1

The beneficial results of choice (or decision/position) A:

____

The beneficial results of choice B:

____

The undesirable results of choice A:

____

The undesirable results of choice B:

____

Format 2

Option (choice/ decision)	Positive personal benefits	Negative personal benefits
1. ____________	1. ____________	1. ____________
2. ____________	2. ____________	2. ____________

Option (choice/ decision)	Positive personal benefits	Negative personal benefits
1. ____________	1. ____________	1. ____________
2. ____________	2. ____________	2. ____________

Format 3

The best choice is ______________________________.

The basis for selecting this choice is

____.

The anticipated positive consequences to me are

____.

The possible negative consequences are

____.

The criteria I would use to justify this choice are

____.

Hawley and Hawley (1975) included two decision-making techniques in their book, *Developing Human Potential,* that are useful in connecting one's values to the available options and end goals. Because decisions are always based on value judgments regarding the available options, understanding one's values in relation to options and end goals can result in more effective and satisfying choices. The techniques used by Hawley and Hawley are Decision Charting and Force-field Analysis.

Table 7.1 is an example of Decision Charting. Any decision can be selected to be used with the chart: to buy a ski boat, where to go on vacation, finding more time in one's schedule for leisure. Once a decision area is selected, the individual and/or group determine and list the possible end goals of that decision (column 2). The end goals are then ranked in order of importance to the individual and/or group. The ranked end goals are then recorded in column 1 in order of priority. The possible options are then identified and entered in column 3. The values the decision maker perceives inherent in each of the options are entered in column 4, under the title "option values."

The decision chart organizes the pertinent information regarding a decision in a clear, concise way that helps decision makers to see the relationship between the end goal, options, and their perceived values of the options.

Table 7.1
Decision Charting

Decision: Buying a Boat

Ranking	End Goal	Options	Option Values
1	Being out of doors on water with family	Pontoon boat	Docking fee, easy to handle, whole family can do
2	Family fun	Fishing boat	Limited recreation use
3	To impress others	Ski boat	No docking fee, exercise, fun, versatility
4	Challenge	Sail boat	Requires skill, difficult, limited use, fun, docking fee

The Force-field Analysis is useful when dealing with either-or choices, such as buying a ski boat or putting the money in savings, taking the family to the beach for the weekend, or working at the office. The Force-field Analysis looks at either-or decisions as a field of opposing forces. Some forces are pulling in one direction, some in the other direction (Hawley & Hawley, 1975). Table 7.2 shows an example of a Force-field Analysis sheet. The individual lists the forces pulling in one direction and then the forces pulling in the other direction. The forces on each list are then ranked in order of importance or strength to the decision maker.

Table 7.2
Force-field Analysis

Decision: Taking Family to Beach for the Weekend	
Forces compelling me to go to the beach:	**Forces compelling me to work:**
1) Family desire/pressure	2) Desire for advancement
3) Need to relax	5) Work hanging over me
4) Need to get away	7) Will impress higher-ups
8) Fun, enjoyment	6) Less to do next week

Information Processing Through Flow Charts

Information processing is another technique useful in educating for leisure. An Information Processing Chart is beneficial because a person can do it alone. Another advantage is that it provides a complete flow from the identification of a topic or problem to its resolution.

The flow chart uses squares to denote tasks. The questions are depicted in circular shapes. Note that every question is a junction point. If an individual's response is yes, he proceeds in one direction; if he answers no, a different direction is taken. An example of an Information Processing Chart is shown in Figure 7.1. This information processing chart focuses on one's leisure outcomes. It should also be apparent that this format of questions could be utilized with a variety of questions regarding leisure.

Counseling

Thus far, there has been no discussion of leisure counseling as such. No doubt there are lingering questions of "Are leisure education and leisure counseling the same thing or are they two different movements?" and "What are the differences and similarities between leisure education and leisure counseling advocates?"

Figure 7.1
Information Processing on Leisure Outcomes

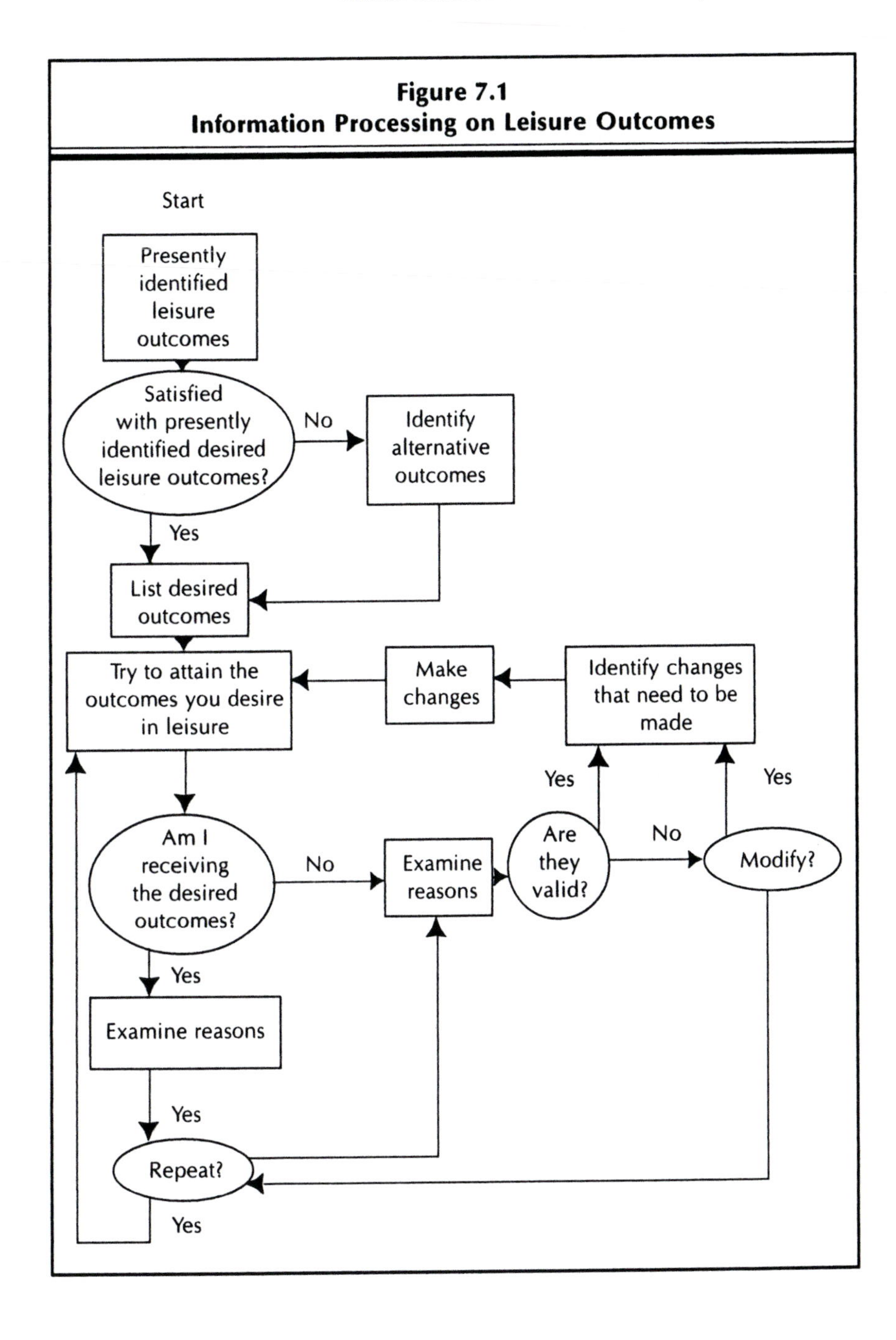

In my opinion, leisure education is a broad, umbrella concept that utilizes many methods, techniques, and processes to educate for leisure. Leisure counseling is a component of leisure education; it is a technique that is effectively utilized in educating people for leisure. Notice, however, that the counseling technique is only *one* of the techniques that can be selected to enable people to have enhancing, meaningful leisure.

The utilization of the counseling technique seems to have national impetus. It is not viewed as a separate movement with different goals and objectives that are in conflict with leisure education goals and objectives; it is viewed as a movement in the development of counseling techniques and strategies that is an effective, viable, successful and, for many professionals, the preferred modality to educate for leisure. It is not uncommon for the term *counseling* to be misused by professionals outside of the counseling field. A frequent misconception is that counseling is simply talking with a person. That is not the view held in this text. The view of counseling held here is that it is a process that utilizes a specific repertoire of techniques, based on various theoretical views of human behavior, to assist individuals in making changes toward more rewarding behavior. Under this approach, the term *counseling* should be reserved for use only by professionals trained in counseling theory and techniques. For this reason, no attempt will made to include counseling techniques in this chapter beyond those included in the General Facilitation Guidelines. This does not negate leisure professionals utilizing the counseling process in educating for leisure. More and more students are being trained in counseling theory and techniques by university counseling departments across the nation. Likewise, counseling majors are being trained in leisure to more effectively deal with this aspect of their clients' lives.

Presentation or Instructional Skills

Presentation or instructional skills as described here include short informal lectures, or mini-lectures, whether the audience is a class, small group, or community group. Short, informal lectures serve a useful function as an auxiliary facilitation technique in the following circumstances:

- when time is an important factor,
- to convey information in an efficient manner,
- to provide a change of pace,
- when the best way to understand a topic is through oral presentation,
- when it is used in conjunction with other techniques such as group discussion,

For example, some of the content in the facilitator's Background Information section of the leisure education units in Chapter 6 is appropriate for a mini-lecture.

Guidelines for Mini-lectures

1. **Create a pleasing physical learning environment.** The placement of furniture should be conducive to group interaction and allow everyone to see the facilitator easily. Try to assure a comfortable level of temperature, lighting, and seating, and minimize distracting sights and sounds.

2. **Support equipment and materials should be prepared and set up in advance.** Have the needed chalkboards, flipcharts, projectors, and handouts ready and waiting.

3. **Know as much as possible about your audience.** This will allow you to relate to them better and tailor your presentation to their interests, needs, and experiences.

4. **Develop objectives.** Develop your objectives in sequence and share them with your audience in both written and oral form.

5. **Be prepared and comfortable with the content.** Do your homework so that you know and are comfortable with the topic. Be accurate and plan a logical sequence and smooth transition from one subtopic to another. Whenever possible, refer to past experiences of the audience; try to link new information to old concepts and understandings. Where possible, go from concrete examples to the abstract.

6. **Give a holistic overview of the session's plan.** This helps the individuals who need to place each activity in context.

It is also a good time to share the objectives with the audience.

7. **Use effective vocal delivery.** Speak clearly and distinctly. Slow down your normal talking speed for an audience. In casual conversation we tend to speak 200-300 words per minute. In a mini-lecture this needs to be reduced to 100-150 words per minute for the best comprehension and attention. Vary your pitch, volume, and speed of talking to claim the listeners' attention. It is difficult to listen attentively to someone who drones on in a monotonous voice with little inflection and no variation in pace. Remember, 38% of what other people gain from your communication comes from your verbal quality and tone of voice; only 7% comes from your actual words.

8. **Use positive body language.** Fifty-five percent of what people get from your communication comes from your nonverbal body language. Your enthusiasm, intensity, and energy will be transmitted through your body language. Remember, gestures can be expressive, communicative, or distracting, so let them be natural. Maintain pleasant facial expressions and try to make eye contact with everyone. Maintain eye contact with someone for five or six seconds and move on to someone else. Speak to all sections of the room. Some movement around the room also helps maintain participant interest.

9. **Change pace frequently.** Attention span for an oral presentation is shorter than most speakers believe. A mini-lecture seldom should exceed 20 minutes. Intersperse the presentation with questions, summarize main points, or carry on a short discussion.

10. **Observe and try to read your audience.** Try to be aware of the audience at all times. Watch for nonverbal behavior to assess whether the activity is being effective. Are they attentive, or are they showing signs of restlessness? You may need to stir them up with voice variations or physical movement, using an example, telling an anecdote, or involving them more directly in the session.

11. **Deliberately plan repetition.** During the early part of a presentation, while curiosity and attention are high, participant comprehension is also usually high. As ideas are added, however, learners tend to lose understanding where there is insufficient time to organize points into a sequential pattern. Therefore, repetition of important points during the body of the presentation is critical.

12. **Enhance listening of the audience.** Use phrases such as "You may want to make a note of this," "This is especially important," or "You may want to pay close attention to . . . ."

13. **Summarize.** Do a brief review of the main point made during the presentation. Allow time for questions for clarification. A question-answer period gives the presenter an opportunity for clarification, correction, elaboration, and permits the presenter to quickly assess the effectiveness of the presentation.

Summary

The strategies and techniques needed to be a facilitator differ from those needed to be a "leader." Facilitating strategies and techniques open communication rather than close it off; they foster self-exploration rather than leader judgments or pronouncements; they produce feelings of empowerment in participants rather than feelings of control in the facilitator. Some of us may have to unlearn other ways of relating to participants than we were taught, that we assimilated though how people worked with us, or that we have observed. While this may require time and effort to develop an expanded repertoire of skills, the payoff in terms of participant development is well worth the effort and is important to move from recreation to leisure education.

Chapter 7 References

Brammer, L.M. (1973). *The helping relationship: Process and skills.* Englewood Cliffs, NJ: Prentice-Hall.

Casteel, D.J., & Stahl, R.J. (1975). *Value clarification in the classroom.* Pacific Palisades, CA: Goodyear Publishing Co., Inc.

Combs, A.W. (1969). Florida studies in the helping professions. Gainesville, FL: University of Florida Press.

Harmin, M., Kirschenbaum, H., & Simon, S.B. (1973). *Clarifying values through subject matter: Applications for the classroom.* Minneapolis, MN: Winston Press.

Hawley, R.C., & Hawley, I.L. (1975). *Developing human potential.* Amherst, MA: ERA Press.

Raths, L.E. (1966). *Values and teaching: Working with values in the classroom.* Columbus, OH: C.E. Merrill Books.

Issues and Special Considerations

Introduction

It has been stated throughout this book that leisure education goals, objectives, processes, and strategies are generic and that professionals working with various groups need only to select and adapt leisure education programs for their specific client populations. To aid in this process, this chapter deals with special issues and considerations in developing and implementing leisure education for persons in therapeutic recreation programs, persons in correctional systems, and aging persons.

Each of the following features (A to C) are written by different authors. While each author deals with a general overview of their specific populations and special issues and considerations when planning leisure education for those populations, there are differences in how the authors deal with the material.

No attempt has been made to alter these differences in order to maintain the integrity of the authors' work.

Feature A:
Issues In Leisure Education for Persons with Disabilities

Dr. Julia Kennon Dunn
Florida State University

Section Overview

This section focuses on the unique needs of persons with disabilities in attaining successful leisure independence. The existence of a disability adds additional challenges to independent functioning in leisure and must be considered in the design and implementation of leisure education programs. This chapter not only looks at the effect of disability on leisure experience, it presents the focus of leisure education as one of overcoming barriers to maximizing leisure independence. Three areas of barriers are discussed: those related to choice, involvement, and independence. In designing individualized leisure education programs, it is critical to understand each of these barrier areas as it applies to the individual participant.

Introduction

Leisure education programs have been an important part of therapeutic recreation services in clinical and community settings in recent years. Most of these programs have focused on the acquisition of predetermined knowledge and skill content. This chapter advocates for a more individualized approach to the design and delivery of leisure education programs for people with disabilities. Here the concept of addressing barriers to leisure involvement caused by the disability is introduced. Discussion of three broad areas of barriers—choice, involvement, and independence—is presented to provide insight into the leisure education needs of individual consumers. These barriers highlight the need to examine what issues need to be addressed by leisure education programs in an individualized plan as well as the need to schedule the presentation at a time when the content will be most beneficial to the consumer.

Leisure education has been an important part of therapeutic recreation services for the past two decades. Though debate has arisen regarding the role of leisure education in therapeutic recreation practice in recent years (Austin, 1991), professionals ascribing to the leisure ability philosophy have readily integrated leisure education into their services. Programs delivered in both the clinical and community setting have been largely based on the leisure education content models (Gunn & Peterson, 1978; Peterson & Gunn, 1984; Mundy & Odum, 1979) and several treatment approaches designed to maximize independence, such as community reintegration and psycho-social rehabilitation. Both the Gunn and Peterson (Peterson & Gunn) Model and the Mundy and Odum Model have relied heavily on content-based objectives with the basic assumption that a person's independence and "leisure lifestyle" can be enhanced with increased self- and leisure-awareness, knowledge of leisure skills and resources, and social interaction and decision-making skills.

These content models influenced the conceptualization and development of the National Therapeutic Recreation Society's philosophy of therapeutic recreation. This philosophy redefined the practice of therapeutic recreation as a continuum of treatment, leisure education, and special recreation (NTRS, 1981). With such a perspective, therapeutic recreation practice included a new focus on leisure lifestyle as a critical element in the quality of life of people with disabilities. This included leisure ability defined by the areas of these content models.

In response to this redefined focus, several model leisure education programs emerged. Ken Joswick's (1989) program is illustrative of the early programs that adapted the content components from the Gunn and Peterson Model (1978) for a particular client group; people with mental retardation. The leisure education program developed for the State Technical Institute in Plainwell, Michigan, provides an excellent example of programs developed to emphasize an individual element of the content models, that of activity skill development in areas designed to provide a balance of skills to maximize participation options (Navar, 1979). An additional contribution of this program was the individualized approach to leisure education programming based on an assessment of activity preference (STILAP) within a variety of participation areas (Navar). More recently, Schleien, Meyer, Heyne, and Brandt (1995) also focused a program on the content area of leisure skills, particularly activity skills for people with developmental disabilities that also includes an assessment component and an emphasis on individualization of the program.

In a different approach to leisure education, Witt and Ellis (1987) developed the Leisure Diagnostic Battery, based on the theoretical foundation of perceived freedom as the indicator of leisure functioning. This effort is significant in that it incorporated leisure theory and defined leisure as experience as opposed to viewing leisure as time or activity. The LDB measures the construct of perceived freedom operationalized by five diagnostic scales that assess the factors of perceived competence, perceived control, ability to meet leisure needs, depth of involvement, and playfulness. In an individually designed leisure education program based on this assessment, the ultimate goal is to remediate problems in perceived freedom. Three remediation scales—knowledge of leisure experiences, leisure preferences, and barriers to leisure involvement—provide the basis for establishing goals and intervention strategies in the individualized plan.

Taken together, the current state of leisure education for people with disabilities can be perceived as educational programs that address predetermined content and programs based on strategies to maximize leisure functioning as defined by perceived freedom. Two recent programs provide evidence of the influence of both the content models as well as the leisure theory approach: the Community/School Leisure Link Leisure Education Program (Bullock, 1992) and the Wake Leisure Education Program (Bedini, Bullock, & Driscoll, 1993).

These programs provide evidence of the influence of leisure lifestyle and therapeutic recreation as an important basis for program development in the enhancement of independence. Other health care professions have also been concerned with client independence and have incorporated programs to address successful discharge, transition, and independent functioning. Many of these programs or program models have been delivered by therapeutic recreation professionals or incorporated into existing leisure education services.

Treatment Programs

In the practice of therapeutic recreation programs in clinical settings, professionals have borrowed heavily from other rehabilitation disciplines to expand the conceptualization of leisure education in their settings. For the most part, these collaborative efforts have focused on increasing the independence of clients involved. The community reintegration programs in physical rehabilitation have often been leisure education programs designed to provide both the leisure and independent living skills for increased independence in the community after accident or injury that necessitated rehabilitation and a change of lifestyle. Community reintegration programs typically are initiated in the clinical setting prior to discharge. Therapeutic recreation can focus on goals such as "a) ameliorate/prevent social isolation, b) develop/maintain social skills, c) develop stigma integration skills, d) develop architectural barrier management skills, and e) develop/maintain a community resource base" (Berryman, James, & Trader, 1991).

In mental health, the community support or psycho-social rehabilitation model has also included many components that overlapped with leisure education goals and programs. Psycho-social rehabilitation emerged as a response to the deinstitutionalization movement as a community-based treatment for the chronically mentally ill. Programs have focused on daily living skills and improved quality of life to support the client in the community. These programs have varied widely but share the philosophy of maximizing independence after discharge and providing support to keep the client in the community rather that being readmitted to inpatient care.

The continuing efforts for least restrictive environment, improved self-help skills, normalization, and mainstreaming have provided great impetus for leisure education programs as part of the ongoing training for individuals with mental retardation both in the residential environment and in community-based therapeutic recreation programs. Many of these programs focus on developing leisure skills to contribute to community integration through specific training techniques (Mahon, 1994; Henderson, 1994), non-disabled peer involvement (Sable, 1995), and at various program locations or classifications such as outdoor or adventure (Dattilo & Murphy, 1987; Sable, 1995) and camping (Sable, 1992).

Most leisure education models and programs are based on the concepts of quality of life as applied to the general population. Often programs developed for specific groups of individuals are designed to adapt to their unique needs either in content or process (Schleien, et al., 1995; Hood & Peterson, 1990) or as with Dattilo and Murphy's work (1991) to provide guidelines for making needed adaptations. These general concepts do apply to people with disabilities. However, the existence of disability may cause additional barriers to the achievement of leisure and thus to leisure's impact on quality of life and must also be addressed as a unique concept. If we are to understand the role of leisure education in providing services for people with disabilities, we must first understand the impact of disability on leisure. This feature shall address some of these barriers to the leisure experience that may be created by the existence of disability.

The Leisure Experience

The leisure experience can be examined in a variety of ways. It has been viewed in temporal phases of anticipation, participation, and reflection (Rossman, 1995). Gunter's work (1987) identified several common properties: "1) a sense of separation from the everyday world, 2) freedom of choice on one's actions, 3) a feeling of pleasure or pleasurable involvement in the event, 4) spontaneity, 5) timelessness, 6) fantasy (creative imagination), 7) a sense of adventure and exploration, and 8) self-realization" (p. 119). Witt and Ellis (1987) see perceived freedom as the essence of leisure functioning, with the factors of perceived competence, perceived control, leisure needs, depth of involvement, and playfulness. Rossman views the leisure experience programmatically as a social occasion, requiring elements of interacting people and as recognition of relationships and place or location, leisure objects, and rules and animation based in the symbolic interactionist theory. He uses this theory as a basis to understand the leisure occasion and to enable programmers to enhance the quality of the participant's experiences.

Kelly (1996) summarizes eight theories of leisure experience to conclude the following:

> freedom is not a simple absence of constraint but is self-determined action that is possible in environments that are always limited . . . leisure is dialectic with essential dimensions of action and of social context . . . leisure is more than a historical phenomenon. It is being and becoming, a possibility of creative actions. (p. 432)

In order to assist anyone with disabilities in experiencing leisure and to enable and empower each to design a leisure experience for her own participation, it is essential that we understand the impact of disability on leisure and the barriers that it can create in experiencing leisure. The foundation of leisure education intervention would then be targeting and overcoming these barriers.

Three areas of interrelated barriers will be examined: those affecting choice, involvement, and independence. Issues related to choice are concerned with the individual's perception of being able to choose, perceived and actual choice options, factors affecting personal choices, skills in choosing, and ability to create or expand choice options. Aspects of engagement or involvement are concerned with the motivation for involvement, the quality and meaningfulness of the involvement, and the anticipated and actual outcomes of a leisure experience. Issues related to independence in leisure can be explored through a redefined concept of independence and freedom. They can further be examined in light of the techniques that can be utilized to maximize independence in various areas of leisure involvement.

Understanding the barriers that may occur in these areas will assist professionals in designing leisure education programs that can address specific content or process needs as well as programs that can be individualized based on the uniqueness of each client and the barriers they have to experiencing leisure. Ultimately, leisure education programs should maximize each individual's independence in leisure, allowing them to achieve the quality experience that they desire, an experience that they can consider leisure. In order to facilitate this, the professional can provide interventions to assist individuals in overcoming barriers to leisure and to learn the skills needed to create personally satisfying leisure experiences, to participate at their highest level of independence.

Issues Related to Choice

At the core of the leisure experience is the perception of freedom. Without this sense of freedom, few experiences, if any, would be characterized as leisure. Perceived freedom can be operationalized in terms of making choices or decisions. For an individual to perceive that choices exist, several conditions must be met: 1) the individual must perceive themselves as having the power to choose 2) realistic options must exist, 3) the individual must recognize these options as realistic for them based on an understanding of self, their abilities, and preferred participation styles, and 4) the individual must have the skills and experiences in the act of choosing and acting on choice options. To further enhance the ability to exercise freedom of choice in leisure, the individual must be internally motivated, empowered to make and be responsible for their choices, and understand that the choices they make are related to meeting needs.

Socialization is a critical determiner in the choice of leisure activities as well as in predicating competence in leisure. In Iso-Ahola's work (1980), the Leisure Socialization Model illustrates the effects of socializing forces and environmental forces in predicting leisure behavior. The participation experiences resulting from leisure behavior consequently affect perceived leisure competence. Leisure competence cycles back to influence future leisure behavior. This process of leisure socialization is lifelong and, as such, continually shapes an individual's leisure behavior. For the person with a disability, the existence of that disabling condition will affect every phase of the leisure socialization process and, thus, their leisure choices.

For choice to exist in the real world, a variety of elements for those choices must be available. Leisure choices consist of leisure activities, supportive activities that allow participation to occur or to expand participation in an area of interest; resources for participation must also exist, such as time, money, activity specific equipment, and supplies; accessible areas; personal resources; and people (leisure partners). The perception of skill and ability to participate is paramount. As indicated by Caldwell and Weissinger (1994), perceived competence is more of a determining factor in engagement than self-determination.

Children with disabilities are exposed to a society who devalues people with disabilities (Vash, 1981) and, thus, their socialization reflects substantially different socialization experiences from non-disabled children (Battle, 1984). Thus, they may begin their socialization without realistic expectations of choice, ability, or effort. They may be socialized to externally attribute success and failure in leisure to effects of the disability rather than other internal attributes that would affect the perception of the experience as leisure. In addition, some children may be exposed to negative parenting from the primary socializing forces, such as overprotection or enabled dependency (Versluys, 1984). In other words, the child with a disability may be socialized without basic leisure choices, play skills, or the ability to make choices independently. This is further compounded by the continuing devaluing messages sent throughout life through the socialization process.

As the issue of disability is defined in terms of the interaction between person and environment (Stolov, 1981), socialization of the individual is affected by the person's immediate environment, family, home, and neighborhood as well as society and the physical environment at large.

Socialization, being a lifelong process, also illustrates the effect of the age of onset of a disability throughout the life span. The occurrence of a disability will determine the socializing agents; new agents may exist (health care system) and previous agents may not be as influential (friends) or may change significantly. Competence in previously experienced leisure involvement may change, usually in a negative direction and, in general, perceived competence will be reduced. In addition, some disabling conditions also affect both the individual's ability to deal with change or his memory or cognitive process in such a way that previous positive socialization experiences are no longer a historical influence. All of these factors have the power to affect an individual's perception of the ability to choose.

In some cases, people who acquire disabling conditions will be resocializing with a new identity, that in which they see themselves as disabled. They may be perceived as different people as a result of loss of skills or abilities, emotional control, ability to manage emotions, loss of cognitive abilities, and/or loss of physical abilities. They may no longer be completely independent and must rely on other people for personal care assistance or supervision. All of these possible results of disability will affect how people see themselves and how society and significant others (socializing influences) react and socialize with them in the future. Each person's understanding of self will affect the choices she makes and whether or not she believes she has choice options.

At the heart of the perception of freedom is the issue of making choices and self-determination. Closely linked to this is the perception of control (attribution theory) and competence (Witt, Compton, Ellis, Aguilar, Forsyth, Niles, & Costilow, 1982). For many individuals the existence of a disability diminishes their perceived control and, in some cases, actual control. This decrease in control, in addition to a reduction in perceived competence, can reduce perceived freedom; this is both in the personal as well as the societal realm. Personally, a variety of disabling conditions may threaten personal control of the outcome of one's own behavior as a result of reduction of cognitive functioning (traumatic brain injury, stroke, dementia, later stages of AIDS, Alzheimer's disease, mental retardation, mental illness). Such symptoms include problems with control of thought processes, intellectual thinking, ability to plan and understand consequences, memory, and emotional control.

Physically disabling conditions or illnesses will affect physical functioning and, in some cases, physical control (for example, multiple sclerosis, muscular dystrophy, cerebral palsy, Parkinson's disease, stroke, and traumatic brain injury). This may be seen in the loss of functioning of a particular body part, as in paralysis or paresis, or in the lack of control, as with spasticity or tremor. Such loss may be overcome with mobility aides or adaptive devices; however, full recovery may not be realized. These physical limitations affect the existence of realistic choice options.

In the process of exercising choice in leisure, individuals typically exercise preference based on a variety of variables. One variable that can be examined is that of personality. Kiersey (1984) states that 75% of the population are considered "extroverts," meaning they get their energy from interaction with other people. Thus, for a satisfying lifestyle (leisure) most people choose activities that involve interactions with others. One major consequence of disability is a reduction of social contact. Isolation has been related to depression, boredom, and unhealthy behaviors.

In our society, in which disability and individuals with disabilities are devalued, the social implications of such disability are pervasive. Interpersonally, the person with a disability may see himself as less socially adept or acceptable, and others may share that view, thus interrupting the relational abilities and potential leisure involvement of the person with a disability. Relationships and friends are a critical element in creating realistic participation choices. Many people use leisure for social contact, and this social contact is critical for the well-being of many people with disabilities. Without friends, or the skills and motivation to develop friendships, leisure participation opportunities are severely limited.

For many who acquire a disability later in life, an established pattern of leisure participation and interest is disrupted by the disability. The significance of this will be determined by the degree to which the disability is related to the body system that is critical to participation (Vash, 1981) and whether an acceptable substitution can be found.

Preferred participation styles may also be affected by certain disabling conditions. If an individual prefers risk and active participation and then develops an illness or disability that does not permit as active a participation style, or the concept of activity is redefined, the level of satisfaction or needs met by that level of participation may decrease. Further adjustment of finding alternative ways to meet needs must occur. An individual severely injured as a result of a mountain climbing accident, whose premorbid leisure participation indicated a preference for high risk activities, may no longer be able to participate in the manner he preferred. Additionally, the entire concept of leisure experience may need to be redefined. An entire adjustment may be required to meet needs previously fulfilled through specific high risk activities. Leisure education programs for this man may include understanding the place of risk in his satisfaction and substituting alternative experiences based on his interests, abilities, and leisure needs.

The specific skills in decision making can be thought of in a developmental sequence. Basic choice between activity and inactivity or between stimulus and no stimulus can be exhibited by individuals with severe mental retardation (Dattilo, 1986; 1987) and by very young children. As development and cognitive ability increase, more options can be evaluated for choice.

Still at a higher level is seeking out choices, evaluating decisions, and planning. The question is not necessarily "Does the individual have the ability to choose, but at what level can they engage in choice and decision making?" The occurrence of disability will affect the level and types of decisions that can be made and give some indication to the potential level of decision making possible. For individuals who have acquired a disability that affects cognitive functioning, the ability to make choices and utilize planning skills may be disrupted or diminished to such a degree that assistance is needed for higher level planning. For an individual who was expected to fulfill a role as a decision maker in a family or leisure network, this will cause major role redefinition or threaten the membership in that group, all of which can contribute to a devaluing and redefinition of identity.

One of the major defining theories of leisure behavior is optimal arousal (Ellis, 1973). The optimal arousal theory basically states that an individual can use leisure activities to maintain an optimal level of arousal, thus contributing to overall life satisfaction. Leisure participation can be used to return a person to an optimal level when they fall below that level by providing stimuli to return then to the optimal level or by providing an escape or coping when they experience hyper-arousal and meet to return to the optimal level. Iso-Ahola (1984) questions the effect of disability on level of arousal. If individuals have been socialized to lower levels of arousal, will the activities and experiences that they select be used to maintain that lower level? Optimal arousal is a major motivating factor to satisfying leisure; therefore, the existence of disability may mediate this level affecting the arousal producing activities available for choice.

Demographic variables will also serve to define choice options available to people with disabilities. In addition to the disability's specific concerns, low income and fewer employment opportunities exist for many, which, in turn, limits discretionary resources (Eisenberg, Glueckauf, & Zaretsky, 1993). Home location and home type impact choice options based on geographically-available and -accessible leisure sites. The type of living situation may limit choices and the ability to exercise those choices. In a supervised home—long term care, residential facility, group home—the care staff and home resources affects the choice options available for residents.

Programs in leisure education have the ability to assist and empower individuals with disabilities to realize that choice and decision making are within their control. Further, such programs can be structured to identify the specific barriers an individual has to making choices and to work with the individual to reduce both the personal and environmental barriers. It is critical to understand the relative importance and interrelationships of these barriers to choice, so that intervention can be appropriately sequenced. Thus, if a person is not choosing leisure involvement because of a perception or lack of competence, a program in community resource awareness will be inefficient and most likely ineffective.

Issues Related to Involvement

The benefits of leisure are numerous and it has been clearly identified that successful leisure involvement can contribute to many aspects of well-being and quality of life. The key here is successful involvement. For an experience to be defined as leisure, there is an expectation that it be intrinsically motivated and pleasurable. Thus, for individuals with disabilities, both barriers related to intrinsic motivation, as well as those related to a satisfying outcome, must be examined. "For leisure activities to become intrinsically motivated, a person has to be able to participate in them freely . . . and must be able to obtain feelings of competence from such engagement" (Iso-Ahola, 1980). As previously seen, perceived competence is a major barrier for people with disabilities. If such a barrier exists for individuals, the quality of experiences can be threatened.

As Iso-Ahola (1980) has discussed, the motivations for leisure participation are many, social contact and enhanced competence among the most significant. Both social contact and enhanced competence are potential benefits of leisure involvement for people with disabilities. It must also be considered that lack of social contacts and poor perception of competence can be major barriers to the initiation of leisure involvement. Both of these are often seen as secondary disabilities for many individualities with disabling conditions. For some individuals with mental illness or head injury, the emotional energy and cognitive functioning level directly affect motivation. In addition, the existence of complications such as stress, pain, and fear divert the focus on motivation to engage in leisure activity.

One motivator that may be in effect is that of escape (Iso-Ahola, 1984). The diversional aspect of leisure involvement allows a participant to "escape" from a current situation or stress level to reenergize—to return to those situations. Some individuals may also seek escape from their disabilities; however, that may not be realistic nor may it be possible in some leisure options. Some symptoms or effects of disability are so pervasive that escape may not be possible with current leisure involvement. Another perspective is the view of healthy leisure involvement that cannot totally consist of attempts to escape the disability, thus using leisure as a continued delay tactic in the adjustment to the disability. Both of these type of experiences detract from the quality of leisure involvement.

Possible side effects of disability are boredom (Caldwell & Weissinger, 1994) and helplessness, which may potentially lead to depression. Both of these situations negatively affect motivation to become involved in leisure or in other life activities. If a person has tried repeatedly to engage and/or become involved without success, or believes that external forces are totally in control of the outcomes of a situation, a condition of learned helplessness may occur, thus further decreasing motivation.

Once an individual does become involved in a leisure experience, the barriers to the quality of that experience must be identified. For total involvement to occur, the individual must be able to focus attention completely on the involvement and become immersed in its progression. The experience of "flow" (Csikszentmihalyi, 1975) or "depth of involvement" (Witt et al., 1982) provides the greatest opportunity for the benefit of leisure to be realized. However, both internal and external factors can inhibit the person with a disability from achieving this "flow" state. This does not imply that the only way to achieve a satisfying leisure experience is to achieve a state of "flow." Even at lower levels of involvement, great benefits can be achieved. Without the ability to feel comfortable with oneself (competence) and one's social and physical environment, and attending to the process of the experience, satisfaction will be reduced. Of particular example here are individuals who are chemically dependent, mentally ill, or have survived specific areas of head injury (Alzheimer's) who have difficulty in experiencing pleasure.

The pleasure or positive perceptions related to engagement in a leisure experience is considered leisure satisfaction (Ragheb & Beard, 1980). Ragheb and Beard have described the elements of satisfaction as including psychological determiners: emotional, social, relaxational, and physiological. Rossman (1983) conceptualized the possible elements of satisfaction as achievement, physical fitness, social enjoyment, family escape, environment, risk, family togetherness, relaxation, fun, and autonomy. With these elements of satisfaction specified, it is easily seen that some symptoms of disability, and adjustment to disability, can inhibit the achievement of satisfaction in leisure involvement. In the cycle of leisure behavior, lack of satisfying leisure involvement will then affect further involvement and add to the perceptions of lack of competence or control. Decreasing involvement means that the person will not receive benefits of leisure.

Another variable in examining barriers related to engagement is knowledge of the potential for leisure in enhancing the quality of life and its possible outcomes. Planning for the use of leisure must start with the recognition that leisure involvement can be beneficial.

Leisure education has great potential is assisting an individual in understanding the factors needed for them to experience leisure. Programs can address the barriers an individual has in experiencing the benefits of leisure engagement and assist them in discovering ways to overcome such barriers. Like the barriers associated with choice, the most salient must be identified and dealt with first if the leisure education intervention is to be a successful one.

Issues Related to Independence

When discussing disabling conditions and leisure, one of the incompatibilities is the notion of independence. For individuals with severe disabilities, independence has a different definition than for those without disabilities. Anthony (1984) has presented a different concept of independence in his discussion of psychiatric rehabilitation. His concept is of a "most facilitative environment," one in which "no unnecessary restrictions are placed on the client's functioning, but in which the client's abilities are accommodated." From this it is possible to see that independence in leisure may exist on a continuum. In some activities, an individual may be completely independent, others may require partial assistance, as when assisting those entering or exiting a swimming pool or assisting in setting up a craft project. Still other activities will require comprehensive assistance or supervision from a family member or caretaker.

So for the individual with a disability, leisure education can provide the opportunity to create opportunities and adaptations which will maximize independent leisure involvement, thus enhancing the perception of freedom in experience. Perceived and actual freedoms are different concepts. Actual freedoms may be limited by the existence of disability. However, the perception of self-determination and involvement may be created within environments that would not typically be considered "free." For some disabled persons, freedom like that known to the nondisabled person may not exist. But within the leisure experience, perceptions of freedom can be created.

The concept of the environment is only one element in the concept of independence. An additional consideration is the ability to interact in an independent situation. For some individuals, the occurrence of disability has restricted them, either as a result of the primary symptom or the socialization from learning independence skills. For example, during adolescence when independence becomes a critical force in development, the disabled adolescent receives the socializing message of dependence rather than support for independence. If independence skills have not been learned throughout childhood, the adolescent is faced with the difficulties of adolescence without the competence and skills to deal with it. Families of individuals who acquire disability later in life may also react by facilitating dependence. Thus, as individuals are resocializing, they may not regain her abilities for independence.

Leisure education has the potential to assist the individual participant in ways to maximize perceptions in a seemingly "unfree" environment. A key issue here is not only independence skills for the participant, but the education of the families and caregivers related to maximizing independence as skills and responsibility increases.

Leisure education has a great potential for assisting individuals with disabilities to increase their well being and ability to benefit form successful leisure involvements. However, leisure education programs should focus on the factors of the leisure experience and the barriers that disability can affect. Such barriers should then be the focus of the content and process of leisure education programs developed with individuals within both the clinical and community therapeutic recreation programs.

Chapter 8: Feature A References

Anthony, W.A. (1984). Explaining "psychiatric rehabilitation" by an analogy to "physical rehabilitation." In R.P. Marinelli, & A.E. Dell Orto (Eds.), *The psychological and social impact of physical disability* (2nd ed.) (pp. 30-38). New York: Springer.

Austin, D.R. (1991). *Therapeutic recreation: Processes and techniques* (2nd ed.). Champaign, IL: Sagamore Publishing.

Battle, C.U. (1984). Disruptions in the socialization of a young severely handicapped child. In R.P. Marinelli, & A.E. Dell Orto (Eds.), *The psychological and social impact of physical disability* (2nd ed.) (pp. 67-85). New York: Springer.

Bedini, L., Bullock, C.C., & Driscoll, L.B. (1993). The effects of leisure education on factors contributing to the successful transition of students with mental retardation from school to adult life. *Therapeutic Recreation Journal, 27*(2), 70-82.

Berryman, D., James, A., & Trader, B. (1991). The benefits of therapeutic recreation in physical medicine. In C.P. Coyle, W.B. Kinney, B. Riley, & J.W. Shank, *Benefits of therapeutic recreation: A consensus view*. Philadelphia: Therapeutic Recreation Program, Temple University.

Bullock, C. (1992). *School-community leisure link.* Chapel Hill, NC: Curriculum in Leisure Studies and Recreation Administration at the University of North Carolina.

Caldwell, L.L., & Weissinger, E. (1994). Factors influencing free time boredom in a sample of persons with spinal cord injuries. *Therapeutic Recreation Journal, 28*(1), 18-24.

Csikszentmihalyi, M. (1975). *Beyond boredom and anxiety.* San Francisco, CA: Jossey-Bass.

Dattilo, J. (1986). Computerized assessment of preferences for persons with severe handicaps. *Journal of Applied Behavioral Analysis, 19*, 445-448.

Dattilo, J. (1987). Computerized assessment of leisure preferences: A replication. *Education and Training in Mental Retardation, 22*(2), 128-133.

Dattilo, J., & Murphy, W.D. (1987). Facilitating the challenge in adventure recreation for persons with disabilities. *Therapeutic Recreation Journal, 21*(3), 14-21.

Dattilo, J., & Murphy, W.D. (1991). *Leisure education program planning: A systematic approach.* State College, PA: Venture.

Eisenberg, M.G., Glueckauf, R.L., & Zaretsky, H.H. (Eds.). (1993). *Medical aspects of disability: A handbook for the rehabilitation professional.* New York: Springer.

Ellis, M.J. (1973). *Why people play.* Englewood Cliffs, NJ: Prentice Hall.

Gunn, S.L., & Peterson, C.A. (1978). *Therapeutic recreation program design: Principles and procedures.* Englewood Cliffs, NJ: Prentice Hall.

Gunter, B.G. (1987). The leisure experience: Selected properties. *Journal of Leisure Research, 19*(2), 115-130.

Henderson, K. (1994). An interpretive analysis of the teaching of decision making in leisure to adolescents with mental retardation. *Therapeutic Recreation Journal,* 28(3), 133-146.

Hood, C.D., & Peterson, C.A. (1990). *Therapeutic recreation treatment needs in chemical dependency treatment.* Champaign, IL: Office of Recreation and Park Resources, University of Illinois.

Iso-Ahola, S.E. (1980). *The social psychology of leisure and recreation.* Dubuque, IA: Wm. C. Brown.

Iso-Ahola, S.E. (1984). Social psychological foundations of leisure and resultant implications for leisure counseling. In E.T. Dowd (Ed.), *Leisure counseling: Concepts and applications.* Springfield, IL: C.C. Thomas.

Joswick, K. (1989). *Leisure counseling program materials for the developmentally disabled.* State College, PA: Venture.

Kelly, J.R. (1996). *Leisure* (3rd ed.). Boston: Allyn & Bacon.

Kiersey, D., & Bates, M.M. (1984). *Please understand me: Character and temperament types* (5th ed.). Del Mar, CA: Gnosology Books.

Mahon, M.J. (1994). The use of self-control techniques to facilitate self-determination skills during leisure in adolescents and young adults with mild and moderate mental retardation. *Therapeutic Recreation Journal, 28*(2), 58-72.

Mundy, J., & Odum, L. (1979). *Leisure education: Theory and practice.* New York: John Wiley & Sons.

National Therapeutic Recreation Society. (1981). *Philosophical position statement of the National Therapeutic Recreation Society.* Arlington, VA: National Recreation and Park Association.

Navar, N. (1979). Leisure skill assessment process in leisure counseling. In D.J. Szymanski, & G.L. Hitzhusen (Eds.), *Expanding Horizons in Therapeutic Recreation VI.* Columbia, MO: Department of Recreation and Park Administration, Extension Division, University of Missouri.

Peterson, C.A., & Gunn, S.L. (1984). *Therapeutic recreation program design: Principles and procedures* (2nd ed.). Englewood Cliffs, NJ: Prentice-Hall.

Ragheb, M.G., & Beard, J.G. (1980). Leisure satisfaction: Concept, theory and measurement. In S.E. Iso-Ahola (Ed.), *Social psychological perspectives on leisure and recreation*. Springfield, IL: C.C. Thomas.

Rossman, J.R. (1983). Participant satisfaction with employee recreation. *Journal of Physical Education Recreation and Dance, 54*(8), 60-62.

Rossman, J.R. (1995). *Recreation programming: Designing leisure experiences.* Champaign, IL: Sagamore.

Sable, J.R. (1992). Collaborating to create an integrated camping program: Design and evaluation. *Therapeutic Recreation Journal, 26*(3), 38-48.

Sable, J.R. (1995). Efficacy of physical integration, disability awareness, and adventure programming on adolescent's acceptance of individuals with disabilities. *Therapeutic Recreation Journal, 29*(3), 206-217.

Schleien, S.J., Meyer, L.H., Heyne, L.A., & Brandt, B.B. (1995). *Lifelong leisure skills and lifestyles for persons with developmental disabilities.* Baltimore: Paul H. Brookes.

Stolov, W.C. (1981). Comprehensive rehabilitation: Evaluation and treatment. In W.C. Stool & M.R. Clowers (Eds.), *Handbook of severe disability.* Washington, D.C.: U.S. Department of Education, Rehabilitative Services Administration.

Vash, C.L. (1981). *The psychology of disability.* New York: Springer.

Versluys, H.P. (1984). Physical rehabilitation and family dynamics. In R.P. Marinelli, & A.E. Dell Orto (Eds.), *The psychological and social impact of physical disability* (2nd ed.) (pp. 102-16). New York: Springer.

Weissinger, E. (1994, March). Recent studies about boredom during free time. *Parks and Recreation, 29*(3), 30, 33-34.

Witt, P.A., & Ellis, G.D. (1987). *The leisure diagnostic users manual.* State College, PA: Venture.

Witt, P.A., Compton, D.M., Ellis, G.D., Aguilar, T., Forsyth, P., Niles, S., & Costilow, A. (1982). *The leisure diagnostic battery: Background, conceptualization, and structure.* Denton, TX: North Texas State University.

Feature B:
Issues In Leisure Education for Persons In Correctional Systems

Dr. Brenda Robertson
Acadia University
Nova Scotia

Section Overview

This section gives a brief historical perspective on recreation and leisure education in correctional (prison) settings. Additionally, it presents specific issues and considerations in each program component (leisure awareness, self-awareness, leisure skills, and leisure resources) to better meet the unique needs of incarcerated individuals in educating them for leisure. Two program delivery models that have been used successfully in prison systems, adventure based programs and marathons, are described. Lastly, issues related to special segments of the prison population, such as older adults, women, and long term inmates, are discussed.

Introduction

Recreation as a part of prison system programs has been in operation since the late 1800s. Whether recreation was instituted as a means of helping control behavior problems, increasing productivity, or as a part of the rehabilitation process, by the turn of the century many prisons provided a wide variety of recreation activities for inmates. However, it wasn't until half a century later, in 1957, that the concept of leisure education in correctional settings was clearly articulated:

> Among the inmates of correctional institutions there are many who have no knowledge or skills which will enable them to make acceptable use of their leisure . . . They cannot play, they do not read, they have no hobbies. In many instances, improper use of leisure is a factor in their criminality. Others lack the ability to engage in any cooperative activity with the

> fellows; teamwork is something foreign to their experiences. Still others lack self-control or a sense of fair play; they cannot engage in competitive activity without losing their heads. If these men are to leave the institutions as stable, well-adjusted individuals, these needs must be filled; the missing interests, knowledge, and skills must be provided. (Heynes, 1957, p. 73)

Today, professionals both inside and outside the prison walls continue to advocate for the inclusion of leisure education as the foundation component of recreation services within correctional institutions. Through leisure education, individuals can learn to cope with the high degree of stress associated with institutional life, as well as obtain the knowledge, attitudes, and skills necessary to cope with the stresses associated with life outside the institution. Individuals can also learn socially acceptable forms of leisure pursuits in order to satisfy their personal needs, the fulfillment of which frequently caused them to come into conflict with the law.

Individuals who are incarcerated in correctional systems, like other special populations, have common and unique characteristics and needs related to leisure education. Likewise, there are different needs and considerations among incarcerated offenders in correctional systems. For example, certain residents may have little education, and as such require a comprehensive leisure education program addressing all aspects of leisure education. Others may possess a high degree of leisure literacy and require a program focusing on how to cope with free time within the confines of the restricted environment. Also, the focus of a leisure education program for an adventure-seeking youth serving a short term sentence for involvement in delinquent activity will differ substantially from a program designed for an elderly individual who is about to return to society after years of incarceration. The services of a highly-trained recreation professional with expertise in leisure education is required if programs are to be developed and delivered in an effective manner.

Specific Issues and Considerations

Leisure awareness

One of the primary issues in leisure education for people who are incarcerated is the issue of perceived freedom, the central determinant of leisure. The restricted environment of correctional systems results in severely limited choices and opportunities for self-determination and control. The environment itself can result in a diminished perception of freedom and, thus, leisure. Leisure education programs can assist individuals in correctional systems in understanding the concept of leisure as a whole. Such programs can also assist them in understanding the choices and opportunities for self-determination and control that are available to them within their confined and restricted environment.

Another issue to be dealt with in addressing leisure awareness with incarcerated individuals is that their personal concept of leisure may well include involvement in delinquent and criminal activities. Recent research has shown that although such activities may have a negative impact upon other people and society in general, such experiences often have all the attributes generally associated with leisure in the minds of the offenders (Robertson, 1993). In these cases, the leisure educator may attempt to foster an understanding of the negative impact of such action on the lives of others in an attempt to discourage such activities. Other components of the leisure education process will assist the individual in substituting negative activities with more socially acceptable ones that will still satisfy his needs.

Another aspect of the leisure awareness component, which is tied with one's perception of freedom, is the issue of self-responsibility. Offenders tend to possess an external locus of control, that is, they believe external factors, conditions, and people are responsible for their behavior and, thus, their lives and what has happened to them. They do not tend to have feelings of personal power and its resulting ability to change and direct their own lives through the choices and decisions that they make.

Some offenders are also of the opinion that it is someone else's responsibility to provide for their leisure, such as government agencies or specific individuals like a family member or friend. Although such groups and individuals may assist in facilitating leisure opportunities, the ultimate responsibility for seeking out and accessing meaningful experiences rests with the individual. Until individuals accept leisure as their responsibility, leisure satisfaction is likely to occur only on a sporadic basis.

Self-awareness

Incarcerated individuals must become aware of their personal needs, the ways in which they have satisfied these needs in the past, and how they can satisfy their needs in the future in ways that are more socially acceptable and personally positive. Understanding the needs that motivate delinquent and criminal behavior can help serve as a basis for behavior that is considered more socially acceptable. For example, a high percentage of individuals who come into conflict with the law experience drug and alcohol addictions. Individuals participating in treatment programs often experience a significant increase in free time. Assistance in identifying meaningful leisure pursuits during time previously devoted to the addiction can greatly assist with the rehabilitation process.

Often, attempts are made to substitute one activity for another to satisfy specific needs based upon the structural similarity of the activities. While this may work in some cases, it is not universally effective. Activity substitution based on the meaning the individual attaches to the activity and the individual needs that it satisfies, rather than structural factors, is more effective.

Examining one's values, attitudes, and beliefs' systems and how they impact decision making and behavior is important for offender populations. Some of their values, attitudes, and beliefs have led to their delinquent and criminal behavior and, therefore, require considerable attention in the leisure education process.

Incarcerated individuals can also have negative attitudes toward specific activities in which they have never participated. Negative attitudes can exist toward activities that are not considered fast enough, thrilling enough, or "cool" enough, even though such pursuits may be readily accessible and hold the potential of satisfying a broad spectrum of personal needs.

Through examining attitudes, and increasing knowledge about the potential benefits that can accrue from certain activities, individuals can greatly expand their repertoire of potential leisure pursuits.

Although certain incarcerated individuals may have a broad range of leisure interests and skills that enable them to access positive leisure pursuits, many have a limited leisure activity repertoire. For those individuals with few interests and skills, fostering new interests, developing leisure activity skills, and providing opportunities to participate in leisure experiences can aid in opening new and satisfying leisure options.

Incarcerated people have faced barriers or constraints to leisure before their incarceration. Whether these constraints are internal or external, constraints such as lack of available opportunities, inability to pay fees, or lack of transportation, assistance in identifying past and potentially future constraints, as well as how to negotiate constraints, is an important part of the leisure education process.

Leisure Skills

Incarcerated individuals frequently have deficits in decision-making and problem solving skills, which in many instances have contributed to their delinquent and criminal behavior. They additionally may lack the ability to foresee the consequences of their decision on other people or themselves.

Consequently, another important set of skills for this population are those related to self-management and behavioral change. The ability of many offenders to live in a socially acceptable, yet personally satisfying, manner depends upon the development and utilization of these particular skills. The inability to affect and manage desired behavioral change may result in a continuation of behaviors that negatively impact the individual and/or other members of society.

Many incarcerated individuals also lack basic social and interpersonal skills as well as pro-social friendship systems. If one returns to social connections that are antisocial, there is a high probability their activities will also revert to being antisocial. Learning basic social and interpersonal skills will be necessary for most offenders to move into a more positive, non-criminal, social environment if they choose to do so.

Leisure Resources

The ability of individuals to identify and access pro-social (as opposed to antisocial) leisure resources is critical to positive leisure functioning. Many incarcerated individuals lack a knowledge of pro-social leisure resources and opportunities, whereas their knowledge of accessibility to antisocial pursuits is more readily accessible (Robertson, 1993). Through leisure education, participants can learn what alternative, pro-social resources are available in their communities and how to access these opportunities.

Program Delivery Models

Many of the options for leisure education program delivery enumerated in earlier chapters are applicable to inmates in prison systems. Systems currently offering leisure education use classroom-based approaches, workshops, and experiential-based programs where participants learn about leisure through participation in activities.

Prisons also use two methods of program delivery not previously mentioned. One method is the adventure-based method. Increasingly, adventure-based programs are being developed for incarcerated individuals. Such programs take place in outdoor settings and involve experiences that range from rope courses to wilderness adventures. The adventure-based programs are designed to take participants out of their personal comfort zone to enhance learning, personal assessment, and reflection. From a leisure education perspective, the long term impact of such programs on the daily leisure lifestyles of participants has been called into question. Psychologically, some of the leisure education objectives may be achieved through such programs but little development of personal activity repertoires may occur. Work is presently underway in a number of cities throughout North America to develop urban-based adventure programs that may have greater carry over in terms of the daily lives of participants.

Marathons have also been used successfully in the delivery of leisure education in a variety of correctional institutions. In such a program, a group of participants meet together for an extended period of time with one or more facilitators. The marathon has a specific theme, such as leisure, which becomes the focus of discussion for as long as the group remains involved in the process. The group shares meals and may spend the night, depending on the duration of the session. Marathons allow participants to remain on a specific topic, such as leisure values, as long as they wish. Likewise, the duration of the entire session is not limited by time constraints. Marathons allow sustained group involvement, momentum, and a sense of long-term commitment. They are particularly well-suited for incarcerated environments where participants do not have time pressures, commitments, or constraints.

Issues Related to Special Segments of the Prison Population

Prisons, like society, have diverse populations. While the populations tend to be predominantly young (early twenties) and male, there are minority segments that include older adults, people with disabilities, women, native peoples, alcohol and drug addicts, and a variety of racial and ethnic groups. For many of these special population segments, leisure needs may not be fully addressed through a generic leisure education program. The following examples outline some special issues related to selected groups:

Older Adults. The mean age of incarcerated offenders is in the early twenties, making an individual in middle adulthood or older considerably older than the majority of the institution population. As a result, they tend to differ from the average population in terms of such factors as the stage in the family life cycle, physical abilities, and work ethic. Programs focused on the needs of the mean population may not satisfy their needs. For example, traditional recreational offerings of baseball, weightlifting, and video games may hold little appeal for older inmates. For a more detailed discussion of issues related to older people, see Feature C.

Women. There are a number of issues related to leisure education for incarcerated women. Two key issues for women are the psychological stress caused by the separation of women from their families and women's lack of sense of entitlement for leisure. Women may value leisure for other members of their family but not for themselves. Prison systems also frequently do not recognize leisure interests and needs of women in regard to recreation activities. Women may be denied access to certain opportunities, such as the gymnasium and the library, because they are located only in the men's area of the facility because the highest percentage of the population is men, who also do not want to surrender time to the women. Therefore, the leisure activity repertoire and opportunities of females, and males, may be severely limited to stereotypical female and male experiences.

Long-Term Inmates. Individuals with long-term sentences may have the most difficult time adjusting to life outside the institution because the world has changed so much since they lived on the outside. Some individuals being released from a correctional institution have never seen a McDonald's restaurant, shopped in a mall, seen a computer, used a bank machine, or held a driver's license. As such, they will need far greater assistance to prepare them to survive in the society that they are about to enter. These people also tend to lack support groups, have few opportunities to obtain full time employment, and have difficulty understanding the norms, values, expectations, and issues of the society they are entering. The leisure lifestyle that these individuals are able to develop may well determine whether they are able to survive in the outside world.

These few examples do not cover the entire range of special segments of the populations of prisons, nor is this their intent. They serve to illustrate some of the special issues of which the facilitator needs to be aware in planning and implementing leisure education programs in prisons. For special issues related to programming leisure education for inmates with disabilities, the reader is referred to Feature A for more in-depth details related to this population.

Chapter 8: Feature B References

Agnew, R. (1990). The origins of delinquent events: An examination of offender accounts. *Journal of Research in Crime and Delinquency, 27*(3), 267-294.

Heynes, G. (1957, September). Penal institutions. *The Annals of the American Academy of Political and Social Science, 313*, p. 73.

Robertson, B.J. (1993). *An investigation of leisure in the lives of adolescents who engage in delinquent activity for fun, thrills, and excitement.* Unpublished doctoral dissertation, University of Oregon, Eugene, OR.

Feature C:
Issues in Leisure Education for Older Adults

Dr. Anne Binkley and
Dr. Terry Seedsman
Footscray Institute of Technology
Melborne, Australia

The tragedy of life is not death, but
what we let die within us while we live.
- *Norman Cousins*

Section Overview

The fact that the global population is aging and that aging people need education for leisure is the basic premise of this section of the text. The section goes on to address specific issues and considerations in designing leisure education programs for adults.

Introduction

Developing leisure opportunities to meet the need of a diverse and expanding older population may be the greatest challenge confronting human service providers in the coming years. It is now well established that the global population is aging. In America, for instance, the National Council on the Aging shows that

- the number of people 65 and older in the United States will number in excess of 70.2 million by the year 2030;
- those aged 85 and over—3.3 million in 1994—are likely to number 9 million in 2030, and perhaps 18.9 million by 2050 (Cohen, 1996, p. 6).

By the time Americans enter the 21st century, the average life expectancy for women is projected to be close to 84 years while for men it will be 77 years. While reference is made to the young old (55-70), and the old (85 plus), the fact remains that chronological age is a poor predictor of human performance. Leisure educators need to fully appreciate that the aged are a diverse population and that heterogeneity rather than homogeneity ought to be the focus in service delivery. A useful way to explore the diverse nature of human aging is to understand that functional age in terms of physical, social, and psychological capabilities is a more realistic interpretation of performance during older age (Seedsman, 1994). Service providers, in addition, need to recognize and appreciate that from a programming and service perspective, the proportion of older women surviving men increases substantially beyond 80 years of age. Research also shows that variations in life expectancy exist when older age cohorts are examined in terms of racial and ethnic differences.

Aging is a process that begins at birth and continues throughout life. Some of the elements surrounding aging are outside our control. We will grow older whether we like it or not, but the overall impact of the aging process on our well-being and our self-image is largely under our own control. Specifically, as we advance in years, most of us find ourselves with more time for leisure. Recent history, however, shows that while the retirement years among older Americans has been set aside for leisure, they have not been adequately prepared for such a major lifestyle transition. It might well be argued that Americans are deceptively unprepared for full-time leisure. Jobes (1986), in an article entitled "Leisure Lifestyles and Satisfaction," provided an important message about retirement that is even more relevant today. He argued that retirement,

> is a period in which people are encouraged, even feel obligated, to reap the rewards they have deferred through years of working, by joining a world of leisure. Though some feel ambivalent or opposed to either retirement or leisure, the themes of "you only live once" and "you are only as old as you think you are" are constant reminders of what they should be feeling. (p. 31)

If we look at leisure in this perspective, we can identify certain life crises that call for a greater or different leisure involvement. Such crises can occur at an early age because of an accident or a debilitating illness. For most people engaged in paid employment, it comes with retirement. With housewives and others whose work activities are less structured, it may come gradually as physical stamina declines with years. Regardless of how it occurs, however, each of us can expect a crisis over which we have no control to impose a changed lifestyle in which leisure, not work, is the characteristic. Macnab (1985) provides a valuable perspective on the challenge of coping with life crises:

> Every day vast amounts of energy are wasted as people try to cope with their hassles and worries, the stressful events of life and those crises that endanger their health and morale, and life itself. Generally, the energy waste is accepted as inevitable and unavoidable. But if this waste could be prevented, and the energy turned to constructive enjoyable objectives and experiences, what a difference this would make to the individuals concerned, their relationships, their way of life, and to the whole human community! (p. 1)

It is the premise of this feature, accordingly, that as we once needed education for a life of work, we now need education for a life of leisure. Through appropriate education for leisure, we will find resources to cope, to adapt, and to continue to live meaningful and creative lives. It cannot be overstressed that for many, perhaps most older people, their own negative presuppositions constitute the biggest obstacles to realizing successful leisure lifestyles. Many older people have been conditioned to believe that they cannot change, that it is too late to attempt new experiences. Fear of the unknown can promote a form of self-sabotage. It can lead to a sense that what remains of life will be mundane and unproductive. This is where education for leisure is particularly important. It helps the retiree to make a successful transition from full-time work to a non-work lifestyle by showing how special knowledge, transferable skills, and personal preferences or needs can still be used in retirement to provide fulfillment and a sense of purpose.

Retirement counselors stress the failure of some older people to recognize the transferable skills they have accumulated in work and life experiences. Bradfield (1988), reporting on decisions related to job change, highlights the tendency of people to neglect accumulated skills such as "organizing, coordinating, learning, repairing . . . A close friend or family member who knows the job seeker can help pinpoint the skill that the person enjoys using and can bring to a new job" (p. 9). Bradfield's comments are equally applicable to a transfer of skills from work to leisure.

In the midst of change, older people are often not strategically placed to understand or value what is taking place. In addition, trying to understand what the changes may mean to them personally, many older people are also trying to determine where they fit into the general scheme of things. Leisure education can help them to anticipate and to recognize the impact of such changes on family and individual lifestyles. It also helps them to cope with change by turning confusion and ambiguity into growth and creativity, thus ensuring a more challenging and stimulating life. The result is to guide people toward that more hopeful arena of searching and finding personal meaning and fulfillment.

Education for leisure must, therefore, begin by evaluating the actual situation of the person who has begun or is soon to begin retirement. The professional must be prepared to deal with a broad range of scenarios that take proper account of the biological, psychological, sociological, and economic dimensions of human aging. Are we dealing with a person unable to work because of an accident, illness, or disability? Or one compulsorily retired at a given age and still physically fit? Or one whose bodily strength and energy are minimal and whose leisure activities are correspondingly limited? In addition, levels of education and lifetime work involving principally either physical or mental activity must all be taken into account. The scenario of leisure for each of these will be significantly different.

There is ample proof to show that we are shaped by what we do and what we love. A wise person will spend life learning new things. Old age is not to be confused with incapacity. Maslow's hierarchy of needs is well known, with the range extending from basic survival needs to the seemingly elusive human need for self-actualization. The fields of psychology and psychiatry are only now recognizing that taking risks is a forgotten human need. In modern society, we find widespread evidence of people who are afraid of risk. Living in the comfort zone where most things are planned and foreseen is to sabotage one's freedom. It is through the risk element that we experience "possibilities for becoming" truly human. Leisure education provides the opportunity for older adults to undertake a sensible engagement with risk, thereby enhancing the potential for the realization of individual autonomy. Very few of us can appreciate that, in order to be free, the human being needs a proper balance between risk and security. The removal of all risk leads to the very extinction of life itself. When older people simply behave like a healthy human being they seem much younger. Far too many older people play the role of being old. The most powerful psychological factor that accounts for human survival is not so much the adoption of the "fighting spirit" but rather a sense of joy with life. This sense of joy with life comes from a positive meaning—seeking engagement in all that we do. Older people should be given the opportunity to thrive, not survive—this is the primary role of leisure education. They need to be encouraged to be people investing in successful aging. Those who wish to pursue successful aging might well consider the relevance of the following viewpoint:

> *How can you fly like an eagle when your attitude places you at the altitude of a turkey? It is attitude not aptitude that will always determine your altitude.*

Leisure education can promote an attitude toward life that incorporates an element of risk taking aimed at enhancing the scope for psychological and emotional maturing.

Specific Issues and Considerations

Self-awareness

Some older adults may need to develop self-awareness, which includes an awareness of their real and perceived physical, cognitive, and psycho-social assets and constraints. While many older adults today are in good health with social supports and adequate financial resources, others may not be as fortunate. Therefore, it is necessary to assist participants in identifying their assets as well as their constraints, and in understanding how to negotiate physical, financial, cognitive, and psychosocial constraints that may exist.

Another issue that may need to be addressed with some older people is an analysis of the myths of aging and their impact upon their thinking. Believing many of the negative stereotypes regarding aging can create artificial constraints on leisure involvement and participation that must be eliminated in order for a satisfying leisure lifestyle to develop.

Older people also need to examine their expectations for their retirement lives and establish goals for this phase of their lives. Assessing one's skills, interests, abilities, resources and knowledge, and how these assets can be used in leisure, can provide a foundation upon which older people can construct positive leisure involvement. It should be noted that people in the 50 to 55 age group frequently have very different expectations and skills than people in the older age groups. Therefore, age group differences need to be taken into account when working in this area.

Leisure awareness

A second cornerstone of the delivery of effective leisure education is leisure awareness. This issue is of particular concern as the older adults of today are a product of life experiences that had little time or interest in the development of a leisure ethic. Many of today's older adults grew up in a world that placed an emphasis and value on hard work and long hours. Little time and support was allocated to the development and pursuit of leisure skills and involvement. For these individuals to overcome their acquired attitudes on the frivolity of leisure, particular attention to the clarification and reassessment of leisure attitudes and values is required. Until older adults are able to successfully develop attitudes and values that are conducive to leisure involvement, they will be unable to see that leisure can play an important role in enhancing the latter stage of their lives. They will also be unable to truly benefit from the last two cornerstones of leisure education—leisure skills and leisure resources.

Leisure Skills and Leisure Resources

There are several issues that must be dealt with regarding leisure skills and leisure resources for older people: 1) the development of new leisure skills, 2) the transfer of existing skills to a leisure context, 3) the development of an awareness of available leisure resources, and 4) the possible need for lower cost, safe, and accessible leisure resources as one ages. Each of these issues has its own special considerations. For example, some older people may not have developed certain leisure skills earlier in their lives and thus have a limited repertoire of skills in their later life. Additionally, older people can be reluctant to undertake the development of certain skills at this point in their lives out of embarrassment, fear, uncertainty, or a belief system that says, "You can't teach an old dog new tricks." Program cost can also be a barrier to instructional classes.

Some older adults may also need to become familiar with new or additional leisure resources that are lower in cost, safe, and accessible. As discretionary income decreases, community crime rates increase, and physical abilities and mobility decreases, the need for different, possibly unfamiliar leisure resources emerges for older people in these kinds of situations.

Summary

The four components of leisure education, as stand-alone elements and as interrelated components, can greatly impact older adults' abilities to achieve optimal life quality. The ideal situation would exist if older adults entered the final stage of their life cycle competent in all four areas of leisure education. Reality, however, does not mirror such a idealized world. Today, in fact, growing numbers of older adults are in need of quality leisure education programs if they are to achieve life satisfaction in the final state of the life cycle. To this end, it is imperative that recreation professionals are conversant with relevant, creative leisure education strategies based on sound theory as well as their own experiential education for leisure.

Leisure education experiences specifically designed to assist older adults with some of the issues included in this chapter can be found in the Appendix.

Older individuals may need leisure education to help them take full advantage of their emerging opportunities for leisure and to explore new and potentially exciting lifestyles. McDowell (1976) argues that individuals unable to establish clear leisure orientations "lack direction in their lives, lack criteria for choosing what to do with their time, their energy, their very being " (p. 40). A willingness to explore new or improved leisure experiences also has implications for fostering improved self-images with older adults. Research supports the belief that improved self-image is an important by-product of participation in meaningful and challenging leisure activities (Leitner & Leitner, 1985). Encouraging older people, from time to time, to be confronted with the opportunity of creating a purposeful life through leisure education enables them to gain a future without the sense of hopelessness and helplessness. Thus, appropriately designed leisure education experiences can help foster belief in an adventurous and vital life after retirement.

Chapter 8: Feature C References

Bradfield, A. (1988, April 11). The job cycle can turn for you. *The Herald*, p. 9.

Cohen, E.D. (1996, Jan.-March). Can research on aging deliver on its promises? *Perspectives on Aging,* XXV(1).

Jobes, P.C. (1986, April) Leisure lifestyles and satisfaction. *World Leisure and Recreation,* pp. 28-31.

Leitner, M., & Leitner, S. (1985). *Leisure in later life.* New York, NY: The Haworth Press.

McDowell, C. (1976) *Leisure counseling: Selected lifestyle processes.* Center of Leisure Studies, University of Oregon.

Macnab, F. (1985). *Coping.* Melbourne: Will of Content Publishing Co.

Seedsman, T.A. (1994). *Aging is negotiable.* St. Kilda, Melbourne: Employ Working Effectively, Inc.

Leisure Education Theory and Practice

Figure 3.1
The Scope and Sequence of Leisure Education

Focus	Level	Self–awareness	Leisure-awareness	Attitudes	Decision Making	Social Interaction	Leisure Skills
Awareness of life activities of self and the familly	Pre-K	Understands the role of self in family activities	Identifies own activities	Recognizes the various activities of the family	Is aware of making choices	Attends, takes turns, begins to share	Participates in leisure experiences in a variety of program areas
		Expands knowledge of self as an individual and as a group member	Identifies life activities of group members (family, school, etc.)	Appreciates activities of each member of the family unit	Is aware of the choices of self and others	Identifies elements that contribute to successful interaction with another individual	Identifies specific leisure activities and relates them to program areas
Leisure and leisure choices and experiences	Level I	Is aware of one's own leisure	Defines the meaning of leisure	Appreciates varying forms of human endeavor	Recognizes the decision-making process in relation to leisure	Identifies possible outcomes, varying types of social interaction, and behavior experiences	Develops basic skills and simple tool handling related to preferred leisure

Figure 3.1 Cont.

Leisure and leisure choices and experiences (cont.)	K-3	Examines the rights and responsibilities of the individual in regard to leisure	Identifies leisure activities of self and others	Appreciates individual differences in regard to leisure patterns and choices	Recognizes outcomes of personal leisure choices	Examines the elements of cooperation and competition and the place of each in one's life	Explores a variety of types of leisure experiences (quiet, active, individual, group)
		Recognizes the capabilities and limitations of self and as a member of society	Identifies the variables upon which leisure experiences depend	Realizes the relationship among family, school, and community leisure experiences	Identifies alternative types of leisure choices		Expands leisure experiences and skills in unfamiliar program areas and activities
			Explores the value of leisure in relation to one's life				
	Level II	Recognizes the value in achieving individual goals	Identifies societal and family factors that influence leisure	Develops an awareness of increasing amounts of leisure and its effect on one's life	Recognizes one's ability to alter amounts of leisure and leisure experiences	Analyzes elements that contribute to successful individual and group interaction	Expands leisure experiences and skills in unfamiliar program areas and activities

Figure 3.1 Cont.

Focus	Level	Self–awareness	Leisure-awareness	Attitudes	Decision Making	Social Interaction	Leisure Skills
Leisure and lifestyle	4-6	Develops an awareness of leisure opportunities and decision-making skills in relation to one's lifestyle	Understands the impact of leisure choice on one's lifestyle, society, and the quality of one's own life	Analyzes advantages and disadvantages of different lifestyles		Identifies possible outcomes of varying types of social interaction and behavior	
		Relates mastery of leisure skills to individual fullfillment	Recognizes levels of satisfaction and proficiency in leisure experiences	Understands the relationship between lifestyles, changing patterns, and growth and development	Applies decision-making process to leisure interest and personal satisfaction	Identifies satisfying patterns of social interaction	Acquires more complex skills in preferred leisure experiences while developing skills basic to new experiences
		Develops an awareness of one's abilities and motivation in leisure experiences	Becomes aware of personal motivation in relation to leisure	Appreciates lifestyles of different individuals and groups	Anzlyzes the selection and rejection of individual leisure choices	Assesses social competence in relation to individual outcomes	Assesses leisure skills and repertoir of experiences in relation to individual outcomes

Figure 3.1 Cont.

Self-understanding and leisure	Level III	Recognizes individual values and their relation to one's life	Understands how values affect, reflect, and determine leisure experiences	Understands the roles of values in one's life	Relates personal value system to leisure choices		Makes necessary plans for alteration based upon one's individual assessment of leisure skills and repertoire of experiences
	7-9	Relates increasing consciousness of personal needs to leisure	Understands the personal nature of leisure experiences	Understands one's attitude as it relates to leisure	Makes leisure decisions related to personal goals	Identifies emotional and social factors affecting styles of interaction	Makes necessary plans for alteration based upon one's individual assessment of leisure skills and repertoire of experiences
		Identifies personal criteria and their relation to criteria of others and society as a whole	Develops criteria related to leisure experiences	Appreciates one's ability to make judgements and establish criteria	Makes decisions related to personal criteria of proficiency, satisfaction, and quality-of-life	Weighs possible long- and short-range effects of personal-social interaction patterns in leisure	Develops competence in preferred leisure experiences

Figure 3.1 Cont.

Focus	Level	Self–awareness	Leisure-awareness	Attitudes	Decision Making	Social Interaction	Leisure Skills
Self-understanding and leisure (cont.)	Level IV	Analyzes the role of leisure in one's present and future lifestyle	Recognizes the relationship of leisure to one's continuous life cycle	Recognizes attitudes, capabilities, and personal development gained through leisure experiences	Applies sound criteria in the selection and use of leisure services and products	Makes necessary plans for alterations based upon one's individual assessment of social competence	Explores in-depth, leisure experiences with carryover values
Leisure and life-long needs	10-12	Realizes one's ability to use leisure to enhance the quality of one's life	Understands the dynamic nature of leisure and the resulting need for continuous exploration and development	Appreciates one's capability to deal effectively with leisure	Weighs a variety of possible long- and short-range effects of leisure alternatives to one's lifestyle. Makes leisure choices related to personal ecosystem and lifestyle		

Figure 3.1 Cont.

Leisure and life-long needs (cont.)	Young adult	Reevaluates one's leisure as it relates to a changing life-style	Recognizes the relationship between changing lifestyle, life situations, and leisure interests	Analyzes lifestyle decisions related to personal goals and attitudes in regard to the family unit	Takes advantage of the flexibility in personal leisure choices	Evaluates social interaction patterns in relation to changing groups, roles, and responsibilities	Utiilizes present leisure skills and expands leisure experiences in relation to new groups and opportunities
Leisure and changing life situations	Adult	Adapts leisure to complement one' present lifestyle	Balances leisure as a meaningful part of one's individual and family life	Integrates personal leisure goals and attitudes into the family unit	Makes meaningful leisure choices for self and family	Enhances the quality of social interaction within the family unit	Exposes family unit to a wide variety of leisure experiences
		Recognizes one's responsibility and role in developing leisure concepts and attitudes within family unit	Accepts responsibility for enriching community leisure resources		Makes decisions regarding the enrichment of community leisure resources		Develops leisure skills within the family unit and carries over leisure experiences from school

Figure 3.1 Cont.

Focus	Level	Self–awareness	Leisure-awareness	Attitudes	Decision Making	Social Interaction	Leisure Skills
Leisure and changing life situations (cont.)	Later maturity	Analyzes the role of leisure in one's life as it relates to preparation for retirement	Explores, expands, and further develops leisure in relation to changing life situations	Recognizes the role of leisure in one's life upon retirement	Applies the decision-making process in preparation for new leisure patterns and preparation for retirement	Reevaluates social interaction patterns in relation to changing groups, roles, and responsibilities	Reintegrates leisure knowledge and skills into changing leisure lifestyles
	Retirement	Uses leisure to maintain a sense of involvement and satisfaction		Adjusts lifestyles to changing roles and increased leisure	Chooses from a multitude of leisure choices, those most personally enhancing and enriching	Maintains and expands social interaction with individuals and groups	Uses skills from work and leisure for self-fulfilling leisure experiences

Password

This game is a modification of the Password television show. The object of the game is to have two to four teams of two people give their partners one-word clues to try to guess the word, activity, or object drawn in the shortest amount of time. (The actual rules of Password can be utilized by substituting or adding a list of words related to leisure and leisure experiences.)

Procedures. This game can have two to four teams comprised of two people each, one designated as Partner A and the other as Partner B. Partner A draws a word written on a slip of paper from a box and gives the other partner one-word clues in order for the partner to guess the word drawn. Once the word is guessed or a predetermined time limit has elapsed, the time is recorded and play proceeds to the next team, who repeats the same process. Once each team has had a turn, the same process is repeated with Partner B, who draws a word and gives the clues while Partner A tries to identify the word selected. After one round of play, the team with the lowest times is declared the winner.

This game can also be played on a noncompetitive basis where one person thinks of a leisure activity, experience, place, or equipment and the other player tries to guess what the word is.

Yes or No

Yes or No is played with two to six people. The object of the game is for one person to think of a leisure-related place, activity, community, resource, or piece of equipment that the other players then question about in order to guess what he is thinking.

Procedures. One person starts the game by thinking of a specific leisure-related place, activity, community, resource, or piece of equipment (or any other category that the participant may think of). The other players then take turns asking the person questions that can be answered with a yes or no response in order to guess what the player has selected. The first few questions should be used to narrow down the category of what the person is thinking of, for example, active-quiet, indoor-outdoor, educational, recreational, public, or private places. The person who guesses correctly then becomes the player to select a leisure-related place, activity, or piece of equipment. This game is also good to play on car trips or bus trips with children.

Leisure Blocks [a]

This particular activity is related to the objective of understanding leisure experiences with a brief focus on leisure satisfaction.

Directions. Under each of the letters that spell "leisure," fill in the block with an experience or emotion that begins with each of the letters. For example, something you do alone—loaf, leather craft, etc.

	L	E	I	S	U	R	E
Something you do alone in leisure							
Something you do with friends in your leisure							
Something you would like to do in your leisure							
Equipment, supplies, and objects you use in your leisure							
Something other people do during their leisure that you don't do							
Some of the feelings you have during leisure							

[a] Developed by Sue Hanlon, assistant professor, Florida State University, Leisure Services and Studies.

I See You

This activity can be used as a mixer with people who do not know each other or who may not know each other very well. The object of the activity is to tell people, from your impression of them, what you see them doing in their leisure. This is a particularly good activity for teenagers and adults.

Procedures. Participants can be seated in a casual circle, and one member of the circle volunteers to begin play. The person to begin play, or the group members, can select a topic or category to focus upon. For example, the first topic could focus on leisure in general. The individual who begins play tells the person on his right what he sees them doing during that person's leisure. I might say to the person on my right, "In leisure, I see you shooting the rapids on a canoe through a mountain river." It is interesting to then tell the person and the group why you associate a certain experience with them. Play then proceeds around the circle until everyone has had a turn. Once the complete circle has been made, a new topic or focus is decided upon and play continues. Topics could be any like the following: " On a summer day . . ."; "If all alone . . ."; "At the beach . . ."; "At home . . ."; "On a trip . . ."

Leisure Chairs [b]

The objective of this activity is to develop an awareness of the variety of leisure activities and experiences.

Participants. Ten 8-year-old boys and girls. (This activity can be used with most any size or age group.)

Equipment. Prepared stories or poems (such as the following) with a variety of leisure activities mentioned within the stories. (The children can write their own stories using leisure activities; this can be an activity in itself.)

Springtime's the best!
No, I like the fall.
But, summer brings fun
What with swimming and all.
Each season of the year brings its own special games.
Now listen to this rhyme.
Can you name their names?
Let's start with the fall when the weather is cool
And it's time for everyone to head back to school.
Hup one! Hup two! Football is here.
And for our favorite team, we'll certainly cheer.
Outdoor camping is another great sport.
Now let's go try our luck out on the basketball court.
The weather gets colder
Our season is changing.
Winter's a good time to learn the art of flower arranging.
Or we can bundle up warmly
And go outside.
Hurry! It's time for the big sleigh ride!
Springtime is here.
A warm breeze is blowing.
Let's go plant a garden
Since everything's growing.
Yes, spring is the season
Which brings a special kind of fun.
You'll often hear the question,
"*Tennis* anyone?"
The weather gets hotter,
Summer is here.
Let's go *fishing* down on the pier.
Decorations and goodies we'll be creating,
It's the Fourth of July *party* that we're celebrating.
Leisure is fun and can be found

Throughout the year.
You may have to travel,
Or it could be quite near.
You're sure to enjoy whatever you choose
It doesn't even matter if you win or you lose.

Formation. The group of children stand on the inside of a circle of chairs. The game begins with the same number of chairs as participants.

Action. One player stands in the center of the circle and reads the story slowly and clearly. The players walk around in a circle as the player reads the story; then, when a leisure activity is mentioned, each player must find a chair and sit down. Each time an activity is mentioned, a chair is removed. The players that do not sit down quickly enough to get a chair when a leisure activity is read, stand on the outside of the circle and listen to and watch the others. It is a fast-moving activity that encourages the children to listen for leisure activities. Also, as new and different activities are introduced, they are more willing to become familiar with the activities; therefore, when they are mentioned again, they will know them. The game is over when just one person is left.

Variations. An innovative facilitator can change this activity for various sized groups, by adding more chairs and removing two chairs at a time and he can adapt the activity for various ages using more varied and different leisure activities. Also, various themes can be introduced (e.g., a *Christmas theme*—activities that often occur during the holidays; selecting *one season's activities*—summer: boating, swimming, picnicking, and so on; or choosing *one category of leisure activities*—arts and crafts: painting, pottery, metal work, etc.).

---

[b] Developed by Jean Keller, Florida State University.

Passport To Leisure

Component: Self-awareness

Subcomponent: Interest, capabilities, needs, expectations, and goals

Program Goal: Participants will become aware of values, attitudes, and interests of their leisure lifestyle and leisure experiences.

Program Objectives:
Participants will:

1. identify past life experiences, both work and leisure.
2. identify contributions that they can make in their future life, and discover who they wish to be.
3. establish expectations and set goals for their retirement, including leisure and possibly work.
4. demonstrate how current skills can be utilized in leisure.
5. create their own leisure portfolio.

Background Information:

An individual needs to develop personal insights into one's attributes and recognize how they may have implications for future leisure behavior.

Program Experiences:

1. Have the participants develop a valid *Passport to Leisure* by first summarizing who they are and formulating who they wish to be. Have them utilize action verbs and accentuate the positive. In other words, have them address both the issue of *what they have to offer retirement* and *what retirement has to offer them.* Are they worthwhile persons only insofar as they can do a full-time job; or can they be worthwhile in other, different ways—as a performer or several other roles? Attempt to avoid the pitfall of self-sabotage. Examples of how this may be done include small-group work, creative writing, and videotaping.

a. Summarize life experiences, both work and leisure.
b. What qualifications do they have?
c. What knowledge and skills did they utilize or still utilize?
d. What attributes and abilities do they have? (e.g., sociability)
e. What are their strengths and weaknesses?
f. What are their needs and wants?

2. Once their initial work is completed, their second stage should be the establishment of expectations for their retirement/later life and setting goals by which they can meet these expectations. Strategies for helping in this area include the following:

   a. Addressing the following questions:

      1) Where do they want to go?
      2) What are their immediate and long-term opportunities?
      3) How can they get there?

   b. Demonstrating how current skills can be utilized in leisure.
   c. Presenting a seminar on *Myths of Aging.*
   d. Providing role models of older adults who have validated their *Leisure Passports.*
   e. Creating their own personal leisure portfolios.

NOTE: For individuals who suffer from dementia-related disorders, the *Passport to Leisure* may take the form of life review/reminiscence, which is a process of reassessing, reorganizing, and reintegrating past and present experiences in order to bridge the gap between the past and the future. This process provides some type of positive closure on the past which, in turn, permits an establishment of the future. This process can involve friends and family members in activities such as development of family trees, slide shows, and photo albums. It should be noted that care must be taken not to reach the obsessive stage with reminiscence/life review. Rather, the goal should be for retention.

Pre-retirement Seminar Quiz [c]

Component: Self-awareness

Subcomponent: Interest, values, attitudes, capabilities, needs

Program Goal: The participant will become informed on present and future status in order to live fully and effectively.

Program Objectives:
Participants will:

1. be encouraged to look ahead at their future leisure and work lifestyles.

2. look at their lifestyles and identify various aspects of their lives that they want to change.

3. become aware of certain "points to ponder," which may help an individual plan for a full and effective life in the future.

Background Information:

These experiences are designed to encourage reflection on real-life issues that significantly impact leisure lifestyles. Individuals need to recognize that they have control over their own well-being as well as their self-image.

Program Experiences:

- It's never too early to look ahead! Do you really want to live fully and effectively, the REST OF YOUR LIFE? Then take stock NOW! Ask participants the following questions:

  a. Does a regular checkup by a doctor let me know how healthy I am?
  b. Do I get physical exercise appropriate for my personal health profile, *every day*?
  c. Do I get some mental stimulation each day?
  d. Have I made friends with persons older and younger, as well as the same age as myself ?
  e. Am I aware of nutritional content of my daily food intake? Do I know anything about the possible interaction of my medicine with certain foods and/or physical activity?

f. Do I have a financial plan that takes possible inflation into account?
g. What kinds of retirement housing would suit me best? How do I find out about those available? What geographic area is best for me?
h. Do I have legal papers "at the ready?"—will? list of securities? pensions? union benefits? insurances? Social Security?
i. Will I need part-time employment in retirement? Can I develop skills now?
j. How will I spend my increased free time? with whom?
k. Which of my organizational contacts will continue after retirement?
l. Would I be happy in volunteer service? what kind?
m. How would my present financial expenditures (clothes, food, entertainment, housing, etc.) change if I retired?

Those are just a few "points to ponder." What others would relate particularly to your circumstances (i.e., married, single, children, no children)?

---

[c] Source: Dr. Janet R. MacLean

Looking Ahead [d]

Component: Self-awareness

Subcomponent: Expectations

Program Goal: Participants will identify realistic leisure expectations.

Program Objectives:
Participants will:

1. clarify values and expectations of their future leisure life expectations.

2. become aware of various leisure skills, experiences, and aspects that they have to offer in retirement.

Background Information:

This exercise is designed to facilitate forward thinking on matters relating to leisure and retirement. It is never too early to prepare for the future. Recognizing future retirement and realizing all of the free time one will have may spark new interests and open up a new leisure lifestyle.

Program Experiences:

- Have the participants look ahead to determine their leisure expectations by answering the following questions:

    a. If you were retired right now, how would you spend your leisure?
    b. Do have some retired relatives or friends who seem to be enjoying their retirement?
    c. Do you have some intellectual and cultural interests that will carry over into your retirement?
    d. Will any of your leisure choices take you out of the house?
    e. How much money will you need to make your leisure choices available?
    f. Are you active in volunteer service to your community? Will that continue or can it broaden in retirement?
    g. Do you want a second career in retirement?
    h. Will your community's attitude toward your leisure choices affect your ability to enjoy your retirement activities?
    i. What leisure interests, skills, or appreciations could you develop *now* that would enhance your retirement years?
    j. Will any of your present leisure skills provide potential for part-time employment?

---

[d] Source: Dr. Janet R. MacLean.

How is Your Leisure Ledger? ©

Component: Self-awareness

Subcomponent: Interests, values, attitudes, capabilities, needs, ____

Program Goal: Participants will become aware of the use of time ____ lives.

Program Objectives:
Participants will:

1. keep a leisure ledger in order to analyze their lifestyles.

2. recognize how much time is spent in leisure, work, free time, ____ sonal maintenance.

3. clarify and look for any changes that they may want to make ____ lifestyles.

Background Information:

It is important to become aware of your ____. Satisfaction, happiness, enjoyment, etc., are very important aspect ____ sure. Through self-awareness activities, individuals can clarify ____ values and use of time in their leisure lifestyle. Individuals ____ have the opportunity to determine if there is a need for change.

Program Experiences:

- Have the participants develop a leisure ledger so that they ____ their leisure choices and resultant satisfaction in order to ____ if there is a need for change.

  a. Keep a log of your activities (by half-hour units) fo____
  b. Beside each block of time in the log, write F for fre____ work, or P for personal maintenance. Indicate with R ____ spent in recreation. You may find that you will have ____ on some time frames.
  c. Chart your time consumption according to total hours ____ category, and the percentage of total available hours ____ total represents. (You have only 168 hours in the we____ remember.)

d. Chart the numbers of hours that you indicated were sp____ recreation. What was the percentage of total free ti____ were your other free-time experiences?

e. Analyze your recreation experiences in the following categories:

   1) How many hours in active participation? as spectator?
   2) How many hours alone? with others?
   3) How many experiences were free? cost money?
   4) How many experiences were primarily mental? physical? social?
   5) How many hours were spent indoors? outdoors?
   6) How many hours used transportation? no transportation?
   7) How many hours used energy resources—gas, electricity, and others?
   8) How many hours were spent with peer groups? others?

f. Critically analyze your week in terms of choices and resultant satisfaction. Is there any need for change? What are your conclusions?

---

[e] Source: Dr. Janet R. MacLean.

Leisure IQ[f]

Component: Self-awareness/Leisure-awareness

Subcomponent: Interests, values, attitudes, capabilities, needs. Relationship to one's life, lifestyle, quality of life, time, expectations, goals.

Program Goals: Participants will evaluate their leisure lifestyles.

Program Objectives:
Participants will:

1. identify how much their leisure has an impact on other areas of their lives.

2. have the opportunity to evaluate their leisure lifestyles.

3. recognize what values and resources are placed on their leisure.

Background Information:

It is important that individuals understand how their interests, values, attitudes, capabilities, and needs interact and impact their leisure and leisure experiences, as well as understanding the concept of leisure and its relationship to other areas of their lives. In addition, it is important to identify realistic leisure expectations for themselves, and to determine and reconcile life and leisure goals.

Program Experiences:

- Have participants determine their Leisure IQ's by asking the following questions:

  a. How much free time do I have each week?
  b. How much of that time is spent in physical activity?
  c. How much is spent in programs that demand mental activity?
  d. How much free time is spent alone? with others?
  e. Do my leisure choices cost much money?
  f. Do my choices use gas? electricity? other natural resources that are getting scarce?
  g. Do my choices need special environments or equipment?

h. What is my favorite leisure choice now?
i Will I be physically able to participate in that choice for the rest of my life? financially able?
j. Do I have broad choices or have I limited my activities?
k. Do I ever try to serve others in my leisure?
l. If I could add one more choice to fill my leisure, what would it be? Do I have the skill for it now? Would I need more? Are necessary facilities now available? *Goals.*

---

[f] Source: Dr. Janet R. MacLean.

About the Author . . .

DR. JEAN MUNDY is a Professor and Chair of the Recreation and Leisure Services Administration Program at Florida State University in Tallahassee, Florida. Dr. Mundy has been a consultant to numerous organizations such as the United Nations, the U.S. Department of the Interior, The Department of Defense, the U.S. Air Force and the U.S. Navy. Dr. Mundy is a noted author and speaker. She has been an invited speaker in Europe, Japan, Korea, the Philippines, Bermuda, Australia, and Canada. Dr. Mundy began her career in therapeutic recreation. She has also worked in public recreation and private recreation, owning her own private corporation, which provided contractual recreation services to persons with disabilities.

Index

A

Acting on one's beliefs, 236-237
Active facilitation, 20
Activity substitution, 273
Addiction, 273
Adolescence, 266
Adventure-based programs, 275
Aging, 280
AIDS, 260
Alzheimer's disease, 260, 264
Anxiety, 13, 35, 42
Art and crafts, 71-72
Attending, 226
Attitudes, 51, 52, 57, 64, 273
Attractiveness of options, 14
Attribution theory, 260

B

Barriers. *See* Leisure, constraints to
Behavior, 215-220
 antecedents of, 216-217, 219
 consequences of, 216-217, 220
Behavioral change, 214-221, 274
Body language, 248
Boredom, 38-39, 45-46, 86, 260, 264
Brochures, 89

C

Calendar of events, 85, 88, 179
Camps, 93
Canadian Ministry of Culture and Recreation, 56
Catastrophizing, 115
Cerebral palsy, 260
Charades, 71
Children with disabilities, 258-259
Choices, 10, 37-38, 55, 180-185, 258-263, 260
 and the incarcerated, 272
Choosing one's beliefs, 235-236
Clarifying, 227
Classes, 83, 84, 93, 96
Cognitive functioning, 262, 263
Communication, 225
Community Organization and Development Component, 95-96
Community reintegration programs, 255
Community/School Leisure Link Leisure Education Program, 254
Competence, perceived, 258, 260, 263
Computer-assisted instruction, 91, 96, 98-99
Constraints. *See* Leisure, constraints to
Contact, 226
Contingencies, 10, 13-14
Counseling, 246. *See also* Leisure counseling
Criminal behavior. *See* Persons in correctional systems
Curriculum- or school-based models, 50-56

D

Dance and creative movement, 73
Decision Charting, 242-243
Decision making, 37-38, 51, 52, 58-66, 93, 96, 104, 105, 180-198, 274
 and persons with disabilities, 262
 process of, 187-188
 styles of, 195-198
Decisions
avoidance of, 187
types of, 186
Declarative statement, 232
Demographic variables, and persons with disabilities, 262
Depression, 35, 42, 83, 260, 264
Delinquent behavior. *See* Persons in correctional systems
Direct strategies, 67, 70, 83-93, 104-105

Disabling conditions. *See* Persons with disabilities
Drama, 72

E
Educational system, 2-3
Education Component, 94-95, 96-97
Environment, 266
Environmental determinists, 10
Escape, 264
Evaluation forms, 81-82
Exercise, 43
Expectations, 65
and older adults, 284
preconceived, 36-37, 44
societal, 128
Expressive art forms, 71-74
External factors influencing the perception of freedom, 13-15
Externals, 11
Extrinsic determination, 16-18
Extroverts, 260

F
Facilitation, 224
techniques of, 223-249
Facilitator, 224
person of, 228
skills of, 231-234
Family unit, 2-3, 10
Fatigue, 35, 42
Fear, 13
Florida Department of Education, 50, 53
Florida State University, 50, 53, 74-75
Flow charts, 244-246
Force-field Analysis, 243-244
Fortune telling, 115
Freedom
concept of, 9-10, 114-117
perception of, 9-15, 64, 65, 256-257, 258, 260, 272
Frustration, 35, 42
of needs, 39

G
Games and activities, 70
Genetics, 10
Gestures, 226
Goal statement, 102
Group discussions, facilitating, 229-234
Guilt, 13, 31, 33-34, 41-42, 83

H
Handouts, 89
Helplessness, 13, 35, 42, 264
Hidden agendas, 233
Home page, 85
Hopelessness, 35, 42

I
I See You, 303
Implementation strategies, 67-100, 104-105
applicability to various program forms, 92
appropriateness for age and special population groups, 90-91
worksheet, 105-107
Inability to discriminate along a continuum, 35-36, 43-44
Independence, 265-267
Individual development models, 21-22, 23-24
Inertia, 34-35, 42-43
Information processing, 244-246
Infusion strategies, 67, 70-82, 104-105
Inmates. *See* Persons in correctional systems
Instructional skills, 246-249
Interjectory statements, 225
Internal factors influencing the perception of freedom, 11-13
Internal motivation, 15, 64, 65, 122, 258
Internals, 11
Internet, 85
Intervention strategies, 40-47
Intrinsic determination, 16, 19-21, 23-24
Invitation to elaborate, 233
Involvement, 263-265

J
Job change, 281-282
Job image, 33

K
Kangaroo Kit, 56, 177

L
Laissez-faire attitude, 19
Leadership, 224
Leader skills, 77-79
Leagues, 92
Learning environment, 247
Least restrictive environment, 255
Leisure
 changing attitudes toward, 18
 constraints to, 64, 65, 104, 172-176, 252-267, 274
 definition of, 5, 112-113
 goals of, 159-160
 and internal motivation, 15
 lack of conscious awareness of, 30-31, 40-41
 needs and motivations for, 151-154
 relationship to quality of life, 145-150
 relationship to time, 123-128
 societal benefits of, 18-19
 "wise" or "worthy" use of, 17
Leisure ability, 57
Leisure assessments, 91, 99
Leisure attitudes, 223, 297-298
Leisure Auction, 84, 141
Leisure awareness, 51, 52, 58-66, 80, 99, 103, 108, 112-150, 313-314
 infusing into recreation and leisure programs, 75
 and older adults, 284
 and persons in correctional systems, 272-273
Leisure Chairs, 304-305
Leisure competence, 258
Leisure content, 70-75
 infusing into existing activities, 70-71, 91
 infusing into expressive art forms, 71-74
 infusing into special events, themes, and productions, 74-75
Leisure counseling, 85, 91, 99, 244-246
Leisure Diagnostic Battery, 254
Leisure education
 activities developed for, 84-87
 components and subcomponents of, 59-66, 103-104
 conceptual models of, 49-66
 definition of, 5-7
 distinguished from traditional recreation services, 7-8
 goals of, 7, 56, 102
 infusing into teachable moments, 76-80
 target groups for, 103-104
Leisure Education Advancement Project (LEAP), 5, 54-56, 177
Leisure Education Curriculum, 56
Leisure ethic, 39-40, 284
Leisure expectations, 64, 310
Leisure experiences, 46, 54-55, 64, 65, 72, 129-144, 256-257
Leisure Fair, 74, 84-85
Leisure hot-line, 85-86, 99
Leisure interests, 46, 161-171, 299-300
Leisure lifestyle, 253
Leisure opportunities, 46, 55, 95
Leisure problems, 29-47
Leisure resource center, 86
Leisure resource guide, 89, 179
Leisure resources, 58-66, 94, 95, 104, 177-179
 and older adults, 284-285
 pro-social, 275
Leisure satisfaction, 151-152, 155-158, 265, 295
Leisure skills, 46, 51, 52, 57, 58-66, 94, 104, 180-221
 and older adults, 284-285
and persons in correctional systems, 274
Leisure Socialization Model, 258
Libertarians, 10
Life expectancy, 279-280
Listening skills, 226
Locus of control, 11-12, 46, 181, 272-273
 lack of, 37-38, 45
Loneliness, 86
Long-term inmates, 277

M
Mainstreaming, 255
Marathons, 275-276
Maslow's hierarchy of needs, 282
Media utilization, 87-90, 96, 98
Meditation, 43
Meet Your Match, 75-76, 84, 141
Membership applications, 80
Mental health, 255
Mental retardation, 78-79, 260, 261
Mind reading, 115
Mini-lectures, 246-249
Mission statement, 101, 103
Modeling, 19-20
Motivation, 15, 122, 173, 263-264, 296
lack of, 34-35
Multiple sclerosis, 260
Muscular dystrophy, 260

N
National Council on the Aging, 279
National Policy and Position Statement on Leisure Education, 50
National Recreation and Park Association, 5-6, 54, 177
National Therapeutic Recreation Society, 253
Normalization, 57, 255

O
Older adults, 279-286
and correctional settings, 276
Optimal arousal, 262
Oral presentations, 89-90
Organizational skills, 46
lack of, 40
Overchoice, 34

P
Paraphrasing, 227, 228
Parkinson's disease, 260
Participant skills, 77-79
Partnerships and collaborations, 96
Password, 301
Perception checking, 228
Personality, 260
Persons in correctional systems, 270-277
Persons with disabilities, 10, 57, 173, 252-267
Peterson's Leisure Education Content Model, 56-57
Physical environment, 24-25
Planning, 105, 202-204
Play, 32-33
Playgrounds, 93
Posture, 226
Presentation skills, 246-249
Prison population. *See* Persons in correctional systems
Prizing one's beliefs and behaviors, 236
Problem solving, 93, 96, 105, 209-213, 274
process of, 210-211
Processes and procedures, 80-82
Program delivery
models, 275-276
systems, 4
Program planning, 101-110
comprehensive, 101-102, 103-107
developing specific programs, 102-103, 107-109
Pro-social friendship systems, 274
Psychosocial factors, 24, 25
Psychosocial rehabilitation, 255
Publications, 89, 96, 98
Publicly affirming, 236
Public recreation and park systems, 69
reconceptualization of, 94-100

R
Radio, 88
Reallocation of staff and resources, 99, 104
Reciprocal determinism, 10
Reflective restatement, 232
Registration forms, 80
Relaxation, 43
Repetition, 249
Resocializing, 260-261
Resource Component, 94, 95, 97, 98
Responsibility-avoiding behaviors, 13
Retirement, 279-286, 306-310

S
Scope and Sequence of Leisure Education, 50-54, 288-294
goals of, 50-51
validation of, 53-54
Self-awareness, 51, 52, 58-66, 94, 104, 151-176, 306-314
and older adults, 283-284
and persons in correctional systems, 273-274
Self-esteem, 31-32, 41
Self-responsibility, 10, 45, 64, 65, 93, 118-122, 272-273
negation of, 37-38, 45
Self-talk, 12-13
Service components, 94-100
Skinner, B. F., 10
Social interaction, 51, 52, 58-66, 205-208, 263
and persons with disabilities, 261
Socialization, 32-34, 41-42, 173, 258, 266
role of family in, 2-3
role of schools in, 2-3
Social skills, 93, 205-208, 255
and persons in correctional systems, 274
Societal expectations, 128
Socio-professional models, 22-23
Special events, themes, and productions, 74-75
Special populations, 90-91, 251-286
Specific programs, development of, 102-103, 107-109
State of mind, 232-233
STILAP, 254
Stimulus-avoidance needs, 154
Stimulus seeking or excitement needs, 153
Stress, 35, 42, 86, 264
and institutional life, 271
Stroke, 260
Success, 33
Support equipment and materials, 247
Systems Approach, 58-66
components of, 58-60, 63
new configuration, 58, 63-66
original model, 58
potential behavioral outcomes, 58, 63-66
subcomponents of, 58, 60-62, 64-66
Systems models, 56-57

T
Target groups, 102, 103-104, 107
Teachable moments, 70, 76-80, 214
Television, 87-88, 104
Tension, 35, 42
Terminal objectives, 50
Therapeutic recreation, 4, 56-57, 69, 108, 252-267
Time, 14-15
lack of, 39-40, 46-47, 83, 173
management of, 46
relationship to leisure, 123-128
Tournaments, 92
Traumatic brain injury, 260

U
Units for implementation, 111-221

V
Value clarification, 64, 66, 199-201, 234-243
basic format, 238
consequential analysis formats, 240-243
forced-choice format, 238-239
learning experiences, 237-243
rank-order format, 239-240
Values, 64, 199-200, 273
conflicting, 200-201
Valuing process, 235-237
Verbal statements, 226
Vocal delivery, 248

W
Wake Leisure Education Program, 254
Women, and correctional settings, 276-277
Work, 32-33, 284
Workshops, 83, 84, 96, 275
Worry, 13, 33, 41-42

Y
Yes or No, 301